MULTICULTURAL MARKETING

MULTICULTURAL MARKETING

SELLING TO THE NEW AMERICA

POSITION YOUR COMPANY TODAY

FOR OPTIMAL SUCCESS

IN THE DIVERSE AMERICA OF TOMORROW

ALFRED L. SCHREIBER

WITH BARRY LENSON

NTC Business Books

NTC/Contemporary Publishing Group

Library of Congress Cataloging-in-Publication Data

Schreiber, Alfred L.
    Multicultural marketing : selling to the new America / Alfred L.
Schreiber, with Barry Lenson.
        p.   cm.
    Includes index.
    ISBN 0-8442-2601-7
    1. Market segmentation—United States.   2. Minority
consumers—United States.   I. Lenson, Barry.   II. Title.
HF5415.127 .S37   2000
658.8′00859′00973—dc21   00-40114

Interior design by Hespenheide Design

Published by NTC Business Books
A division of NTC/Contemporary Publishing Group, Inc.
4255 West Touhy Avenue, Lincolnwood (Chicago), Illinois 60712-1975 U.S.A.
Copyright © 2001 by NTC/Contemporary Publishing Group, Inc.
Printed in the United States of America
International Standard Book Number: 0-8442-2601-7
01 02 03 04 05 06 LB 19 18 17 16 15 14 13 12 11 10 9 8 7 6 5 4 3 2 1

For Amanda, Scott,
and Suri . . . with love

CONTENTS

Seven Truths About the Changing Face of America

1. By the year 2005, people of color will represent one in three Americans. By 2050, they will represent 55 percent of the population.

2. Ethnic Americans—African-, Hispanic-, and Asian-Pacific-Americans—are increasing in populations seven times as fast as the nonethnic majority.

3. Ethnic Americans have economic clout. Their spending power has doubled in the past decade and is now over $1 trillion. They are rapidly opening businesses, buying homes, going to college, and living the American Dream at rates that outpace "mainstream" white Americans by almost 350 percent.

4. Of the over $200 billion spent annually against domestic paid media, only about 1–2 percent are currently dedicated to targeted ethnic media.

5. Today's emerging ethnic consumers represent the largest, most overlooked market in America. Companies who capture the attention and brand loyalty of this market today will position themselves for security and success in the years to come.

6. Many of today's ethnic Americans can be effectively reached at less cost than mainstream consumers. Many live in well-defined areas, consume well-defined media, and shop in certain retail outlets. In sum, there is greater return on investment (ROI) to be found in addressing the ethnic markets than in the traditional mainstream mass markets.

7. Diversity is the hidden key to being a successful business in the changing America. Ads alone will not do it. Neither will "window dressing" efforts that build a false image of diversity for a company. To become successful in the new, diverse America, your company must *become* the new America. When your workforce is part of the changing picture and imbues your organization with the views and outlooks of the new America, you position yourself for growth.

The face of today's American consumer looks dramatically different than it did ten years ago—but have marketers kept pace? Despite growing attention to the issue and criticism from outside the business, the answer is no. Consider again this disparity: of the over $200 billion spent annually against domestic paid media, only $2.5 billion, or 1.3 percent, are currently dedicated to targeted ethnic media markets—Hispanic,- African-, and Asian-Pacific-Americans—who as a whole are increasing in population seven times as fast as the nonethnic majority.

A Pivotal Moment

This is a critical moment for American business. It is time to ask ourselves "Who are we marketing to?" Are we really addressing the people who make up our country today, or are we devoting most of our energies to yesterday's audience? Are we taking the necessary steps to ensure market expansion?

These profound demographic changes offer companies the chance to play a pivotal role in advancing the national discussion on race, thereby furthering their status not only as leading-edge businesses but also as valued corporate citizens.

We as an industry must make conscientious efforts to create a business environment that reflects the face of America today, including internal recruitment, retention strategies, and internal communications, and develop business strategies that recognize the impact and influence of ethnic growth markets. By narrowing the mainstream-versus-ethnic business gap, companies can make great strides in narrowing the nation's cultural gap as well.

All the aforementioned factors add up to a textbook case wherein operating from enlightened self-interest makes superb business sense. The combined buying power of America's racial and ethnic groups—currently over $1 trillion—has reached an all-time high and continues to skyrocket.

Parity by 2007

According to the Multicultural American Dream Index, a recent groundbreaking study that will be explored in Chapter 1, if current trends continue, ethnic Americans will achieve proportional economic parity with nonethnic Americans by the year 2007, if not sooner.

In some cases, the economic impact of ethnic Americans already exceeds their percentage of the population. The growth rate of African-Americans purchasing new cars has been twelve times that of non-African-American auto purchasers over the last decade. African-American per capita spending is now virtually equal to non-African-American spending in the major household appliance, furniture, and grocery categories. The statistics for Hispanic-Americans and Asian-Pacific-Americans are similarly high.

It's no coincidence that the slow-rolling trend away from mass media and toward more targeted delivery vehicles has picked up steam as these markets have bulged in numbers and economic power. By beefing up their ad presence in first-class ethnic media vehicles, including long-standing cable TV channels such as Black Entertainment Television and Telemundo; new publications such as *Latina*, *Vibe*, *Emerge,* and *The Source*; and websites such as the Chinese-language SinaNet (http://www.sinanet.com), forward-thinking marketers have found they can get a leg up on earning recognition and brand loyalty from the new America.

The Ubiquitous Force of Media

Advertising is the most ubiquitous media force in the day-to-day lives of most Americans. Advertisers and agencies possess tremendous power to persuade Americans not only about what to buy but also what to think about themselves, their neighbors, their communities, and the world we all live in. It's the power clients look for in agencies when investing in multimillion-dollar ad budgets.

It's up to marketers to use that power to put a realistic face on the new America. When ethnic Americans see themselves and their lives portrayed in ad campaigns, it makes people of all races feel they're part of a greater whole and fosters a sense of inclusion among our society's broad racial spectrum.

Here's the challenge for corporate decision makers: develop a corporate culture that acknowledges, respects, and reflects the distinct heritage of the American mosaic. By doing so, you will help not only ethnic Americans but all Americans feel more enfranchised in the American Dream, a dream that includes opportunity for all. You will then create a climate that encourages other companies to come on board and build a stronger dialogue with today's consumer.

A Critical Edge

Companies that build positive connections with the new America can earn recognition and brand loyalty that can provide a critical edge for expanding their businesses in this millennium. Perhaps more important, they can be in the vanguard of corporate citizens taking part in what may be the most crucial national dialogue of this century.

For American business, the time to act is now. The stakes for our businesses and for our society are too high to ignore.

MULTICULTURAL MARKETING

CHAPTER One

A ROAD MAP
OF THE NEW AMERICA

Building one America is our most important mission. Money cannot buy it. Power cannot compel it. Technology cannot create it. It can only come from the human spirit.

—President Bill Clinton, speaking on the
President's Initiative on Race, June 14, 1997

America is now undergoing the most profound demographic shift since the dawn of the twentieth century. People of color now represent more than one in four Americans. By the year 2005, they will represent one in three. And by the year 2050, people of color will make up 55 percent of the U.S. population.

Growth markets comprised of African-, Asian-Pacific-, and Hispanic-Americans now represent a combined buying power of over $1 trillion, up from $500 billion in the last decade. The economic clout of this segment is predicted to grow 25 percent—over $1 trillion—by the year 2005. It's time for American businesses to recognize and accept this new reality. But as of this writing, that is still to happen. The new America isn't coming five or ten years down the road. It's on our doorstep right now.

The Opportunity

What is this new America? It's where we all live. For the purposes of this book, it is particularly the place where American businesses and corporations will continue to conduct business in the coming decades.

For marketers and for anyone whose existence depends on selling to the citizens of this rapidly changing demographic landscape, this is the moment to ask ourselves two critical questions.

1. To whom are we selling our products and services *today*? Are we really addressing the people who live here now—the people who make up America? Or are we talking to *yesterday's* audience?
2. To whom will we be selling tomorrow? What's the shape of tomorrow's demographic landscape, and what should we be doing now to prepare for it?

To remain successful and competitive, we need to make conscientious efforts to create advertising that accurately reflects the way America looks today—not yesterday—and to develop media strategies that recognize the impact and influence of our ethnic growth markets.

Enlightened Self-Interest

Why are America's marketers lagging so far behind in their spending on the emerging ethnic sectors of our population? Some may simply not be aware of the magnitude of the changes sweeping across America. Others, watching the success of their efforts month by month and year by year, may be taking too short a view of what is coming. They're saying, in essence, "As long as this year's campaigns appear to be working and our sales remain strong, that's enough for the moment." If it's not broken, why fix it? They're planning to adapt gradually over the years and grow into the new America. These members of the advertising, marketing, and business communities protest that applying long-range vision isn't part of their jobs. They're too involved in planning campaigns for the next six months, the next year, or even the next five years.

However, a growing body of evidence supports the view that a significant opportunity is knocking at their doors. Marketers with the foresight to build positive connections with the "new" consumers can earn the recognition and brand loyalty to provide a critical edge for their businesses in the decades ahead.

Findings of the Multicultural American Dream Index

The findings of a recent research study entitled the Multicultural American Dream (MCAD) Index[1] reveal the astounding rate at which Asian-Pacific-, Hispanic-, and African-Americans are accessing the means to prosperity. Based on 1985–1996 compound annual growth rates, MCAD finds that these consumers are increasing their household incomes, obtaining mortgages, owning small businesses, and earning college degrees at a rate that's growing *two to three times as fast as that of nonethnic Americans*[2] (see Figure 1.1). The MCAD Index further predicts that if

Figure 1.1　Minorities' Growth Rates Are Mostly Two to Three Times Those of Whites

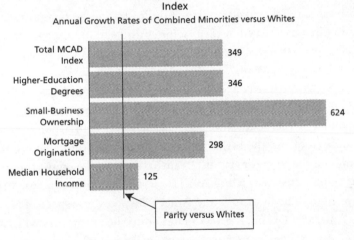

Index
Annual Growth Rates of Combined Minorities versus Whites

	Index
Total MCAD Index	349
Higher-Education Degrees	346
Small-Business Ownership	624
Mortgage Originations	298
Median Household Income	125

Parity versus Whites

Sources: U.S. Census Bureau; National Center for Education Statistics; MCAD Index projections

1. Commissioned by Graham Gregory Bozell and conducted by Market Segment Research and Teller Group Consulting.
2. MCAD demonstrates that the new ethnic market growth is based on more than just population growth in ethnic segments. It is based on an analysis of four categories of economic indicators: median household income, home ownership (represented by the number of mortgage originations), small-business ownership, and education (based on numbers obtaining college degrees).

current trends continue ethnic Americans will achieve proportional economic parity with nonethnic Americans by the year 2007, if not sooner.

In some cases, the economic impact of ethnic Americans already
well exceeds their percentage of the population. For example, between
the years 1987 and 1997, the growth rate of African-Americans purchasing new cars was twelve times that of non-African-American
purchasers. The latest figures also show that African-American per capita
spending is virtually equal to non-African-American spending in key
categories such as major household appliances, furniture, and groceries.

A closer look at some of the findings and implications of the
MCAD study reveals significant information. Data was obtained from
the U.S. Census Bureau, the Home Mortgage Disclosure Act (HMDA),
the Federal Financial Institutions Examination Council (FFIEC), the
National Center for Education Statistics, the survey of Minority Owned
Businesses, and the Small Business Administration, and projections were
made when necessary. For each factor considered (housing originations,
educational attainment, etc.), MCAD determined the average annual
growth rate as contrasted to that of white Americans.

MCAD focused on four key American Dream goals (see Figure 1.2):
owning a home (see Figure 1.3), owning a business (see Figure 1.4),
obtaining higher education (see Figure 1.5), and having sufficient
income to obtain the basics and some luxuries. Ethnic Americans are
obtaining the four American Dream goals at a rate almost three and a
half times faster than white Americans. In fact, minorities are making
gains more quickly than white Americans in every aspect of reaching
the American Dream. If growth rates continue, minorities will achieve
equal representation in mortgage originations, education, and small-
business ownership no later than 2007.

Mortgage Originations
- Minorities accounted for 16 percent of all mortgages—more
  than two million—issued from 1993 through 1996.
- The proportion of minority mortgages issued (16 percent)
  almost equaled its representation of U.S. households (20 percent). Growth rates continued until parity occurred in 1999
  (see Figure 1.6).

Figure 1.2   Minorities Outpace Whites in Every Category

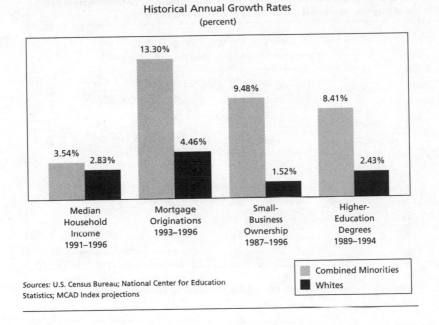

Historical Annual Growth Rates
(percent)

Sources: U.S. Census Bureau; National Center for Education
Statistics; MCAD Index projections

- Growth rates among minorities for obtaining mortgages far exceed those of the white population.

Small-Business Ownership (see Figure 1.7)
- In 1996, minorities owned almost three million small businesses.
- Of those businesses, 816,295 (28 percent) were owned by African-Americans; 779,143 (27 percent) were owned by Asian-Pacific-Americans; and 1,342,426 (45 percent) were owned by Hispanic-Americans.
- By the year 2007, ethnic Americans will own 23 percent of all U.S. small businesses (see Figure 1.8).

Higher Education (see Figures 1.9 and 1.10)
- In 1996, minority students were awarded more than 400,000 degrees of higher learning (including two-year Associate degrees).
- Minorities accounted for about 19 percent of all degrees of higher learning granted in the United States in 1996.

Figure 1.3   Mortgage Originations

All groups' growth rates are higher than white Americans'; African-Americans and Hispanic-Americans are growing almost four times faster.

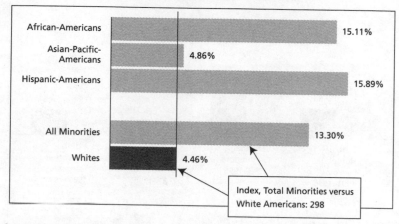

Growth in Mortgage Originations
Annual Growth Rates of Mortgages Issued, 1993–1996

Sources: U.S. Census Bureau; National Center for Education Statistics; MCAD Index projections

Figure 1.4   Small-Business Ownership

Minorities' growth rates far outstrip white Americans'.

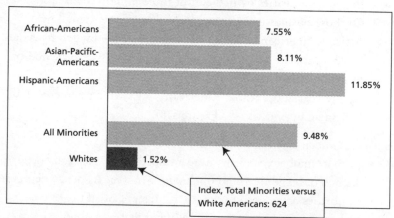

Growth in Small-Business Ownership
Annual Growth Rates, 1987–1996

Sources: U.S. Census Bureau; National Center for Education Statistics; MCAD Index projections

Figure 1.5   Higher Education

All minorities have high growth rates.

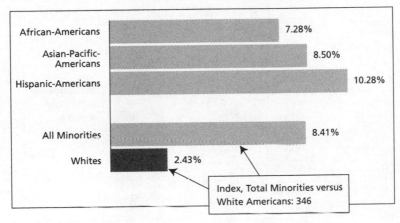

Growth in Postsecondary Degrees
Annual Growth Rates, 1989–1996

African-Americans — 7.28%
Asian-Pacific-Americans — 8.50%
Hispanic-Americans — 10.28%
All Minorities — 8.41%
Whites — 2.43%

Index, Total Minorities versus White Americans: 346

Sources: U.S. Census Bureau; National Center for Education Statistics; MCAD Index projections

Figure 1.6   Parity in Mortgage Originations

The percentage of originations accounted for by minorities equaled its representation of U.S. households in mid-1999.

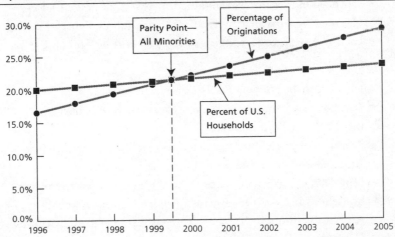

Parity Point— All Minorities

Percentage of Originations

Percent of U.S. Households

Sources: U.S. Census Bureau; National Center for Education Statistics; MCAD Index projections

Figure 1.7   Small-Business Ownership: Overview

Based on our projections, in 1996, minorities owned almost three million small businesses, with Hispanic-Americans accounting for almost half.

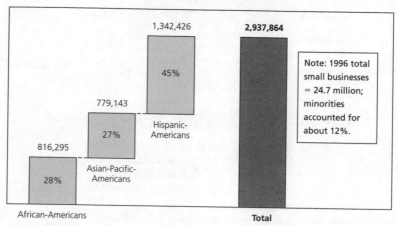

Minority Small-Business Ownership
Number of Small Businesses, 1996

Note: 1996 total small businesses = 24.7 million; minorities accounted for about 12%.

Sources: 1987, 1992 Survey of Minority Owned Businesses; Small Business Administration; MCAD Index projections

(Note: The total number of degrees awarded in the United States in 1996 was 2,197,023.)

- Of those higher degrees obtained, 181,613 (44 percent) were obtained by African-Americans; 114,783 (28 percent) by Asian-Pacific-Americans; and 119,949 (29 percent) by Hispanic-Americans.

Economic Growth and Buying Power (see Figure 1.11)

- Asian-Pacific-Americans already exceed white Americans' median household income.
- African-Americans are projected to reach parity with white Americans' median household income by 2027.
- However, the gap will continue to widen between the median household income for Hispanic-Americans and African-Americans through the year 2027—a trend partially driven by Hispanic-Americans' high rates of immigration.

Figure 1.8 When Will Minorities Catch Up?

If these growth rates continue, minorities will achieve parity in small-business ownership by 2007.

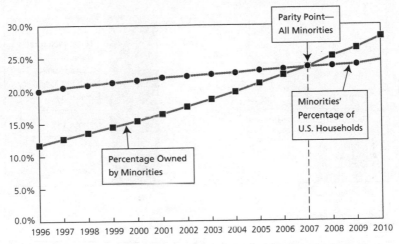

Projections: Small-Business Ownership
When the percentage of small businesses owned by minorities
will equal its representation of U.S. households

Sources: U.S. Census Bureau; National Center for Education Statistics; MCAD Index projections

Clearly, building relationships with America's growth markets can represent the key to survival in the coming millennium. It's no coincidence that the slow-rolling trend away from mass media toward more targeted delivery vehicles has picked up steam as ethnic growth markets have bulged in both numbers and economic power.

Expanding Markets

In later chapters, we'll take an in-depth look at three specific ethnic markets poised for significant economic and consumer growth—the growth markets of the coming decades. They are African-Americans, Hispanic-Americans, and Asian-Pacific-Americans. For the purpose of this chapter, let's take a preliminary glance at what's taking place in those key market segments.

Figure 1.9 Higher Education: Overview

In 1996, we estimate that minority students were awarded over 400,000 degrees of higher learning.* African-Americans accounted for more than four out of ten.

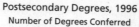

Postsecondary Degrees, 1996
Number of Degrees Conferred

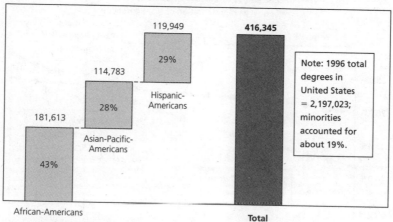

119,949

416,345

29%

114,783

Hispanic-
Americans

Note: 1996 total
degrees in
United States
= 2,197,023;
minorities
accounted for
about 19%.

28%

181,613

Asian-Pacific-
Americans

43%

African-Americans

Total

*Includes two-year Associate degrees
Sources: U.S. Census Bureau; National Center for Education Statistics; MCAD Index projections

African-Americans make up the largest ethnic group in America, with 33 million people at the time of the last census in 1994. African-Americans represent the majority of consumers in many U.S. cities, including Atlanta (67.1 percent), Baltimore (59.2 percent), Detroit (75.7 percent), New Orleans (61.9 percent), and Washington, D.C. (65.8 percent). The buying power of African-Americans is soaring. It now stands at $460 billion annually—up 54 percent since 1990. The African-American population is growing at twice the rate of the white American population, and African-American growth will account for 30 percent of the total U.S. population growth through 2005. (See Figure 1.12 for projected African-American population in 2001.)

More interesting, perhaps, are these 1997 figures:[3]

---

3. Based on research conducted by the Securities Industry Association in 1997.

Figure 1.10 When Will Minorities Catch Up?

If these growth rates continue, minorities will achieve parity in obtaining postsecondary degrees by mid-2005.

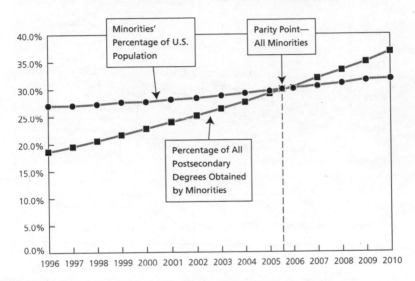

Projections: Postsecondary Degrees
When the percentage of postsecondary degrees obtained by minorities
will equal its representation of the total U.S. population

Sources: U.S. Census Bureau; National Center for Education Statistics; MCAD Index projections

- There are 259,000 African-American households with annual incomes exceeding $100,000.
- The number of those affluent households tripled between 1994 and 1997.
- The total buying power of African-Americans is $400 billion.
- The top African-American markets are New York; Philadelphia; Washington, D.C.; Baltimore; Atlanta; Chicago; Detroit; Dallas–Fort Worth; Los Angeles; Oakland; and Miami.

Asian-Pacific-Americans (comprised of Chinese, Japanese, Koreans, Filipinos, and Asian-Indians) are the fastest-growing of all ethnic groups, projected to reach 11 million by the year 2000 and 21 million by 2020. (See Figure 1.13 for projected Asian-Pacific-American

Figure 1.11 When Will Minorities Catch Up?

Asian-Pacific-Americans already exceed whites' median household (HH) income; African-Americans will cross in 2027; gap widens for Hispanic-Americans.

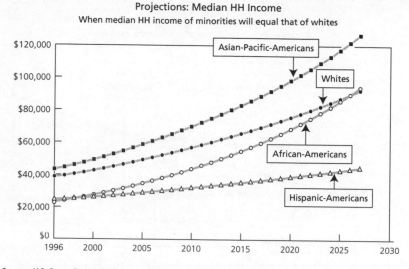

Projections: Median HH Income
When median HH income of minorities will equal that of whites

Sources: U.S. Census Bureau; National Center for Education Statistics; MCAD Index projections

population in 2001.) Enjoying a median household income of $40,000—20 percent higher than the rest of the U.S. population—they heft formidable economic clout:

- There are 111,000 Asian-Pacific-American households with annual incomes exceeding $100,000.
- The Asian-Pacific-American segment is the most affluent of any American grouping—including white Americans—with median incomes 23 percent higher than the rest of the population.
- The total buying power of Asian-Pacific-Americans is $220 billion.
- The top Asian-Pacific-American markets are Los Angeles, the San Francisco Bay Area, New York, and Seattle. Over 70 percent of Asian-Pacific-American consumers are concentrated in ten market areas (in descending order of population density):

Figure 1.12

Affluent African-Americans are finding the good life in southern cities, and lower-income African-Americans are looking for a better life in the land of their grandparents.

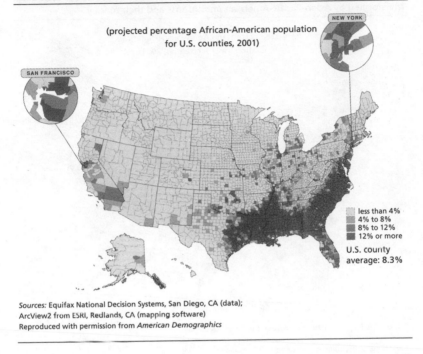

(projected percentage African-American population for U.S. counties, 2001)

NEW YORK

SAN FRANCISCO

less than 4%
4% to 8%
8% to 12%
12% or more

U.S. county
average: 8.3%

Sources: Equifax National Decision Systems, San Diego, CA (data);
ArcView2 from ESRI, Redlands, CA (mapping software)
Reproduced with permission from *American Demographics*

California, New York, Texas, New Jersey, Illinois, Washington, Florida, Virginia, Maryland, and Massachusetts.

Hispanic-Americans (about 30 million in 1996, or a population roughly equal to that of Canada) are our third rapidly expanding group of consumers. The U.S. Census Bureau projects a 25 percent growth rate for Hispanic-Americans over the next ten years. That's in marked contrast to the growth rate for white Americans, which is projected to decrease 14.6 percent. (See Figure 1.14 for projected Hispanic-American population in 2001.)

- There are more than 193,000 Hispanic-American households with annual incomes exceeding $100,000.

Figure 1.13

Asian-Pacific-Americans are a significant presence in only a handful of U.S. counties.
But don't be fooled by the map: America's largest and wealthiest metros are being
transformed by Asian-Pacific-American immigrants and their money.

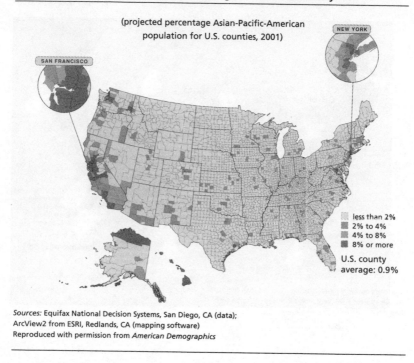

(projected percentage Asian-Pacific-American
population for U.S. counties, 2001)

Sources: Equifax National Decision Systems, San Diego, CA (data);
ArcView2 from ESRI, Redlands, CA (mapping software)
Reproduced with permission from *American Demographics*

- The total buying power of Hispanic–Americans reached $270 billion in 1997, representing a growth of 150 percent since 1973.
- The top Hispanic-American markets are Los Angeles, Houston, New York, Miami, the San Francisco Bay Area, and Chicago.

Seizing the Opportunity

By beefing up their ad presence in the wave of first-class ethnic media vehicles that have emerged in recent years, forward-thinking companies have already found they can get a leg up on earning recognition and loyalty from the new America.

Figure 1.14

Some Hispanic-Americans have immigrated to the United States; others have resided here since colonial times. They are a rich presence in many counties from coast to coast.

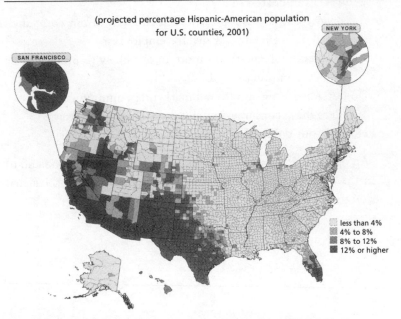

(projected percentage Hispanic-American population for U.S. counties, 2001)

less than 4%
4% to 8%
8% to 12%
12% or higher

Sources: Equifax National Decision Systems, San Diego, CA (data); ArcView2 from ESRI, Redlands, CA (mapping software); Valdes and Sedane, *Hispanic Market Handbook* (1995: Gale Research, Detroit, MI) Reproduced with permission from *American Demographics*

Building business in America's new multicultural century requires that successful companies begin to include a strategic multicultural perspective in their overall business planning processes. Questions such as the following must be addressed and answered:

What is our business opportunity in the multicultural workplace?
What are the underlying economics?
Who are our multicultural consumers, and why?
How unique is our opportunity?
How can we leverage our existing infrastructure?
What is the optimal go-to-market approach?

What can we expect in terms of return on investment?

How are we handling diversity?

How well have we done in recruiting the best and brightest diverse candidates?

Are diverse employees represented at all levels of our company?

How well do we retain our diverse employees?

Are multicultural Americans more or less likely to purchase our product than other brands?

Do our advertising and overall marketing communications reflect these consumers in culturally appropriate ways?

How are our competitors addressing these consumers?

An opportunity is waiting at our doors—both to do good and to sell. In the chapters that follow, we'll see just how we can seize that opportunity.

EIGHT KEYS TO BECOMING A TWENTY-FIRST-CENTURY MARKETER

It seems many marketers today seem to be living in the past. They believe they don't have to direct specialized efforts toward minority markets or apply any kind of unusual expertise. They say, "Oh, our mainstream advertising is good and it will pick up those ethnic consumers along with everyone else."

What a missed opportunity! The opportunities for return on invest-ment, advertising dollar for advertising dollar, can be substantial when ethnic consumers are targeted directly. Plus, there's the long-term equity of positioning yourself for growth in the ethnic markets, with their sub-stantially higher rate of growth.

—Dr. Andrew Erlich, president, Erlich
Transcultural Consultants, in an interview with
Barry Lenson, January 1999

Before we get into the specifics on techniques to be used in reaching the new American marketplace, we will briefly reflect on some more basic concerns. For marketers to succeed,

- What kind of thinking is needed?
- Which attitudes that succeeded in traditional marketing to the white marketplace will serve marketers today and which will not?
- What are the principal pitfalls to overcome?

Let's take a closer look at the eight keys to becoming a twenty-first-century marketer.

Key #1—Avoid Monolithic Thinking

Avoid thinking monolithically!

—Verdia Johnson, president, Footsteps, the ethnic
marketing division of Omnicom

By "monolithic," Ms. Johnson means "seeing all the members of your target audience as one huge, undifferentiated mass with no characteristics that differentiate them as individuals." Time and again, we see monolithic thinking at work in marketing efforts directed at the multicultural and ethnic markets.

Not long ago, for example, a large packaged-goods manufacturer met with a large ad agency, expressing interest in creating television ads to sell one of its laundry detergent brands to African-Americans. They said, "We want to reach more African-American consumers. We were thinking about our ad message and we'd like to ask, what do you think about an ad that centers on the depiction of African-American women, slightly overweight, attending a church service?"

When agency execs said there might be alternative approaches that would play less to stereotypes, the packaged-goods folks responded, "Well, we were looking for an image that would be inclusive of the largest possible number of African-Americans." It took a lot of arguing to convince them that showing African-Americans as individuals going about their daily lives is more effective than a "scattergun" approach to hit as many of them as possible with a single ad.

Or consider the story of a brand of sports apparel that alienated many young urban black New Yorkers this year by running ads in subways that showed roomfuls of young African-American party-goers. One African-American colleague of mine said, "Those ads, which are supposed to be inclusive of as many of us as possible, turn everyone off by playing to the stereotype of blacks as people who don't do anything but party, party, party. We ride the trains and look at those ads and laugh!"

What approach would be better? My colleague offers this advice. "Just show us as individuals. We get up in the morning, get breakfast on the table, go shopping for a car, have our kids get sick. What's the big problem about finding something that plays well with us? I don't understand! When ads try to play up our supposed shared traits, it only turns us off."

The end result of monolithic thinking can be a lack of authenticity and credibility within the target group you are trying to reach. Even when the results are not that bad—for example, the marketplace is merely uninterested and unengaged by your ads—you are still failing to get the best return for your marketing dollar.

Showing concern for the individual in advertising is almost always more effective than trying to be all-inclusive. "Something for everyone" doesn't sell any better in the ethnic marketplace than it does in the mainstream. You have to speak to people's interests, needs, problems, and concerns.

Key #2—Talk to Your Consumers

> So many marketers spend time trying to decode the psychographics of various minority segments. They'll say, "Isn't it true that Hispanic consumers are very family oriented?" or "Aren't Asian consumers generally very entrepreneurial?" That kind of thinking is all well and fine, but a bigger question is, "Are you talking to them at all?" You don't have to understand everything about the segments you are trying to reach, but one thing is for sure. You do need to be talking to them.
>
> —Jeff Symon, president, Alternative & Innovative
> Marketing, Escondido, California

My colleague Jeff is right on the mark with his observation. All the decoding, probing, and psychographic thinking in the world won't boost your sales unless you are making contact with consumers—in Jeff's parlance, "talking to them." That might mean placing an ad in a Chinese-language newspaper, or sponsoring the Hispanic-American Chamber of Commerce, or creating in-language radio ads for the Hispanic-American market. You don't have to do everything right, but you do have to do *something*. After all, very few marketers could point to many marketing efforts that did everything right.

Dwelling on the many complications and complexities of multicultural marketing—or worse yet, sitting on your hands and doing nothing because you are afraid to make a mistake—only allows significant opportunities to pass by your doorstep.

Later in Chapter 7 on diversity, you'll read about a car dealership that, although it was located in a Pennsylvania city with a tremendous number of Hispanic-American citizens, had no Latino salespeople on staff. When it finally hired one Latino salesperson, he became the dealership's top-producing salesperson within one month.

This is an excellent microcosmic example of the power of doing something. The car dealership could have agonized about whether to run in-language ads on local Spanish-language radio. It could have hired an agency. It could have sponsored an event or supported an organization important to the Hispanic-American citizens in its locale. It can still do all those things. But it took one small step to speak to the constituency it was trying to reach. And the results exceeded all expectations.

Key #3—Stop Using Dustbin Logic

> Many marketers believe they don't have to direct specialized efforts toward minority markets. They say, "Oh, we'll just pick them up as we go along with the rest of our advertising."
>
> —Dr. Andrew Erlich, president, Erlich
> Transcultural Consultants

Many mainstream marketers subscribe to this kind of fallacious thinking. I call it dustbin logic because it implies that consumers, like so many grains of dust, simply get swept into the bin by any marketing campaign. It's perfectly true that minority consumers get swept along in mainstream marketing. But allowing this dustbin principle to serve as the main medium for winning their business overlooks a real opportunity.

Why is the "sweep-along" principle fallacious? Because it overlooks a highly effective use of marketing dollars. Marketing targeted at America's emerging ethnic and minority markets offers a higher return on investment (ROI) than mass marketing to the general audience.

Consider the California bank that was using English-speaking telemarketers to call Chinese-Americans. As an experiment, they decided to hire some telemarketers who were native speakers of Mandarin and Cantonese. These telemarketers soon were winning new customers in

8 out of every 100 calls made—more than a sixteenfold improvement over their success rate with English-speaking telemarketers.

So although some consumers might get swept along into the bin with general marketing efforts, targeted minority marketing will bring a higher percentage of consumers in focused segments into the fold.

Especially in Hispanic- and Asian-Pacific-American markets, the opportunities for high ROI are remarkable, as we will discover in later chapters of this book. These consumer groups live in well-defined areas. They are the beneficiaries of media—TV, radio, and print—that are very well defined and easy to find. And they respond remarkably well to in-language advertising. For the most part, they reside in larger households than traditional white consumers; so once you have secured their brand loyalty, you have gotten more "bang for the buck" than you might get elsewhere.

The choice is yours whether to seize the greatest possible return on investment to be gained in multicultural efforts or to let those consumers go to someone else with mass marketing.

Key #4—Maintain Workforce Diversity

Chapter 7 is devoted to the question of diversity. Diversity is imperative for survival in the coming decades.

Consider the cost-effectiveness of diversity. Here are just a few of the benefits:

- A diverse company doesn't need to go to outside consultants and agencies to understand the fundamentals of what ethnic and minority consumers are thinking and buying. That expertise is already resident in house.
- An internally diverse company is far better equipped to sell to the emerging markets. Ethnic and minority consumers are far more likely to respond positively to salespeople who speak their language or share their background.
- An internally diverse company "resonates" with the new marketplace. When consumers call, when reporters write about your company, when executives from other companies visit your offices, they clearly will see that your organization is part

of the changing fabric of American life. Your company doesn't need as much outreach to demonstrate that it is attuned to the lives of ethnic consumers, because its involvement in their lives is internal and dynamic.

The message is clear that diversity is another imperative—an internal one—that attunes a company organically to the changing shape of American life.

Key #5—Market to Urban Teens

Mainstream marketing people say they don't understand today's hip-hop culture. They don't understand what urban youth is wearing, what it is doing. They don't understand the music. They don't understand the words of the songs these young people are listening to. They say that the members of this cohort are earning so little money, there's no point in trying to sell to them. Better, they say, to go after the more lucrative markets—the boomers, the people in their prime earning years.

This is shortsighted thinking. When has it been advisable to completely ignore the opportunity to build credibility and presence in an entire market segment that is sure to, in the next two decades, become the principal consumer group within the entire United States? When has it been right to turn your back on an opportunity of that kind of scope? Is it a good idea to overlook the fact that the baby boomers, who are today our prime consumers, were not that long ago also misunderstood, disliked, and ignored? Yet that is exactly what some of today's mainstream marketers, corporate marketers especially, are still doing today. It represents one of the most extraordinary examples of mass corporate amnesia anyone could point to today.

—La Ron Batchelor, partner, Star Power

Mr. Batchelor has spoken volumes with these words. When we ignore today's urban, hip-hop youth segments because we don't understand them, or because they earn too little, we adopt the worst of ostrich thinking in regard to our emerging markets.

He is absolutely right—establishing brand loyalty in the urban segments is yet another of the imperatives we are exploring in this chap-

ter. Here are a few extra considerations to add to the compelling ones
he has just outlined:

- Selling to urban youth sells to more than urban youth. Have
  you visited the affluent suburbs and taken a good look at the
  kids of upscale, high-income parents? If so, you see that these
  upscale kids, for the most part, have adopted the style and
  music of inner-city and hip-hop youth. In today's America,
  urban styles drive the entire youth culture. In fact, it is a docu-
  mented reality that hip-hop styles sell more in the suburbs than
  in the inner cities.

  For that matter, have you visited Tokyo, Hamburg, or Paris
  lately and noticed that urban American style has also become
  the style of the most with-it, up-to-date young people there?
  Have you seen the youngsters there wearing dreadlocks,
  American-style street jeans, and other trappings of American
  urban life? Establishing your product or brand in youth-
  oriented American markets can be the key to success in many
  secondary—and often unexpected—lucrative endeavors. As
  America goes, so goes the world.
- Adherents of contemporary urban style spend large sums on
  clothing, music, entertainment, and other key areas. Despite
  their urban status, these consumers buy well beyond their
  means, and they are intensely brand loyal. We can't take them at
  face value. Their purchases seem to defy their incomes.

  Moreover, many consumers in their twenties and even early
  thirties are attuned to the youthful styles of the teen generation. Many young affluent urbanites, when they leave their
  offices for the day, listen to the new music, attend the new
  clubs, and wear the new clothes of urban youth. This segment
  has a lot of money; these people are about to enter their prime
  earning and spending years. We ignore them at our peril.
- The chances of a large rate of return are extraordinary.
  Individually, hip-hop inner-city kids may not have a lot of
  money to spend. But we must consider their aggregate buying
  power and their ability to make or break brands.

Some brands experienced remarkable windfalls by "speaking" to the youth-oriented urban marketplace. Tommy Hilfiger, a brand that not long ago spoke to yuppie Anglo consumers, had the courage to talk to urban youngsters after noticing their attraction to Hilfiger clothes. The results were historic: Hilfiger entered the international marketplace. Also consider the Coach brand of products—or Timberland or Polo. Who would have predicted that hip-hop kids would suddenly flock to this brand of upscale leather products that seemingly only upscale professionals might like? Again, the results speak for themselves.

A small effort to build credibility for young and style-conscious consumers can produce many benefits, even sudden windfalls of opportunity.

How do you do it?

- Use highly targeted delivery media. Street marketing is a technique that takes products "to the street" to urban youth. Many companies now offer this kind of marketing service, which sends product-promoting vans to the areas where urban kids spend their time and dollars. Urban kids are hired to distribute samples, give demonstrations, and talk to the new consumers where they live. Again, this kind of marketing vehicle might be one you do not understand—but does that mean you should overlook it?
- Make good use of youth-oriented print media. It may come as a surprise to you, but a relatively new hip-hop magazine called *The Source* is now the number one magazine in America in newsstand sales. Not *People*, not *Time*, not *Forbes*, but *The Source*. Another success story is a magazine called *Vibe*—often called the bible of hip-hop music and fashion. There are others, too, and we should all get to know them. First, they serve as a formidable tool for understanding urban youth—whom they listen to, what they wear, what they are thinking. Second, they offer another opportunity for highly targeted marketing to urban youth.

- Make use of urban radio. Listen to it, advertise on it. It is the gateway to the hip-hop marketplace.
- Let music serve as your gateway to this market. "The music is what drives this market segment," says La Ron Batchelor, and he is right. When you hire a hip-hop artist to promote your products—to appear in ads or onstage wearing your clothes, for instance—you can quickly establish credibility with this cohort.

Of course, building credibility with urban youth is not a one-shot thing. You can't have one artist appear in your clothes and expect consumers to flock to your door. As in any other marketing effort, your presence needs to be reinforced and built through a marketing mix that might include print ads, radio ads, promotions, event sponsorships, and the rest. Yet a truly formidable opportunity is there. Turning your back on urban culture because it seems alien, threatening, or strange can be a highly costly strategic blunder that can result in lost opportunity in the coming years.

Key #6—Transform Your Company Culture

Many companies, going into focus groups, say, "We have a Spanish-speaking executive right here in our company! He can translate the materials for us. He can go into our focus groups and let us know what is being said there."

Well, that might be a good idea. But there are bigger questions. Translation is not just a matter of moving words from one language to another. It's the culture. It is both a science and an art. Where marketing materials and questionnaires are involved, using just the right words in the right way can make all the difference in the quality of responses you are going to get. And is that person, even though he speaks Spanish, the right person to evaluate what is going on in the focus groups? Just because he speaks Spanish doesn't mean he possesses the knowledge of an experienced market researcher.

Yet many marketers, where ethnic research is involved, take the easy way out. They say, "We can do it easily, on the cheap, because we have this Hispanic colleague [or this Japanese-American or this African-American] who will serve as our point of entry into this market. And we can save a lot of money."

—Richard Mascolo, president, Skunkworks

Well said, indeed! And the problems and the attitude that Mr. Mascolo's words reveal have implications and resonance in many marketing areas, not only market research.

Too many ethnic marketers seem painfully unwilling to confront their own lack of expertise about the markets they are reaching. Some astonishing statements have been made over the years that reflect this myopic thinking:

- "Black consumers are just dark-skinned white people."
- "This is America. We speak English. Latinos watch the same TV programs as everyone else, so why do we need specialized marketing to reach them?"
- "Hispanics and whites use laundry detergent to wash their clothes. So why do they need to hear a different kind of marketing message in order to make the same buying decision?"
- "Let's just dub our current general-market TV commercials in Spanish. They've worked well for us in the general marketplace. What's the big deal?"
- "Isn't America supposed to be a melting pot? When did we stop melting?"

Addressing the new multicultural marketplace, however, requires the courage to set aside many of our most cherished perceptions, prejudices, and beliefs. Dubbing ads into Spanish might work well. But some research to assess that assumption is vital before taking the plunge. After all, the wrong kind of ad can do damage—and it is very difficult to regain the allegiance of a consumer group once it has been lost.

Yes, both blacks and whites use detergent to wash their clothes. Yet research shows that these groups base their buying decisions on quite different criteria. There are no easy answers.

The bottom line is it is often necessary to spend money to hire an advertising agency with demonstrated expertise in addressing the ethnic markets. That can take the courage to doubt yourself and question the techniques that have worked reliably for you in the past.

Whether you are starting focus groups or drumming up creative ad concepts, you need to take not just easy or cost-cutting approaches but the *right* approaches. If marketing to the new, culturally diverse America is worth doing, it is worth doing well. A dollar effectively spent today can repay you with many more tomorrow.

Key #7—Obtain Expert Help

I have seen so many cases where an ad generated for African-Americans is just plain wrong. Sometimes, it is downright offensive, completely overlooking some area of sensitivity among the people it is trying to address. But more often, the problems are more subtle than that. Many ads simply fall flat with the intended target audience because they are nonresonant with the target audience—with the beliefs, style of making buying decisions, family values, motivations, lifestyles. All such questions could be resolved if the marketers in question had the courage to go to agencies with demonstrated expertise in addressing the market segments they want to reach.

I hope that, in your book, you are not only going to tell readers how to do things themselves. I also hope that you intend to point out the necessity of getting some expert help where the ethnic markets are concerned. Because the fact is, people who have been doing this kind of advertising for years have a body of knowledge—and a sense of the pitfalls—that can save a lot of money, and mistakes, in the end.

—Verdia Johnson, president, Footsteps, the ethnic
marketing division of Omnicom

The costs of ethnic marketing are not inherently greater than the costs of any other kind of marketing—research, creative, and the rest. In fact, it is more cost-efficient. But the money to be spent must be separate and earmarked for multicultural efforts alone.

Ms. Johnson is right. The very agency that has done right by you in creating ads for white consumers probably lacks the sensitivity and expertise you need to penetrate the African-, Hispanic-, or Asian-Pacific-American markets. A dollar spent obtaining the right kind of expertise can often go farther than the same dollar spent on advice from an agency with only limited knowledge of the constituency you are addressing.

As mentioned earlier, it is often essential to confront and question your own beliefs and experience where ethnic marketing is in question. That principle holds equally true in regard to areas where your money is to be spent—on the market-research firm, ad agency, diversity recruiter, and the rest. The entities who served you so effectively in the past might not be equally equipped to bring you success with ethnic and minority consumers.

Key #8—Understand Your Media

Not every dollar spent on a print ad is the same, for many reasons. The whole question is highly complex. Consider my observation that African-Americans, who of course read everything from the *New York Times* to *People* to *Time*, don't base their world outlook on what those publications say. They read those publications for information, but they read African-American publications to help form their opinions on key issues that are confronting them. So it is logical to believe, by extension, that the power of the ad you place in the *New York Times* versus the one you place in *Ebony* is going to be quite different, both qualitatively and in terms of the return you might expect. So might an ad you place in the *Amsterdam News* in New York.

Oh, you will look at circulation figures and determine that such and such a number of Asian-Americans or African-Americans or Asian-Pacific consumers will see your ad in such and such publications. Yet unless you get beneath the surface and look at the intangible extra considerations of the media you choose, you are not going to understand the potential effectiveness of your efforts.

—Advertising agency executive who wished to be quoted anonymously

People do use media in different ways. And easy assumptions can be very misleading where minority and ethnic segments are being addressed.

- "I can reach Chinese-American consumers through an ad in a Chinese-language newspaper," a marketer opines. She is right, of course. Putting an ad in that newspaper will reach Chinese-Americans. Yet will it reach the kind of Chinese-American customers the marketer is trying to address?

Probing into the question of who reads which kind of media will reveal, for example, that the Chinese-Americans who read in-language newspapers are predominantly recent immigrants and older Chinese-Americans. If you expect your ad to reach affluent, professional Chinese-Americans in their prime buying years, your ad in a Chinese newspaper will substantially fail to do so. Middle-class, middle-aged Chinese-Americans are principally consumers of English-language print media.

- "I can motivate African-Americans to buy my cars by putting an ad in *Black Enterprise*," says an automobile manufacturer. Yes, he probably can. Yet, to understand just how well the ad might do placed there, more needs to be known about a diverse range of factors, including the buying patterns of African-Americans regarding automobiles (they individually buy more luxury cars, on average, than white consumers); demographic information about the magazine's readership; even, if possible, the success that makers of various kinds of cars have achieved through ads in *Black Enterprise*.

You might also need to go into your focus groups to ask groups of African-American consumers such questions as

- "Here's my ad. Would you respond to it favorably if you were to see it in *Black Enterprise*? In *Essence*? In the *Wall Street Journal*? Which publication would add the most credibility to my product? Which would motivate you most strongly to go to one of our showrooms for a test drive?"
- "You were invited here because you subscribe to *Black Enterprise*. Do you remember seeing ads for any of the following products or brands in that publication? Did any of those ads result in a decision to buy?" (A list of products for respondents to check should follow.) Such questions can help determine how readers use a publication's ads to make buying decisions—even whether they remember seeing a company's ads there.

- "You were invited here because you subscribe to *Black Enterprise*. What kind of car do you drive now? Was your decision to purchase that car based on . . . ?" (A list of responses for the respondent to check, such as "referral of friend," "saw ad," "previous ownership of this brand," should follow.)

Such research is required to understand how well your media will work for you. Questions such as "What do you read?" or "How many Asian-Pacific-Americans subscribe to your newspaper?" only scratch the surface. To get more from your ethnic marketing efforts, you need to dig deeper.

A Quick Disclaimer

In the chapters that follow we will by necessity make some generalizations about African-, Hispanic-, and Asian-Pacific-Americans. We know that generalizations are often open to attack, as well they should be.

When we say that African-Americans respond to "respect" in advertising, for example, we are stating a generality that may well overlook how many African-Americans think. Similarly, when we say that many Hispanic-Americans are family oriented and entrepreneurial, we fail to acknowledge the many, many Latinos who do not fit that mold.

We apologize for and acknowledge the fact that such abstractions fail to encompass many, many consumers. Yet for the big picture of these market segments to emerge in this book, we need to infer certain shared characteristics of each group.

Not all white Americans buy the same way and neither do members of the three constituencies we are exploring in this book.

CHAPTER Three

MARKETING TO AFRICAN-AMERICANS

We gather here on the eve of a new century, indeed a new millennium. It's a fitting time to reflect on whence we've come and where we're headed as a people. A century ago, black folk who migrated from southern farms to cities often lived in squalor. Our men were denied decent jobs and steered into menial labor. Teenage girls were lured to the big city with bogus promises of work, only to be forced into prostitution, destitution and servitude. So the National Urban League was founded in 1910 to lead the struggle for social and economic opportunity for urban blacks.

A century ago, Jim Crow confined our families—and our dreams—to urban ghettos and rural backwaters that were wracked with poverty and bereft of hope.

Segregation blocked every escape route. We were barred from the voting booth and restaurants. Marauding white thugs lynched our young men and burned crosses in our yards. That's why, in 1909, the NAACP [National Association for the Advancement of Colored People] was formed to spearhead the fight for equal rights.

In the nineteenth century, we shed the shackles of slavery. This century, we whipped Jim Crow in many realms of American life. We won the right to vote, the right to eat and shop wherever we want, the right to live anywhere we can afford. So the last two centuries laid down the foundation of basic freedom.

It's clear from all the statistics that we're making steady progress. Unemployment and poverty recently hit record lows. Out-of-wedlock births have dipped to the lowest level in four decades. Household

income and homeownership rates have reached all-time highs. The earnings of many low-wage workers are rising again, while the black middle class has more than doubled in the last generation.

The racism that locked millions of our young men out of the job market for years is dissolving slowly. Employers are laying out the welcome mat
because they need eager workers and our young men are eager to work.

Businesses that abandoned inner cities a generation ago are scrambling
to open up shop and capture a share of these rediscovered urban markets.

You may remember that movie called *Cotton Comes to Harlem*. Well,
the sequel today would be titled *Home Depot Comes to Harlem*.

> —from "Destination: The American Dream," the
> keynote address delivered by Hugh B. Price,
> president, National Urban League, at the eighty-
> ninth Annual Urban League Conference,
> Houston, Texas, August 9, 1999[1]

When this nation's current minorities eventually become the majority,
ignoring the rules of marketing to the new America will not be an
option. It's best to get started building your base right now.

African-Americans are today's dominant ethnic group. There are
currently over 34 million African-American consumers (see Table 3.1),
and this number is expected to grow at a rate of 44 percent over the next
twenty-five years—doubling the projected growth rate of nonethnic

**Table 3.1 Estimates of the Total Population and African-American
Population of the United States and States, 1990 and 1999**

Area	Total Population in 1990	Total African-American Population in 1990	Total Population in 1999	Total African-American Population in 1999
United States	249,397,990	30,598,109	272,423,443	34,892,050
Alabama	4,048,317	1,023,407	4,391,822	1,134,180
Alaska	553,102	22,991	633,763	24,904
Arizona	3,679,370	115,711	4,784,307	172,734
Arkansas	2,354,301	375,346	2,596,749	412,613
California	29,901,421	2,302,639	32,435,218	2,377,770
Colorado	3,304,004	136,702	4,075,261	182,894
Connecticut	3,288,975	282,619	3,279,105	312,067

1. Reproduced with permission from Hugh B. Price, president, National Urban League.

Area	Total Population in 1990	Total African-American Population in 1990	Total Population in 1999	Total African-American Population in 1999
Delaware	669,071	114,137	756,190	145,802
District of Columbia	603,792	399,097	522,624	322,496
Florida	13,018,496	1,792,915	15,045,138	2,324,281
Georgia	6,506,509	1,761,503	7,758,907	2,230,942
Hawaii	1,112,646	27,867	1,223,955	36,964
Idaho	1,011,904	3,540	1,297,421	7,651
Illinois	11,446,801	1,710,695	11,977,943	1,837,820
Indiana	5,555,019	435,309	5,985,033	496,560
Iowa	2,779,652	48,531	2,885,631	58,513
Kansas	2,480,630	145,108	2,633,180	160,676
Kentucky	3,692,529	264,792	3,964,108	287,825
Louisiana	4,217,362	1,300,713	4,398,995	1,433,239
Maine	1,231,284	5,206	1,253,513	5,729
Maryland	4,797,676	1,202,070	5,210,222	1,458,235
Massachusetts	6,018,305	328,142	6,167,126	403,850
Michigan	9,310,677	1,302,381	9,671,908	1,401,890
Minnesota	4,387,209	96,632	4,791,064	145,986
Mississippi	2,577,213	917,021	2,786,922	1,013,571
Missouri	5,126,241	551,563	5,488,053	621,000
Montana	799,826	2,425	926,357	3,216
Nebraska	1,580,648	58,033	1,693,860	69,709
Nevada	1,218,702	81,458	1,810,356	136,449
New Hampshire	1,111,861	7,374	1,208,179	8,657
New Jersey	7,739,502	1,069,466	8,125,939	1,209,470
New Mexico	1,520,039	31,759	1,819,483	47,266
New York	18,002,719	3,071,062	18,194,553	3,262,136
North Carolina	6,657,040	1,469,587	7,674,793	1,708,201
North Dakota	637,369	3,543	657,282	5,585
Ohio	10,861,875	1,162,475	11,271,070	1,306,516
Oklahoma	3,147,095	236,262	3,358,324	267,829
Oregon	2,858,757	47,459	3,359,612	63,154
Pennsylvania	11,895,491	1,107,973	12,133,727	1,195,589
Rhode Island	1,004,665	43,446	993,984	50,495
South Carolina	3,498,970	1,045,811	3,808,829	1,147,738
South Dakota	696,636	3,294	760,896	6,171
Tennessee	4,890,621	782,351	5,560,645	920,546
Texas	17,046,399	2,056,802	19,974,760	2,486,466
Utah	1,729,784	12,139	2,152,892	18,890
Vermont	564,489	1,977	608,011	3,500
Virginia	6,213,684	1,174,475	6,902,643	1,393,611
Washington	4,901,289	154,152	5,788,516	196,713
West Virginia	1,792,429	56,423	1,833,457	58,204
Wisconsin	4,902,197	248,005	5,282,728	309,556
Wyoming	453,397	3,721	508,392	6,187

Sources: Estimates for 1990 were obtained from the U.S. Census Bureau (Internet release date: December 18, 1997). Estimates for 1999 were prepared by the Selig Center for Economic Growth, Terry College of Business, University of Georgia, 1998.

Americans. African-Americans alone will account for 30 percent of the total U.S. population growth through 2005. And nearly 50 percent of African-American consumers can be considered middle class (up from 16 percent in 1990). The sheer magnitude of these numbers testifies that the African-American marketplace offers significant opportunity for businesses that are willing to address them directly.

Wielding a staggering annual buying power, the African-American market is the fastest-growing economic segment in the U.S. economy. Over the past decade, African-Americans have demonstrated a remarkable increase in spending power. Although the group as a whole has not achieved parity with nonethnic consumers in disposable income or per capita spending, African-Americans have been responsible for a share of retail sales growth well exceeding their percentage of the population in significant retail categories, including new car purchases, household appliances, apparel, personal products, and the purchase of food away from home. The growth rate of African-Americans purchasing new cars is twelve times the growth rate of non-African-American purchasers over the last decade. The latest figures also show African-American per capita spending is virtually equal to non-African-American spending in the major household appliance, furniture, and grocery categories. Additionally, along with their buying power, these consumers have new saving power and are rapidly becoming an attractive new market for financial services.

This indicates a tremendously viable market segment that is strong today and poised for enormous growth in the future. The African-American marketplace profile in brief:

- There are 259,000 households with an annual income of $100,000—a threefold increase since 1994.
- It is the largest ethnic group in America, with 33,000,000 people.
- In deciding where to do business, the number one reason is competitive pricing; the number two reason is "respect."
- The most lucrative African-American markets are centered in Atlanta, Baltimore, Chicago, Dallas–Fort Worth, Detroit, Los Angeles, Miami, New York, Oakland, Philadelphia, and Washington, D.C.

- African-Americans have larger households. The average number of persons in an African-American household is 3.5, compared with 3.2 for the total U.S. population.
- African-Americans are a youthful market segment. The average age of African-Americans is 29, compared to 34 for the total U.S. population.

What MCAD Tells Us About Marketing to African-Americans

As discussed earlier, the Multicultural American Dream (MCAD) Index was a groundbreaking study presented to the White House. Based on data from the U.S. Census Bureau and other government sources, as well as the National Center for Education Statistics, MCAD reveals the astounding rate at which Asian-Pacific-, Hispanic-, and African-Americans are accessing the means to prosperity.

These consumers are increasing their household incomes, obtaining mortgages, owning small businesses, and earning college degrees at a rate that's growing *two to three times as fast as that of nonethnic Americans*.[2] If current trends continue, MCAD predicts that ethnic Americans will achieve proportional economic parity with nonethnic Americans by the year 2007, or sooner.

Yet what does MCAD tell us specifically about the growth of the African-American market segment?

- **Mortgage Originations**
  African-Americans are obtaining new mortgages in increasing numbers. The growth rate of new mortgage originations among African-Americans is four times faster than that of the rest of the population and is on a par with new mortgage originations among Hispanic-Americans.

---

2. MCAD demonstrates that the new ethnic market growth is based on more than just population growth in ethnic segments. It is based on an analysis of four categories of economic indicators: median household income, home ownership (represented by the number of mortgage originations), small-business ownership, and education (based on numbers obtaining college degrees).

- **Small-Business Ownership**
  In 1996, there were 24.7 million small businesses in America.
  Of these, nearly three million were owned by minorities. In
  that year, 28 percent (816,295) of minority-owned small businesses were in the hands of African-Americans. In comparison,
  Hispanic-Americans owned 45 percent (1,342,426) of
  minority-owned small enterprises. And the rate at which
  African-Americans are starting or acquiring small businesses is
  increasing at five times the rate among the white American
  population. The MCAD projects that minorities will own half
  of all American businesses by the year 2007.

- **Higher Education**
  In 1996, African-Americans obtained 40 percent of all degrees
  of higher learning, including Associate, undergraduate, and
  postgraduate. In all, 181,613 African-Americans obtained such
  degrees, compared to 2,197,023 for the general population and
  416,345 among all minorities. The growth rate for obtaining
  postsecondary degrees among African-Americans is increasing
  at a rate five times faster than among the general population.
      The percentage of ethnic Americans who are obtaining
  postsecondary degrees is increasing at a rate three and a half
  times greater than for white Americans. (MCAD projects that
  in 2005, ethnic Americans will be obtaining as many postsecondary degrees as white Americans.)

- **Median Household Income**
  Overall, minorities' median household income is growing faster
  than that of white Americans, and there are significant differences among minorities. The income of African-Americans
  (and Hispanic-Americans) lags behind whites' median household income significantly, while Asian-Pacific-Americans'
  median household income is far higher. However, the median
  household income for African-Americans is increasing at the
  rate of 4.54 percent annually, in contrast to 2.83 percent for
  white Americans and 3.54 percent for all minorities. And even
  more significantly, MCAD projects that the median household

income of both white Americans and African-Americans will equalize by the year 2025, at about $80,000.

So, to summarize

- African-Americans and other minorities are attaining the American Dream at a faster rate than white Americans.
- If current growth rates continue, African-Americans are well on their way to attaining parity in the American Dream.
- The growth in participation in the American Dream and consumer spending is being driven not by population increases but by increased participation and spending.

Demographic Outline and Economic Power: Findings from the University of Georgia's Terry College of Business

We are grateful to the Terry College of Business at the University of Georgia and, most especially, to their discerning demographic expert, Dr. Jeffrey M. Humphreys, for granting us permission to present here selected graphs, tables, and other portions of the groundbreaking study, "African-American Buying Power by Place of Residence: 1990–1999."

> As African-Americans increase in number and purchasing power, their share of the U.S. consumer market draws more and more attention from producers and retailers alike. The black buying power estimates . . . suggest that one general advertisement or product geared for all consumers misses many potentially profitable market opportunities. As the consumer market becomes more diverse, advertising, products, and media must be tailored to each market segment. With this in mind, entrepreneurs, marketing specialists, economic development organizations, and area chambers of commerce all have sought estimates of black buying power. Going beyond the intuitive approaches often used, such estimates provide a timely, cost-efficient, and quantitative way to assess the size of . . . African-American markets.

> Simply defined, black buying power is the total personal income of black residents that is available, after taxes, for spending on goods and

services—the disposable personal income of the black residents of a specified geographic area. Unfortunately, geographically precise data reflecting annual expenditure and income surveys of African-Americans are
unavailable, and even estimates of black buying power are difficult to
find, especially for individual states.

> —Dr. Jeffrey M. Humphreys, "African-American
> Buying Power by Place of Residence: 1990–1999"

Dr. Humphreys's study offers the following information:

- The University of Georgia's Selig Center projects that the
  nation's African-American buying power will have risen from
  $308 billion in 1990 to $533 billion in 1999, up by 72.9 percent
  in nine years at a compound annual rate of growth of 6.3 percent (see Tables 3.2 and 3.3).
- This percentage gain far outstrips both the 56.7 percent increase
  projected for total buying power, the 55.3 percent increase projected for nominal gross domestic product, and the 14 percent
  increase projected in the African-American population.
- The U.S. Consumer Price Index will increase 28.7 percent during this same period, but African-American buying power will
  grow more than two and a half times as fast as inflation.
  Substantially above-average growth in African-American buying
  power demonstrates the growing importance of African-
  American consumers and should create tremendous opportunities for businesses that pay attention to African-American needs.
- Because of differences in per capita income, wealth, demographics, and culture, the spending habits of African-Americans

**Table 3.2 African-American Buying Power by Place of Residence for
United States and States, 1990 and 1995–1999 (millions of dollars)**

Area	1990	1995	1996	1997	1998	1999
United States	308,096	422,164	450,130	475,137	501,983	532,667
Alabama	7,824	11,012	11,695	12,189	12,737	13,398
Alaska	303	374	373	386	399	419
Arizona	1,161	1,853	2,052	2,220	2,399	2,602
Arkansas	2,565	3,626	3,908	4,072	4,250	4,449

Area	1990	1995	1996	1997	1998	1999
California	27,528	33,441	35,262	36,961	38,839	40,925
Colorado	1,617	2,460	2,641	2,820	3,003	3,206
Connecticut	3,673	4,720	4,996	5,361	5,718	6,127
Delaware	1,285	1,874	2,054	2,185	2,337	2,485
District of Columbia	5,485	6,232	6,406	6,562	6,716	6,920
Florida	15,487	23,001	25,041	26,708	28,641	30,686
Georgia	15,710	23,497	25,484	27,248	28,714	30,374
Hawaii	342	533	553	565	587	617
Idaho	36	81	87	94	101	108
Illinois	17,376	23,536	25,015	26,309	27,714	29,389
Indiana	4,325	6,078	6,444	6,748	7,078	7,453
Iowa	450	646	710	752	797	856
Kansas	1,432	1,895	2,010	2,116	2,237	2,379
Kentucky	2,345	3,169	3,379	3,555	3,745	3,969
Louisiana	9,238	13,174	13,963	14,615	15,232	15,966
Maine	61	77	86	89	93	97
Maryland	15,989	21,926	23,463	24,884	26,305	27,939
Massachusetts	4,052	5,729	6,143	6,640	7,154	7,687
Michigan	13,733	18,958	19,886	20,726	21,676	22,887
Minnesota	968	1,574	1,755	1,888	2,050	2,236
Mississippi	5,719	8,373	9,016	9,376	9,774	10,248
Missouri	5,629	7,719	8,270	8,723	9,197	9,771
Montana	22	36	39	39	41	42
Nebraska	563	776	856	914	970	1,039
Nevada	863	1,505	1,680	1,819	1,974	2,131
New Hampshire	107	141	154	163	172	184
New Jersey	13,973	18,539	19,613	20,709	22,003	23,375
New Mexico	297	502	543	572	609	656
New York	37,398	48,429	51,388	54,173	57,306	60,906
North Carolina	13,157	18,771	20,145	21,388	22,618	24,123
North Dakota	34	48	56	64	73	85
Ohio	11,859	16,286	17,254	18,083	19,071	20,287
Oklahoma	1,980	2,650	2,816	2,978	3,124	3,284
Oregon	437	658	725	780	842	913
Pennsylvania	12,114	15,926	16,913	17,764	18,758	19,789
Rhode Island	449	596	634	675	749	768
South Carolina	8,168	11,120	11,807	12,431	13,097	13,825
South Dakota	35	56	68	78	89	103
Tennessee	6,960	10,267	10,875	11,451	12,055	12,762
Texas	18,629	26,726	28,647	30,583	32,860	35,273
Utah	114	198	221	241	261	282
Vermont	20	42	48	49	51	53
Virginia	12,208	16,933	18,040	19,012	19,893	21,137
Washington	1,836	2,757	3,021	3,231	3,451	3,673
West Virginia	504	655	684	706	743	778
Wisconsin	1,999	2,934	3,156	3,377	3,633	3,916
Wyoming	39	52	55	65	76	89

Source: Selig Center for Economic Growth, Terry College of Business, University of Georgia, 1998

Table 3.3 Percentage Change in African-American Buying Power and Rank of Percentage Change, 1990–1999, by State

Area	Percentage Change in Total Buying Power 1990–99	Rank*	Area	Percentage Change in Total Buying Power 1990–99	Rank*
United States	72.9	—	Missouri	73.6	28
Alabama	71.3	33	Montana	95.1	16
Alaska	38.4	50	Nebraska	84.6	22
Arizona	124.0	9	Nevada	147.0	6
Arkansas	73.4	29	New Hampshire	71.0	36
California	48.7	49	New Jersey	67.3	40
Colorado	98.3	13	New Mexico	120.8	10
Connecticut	66.8	41	New York	62.9	46
Delaware	93.3	17	North Carolina	83.3	24
District of Columbia	26.2	51	North Dakota	149.4	4
Florida	98.1	14	Ohio	71.1	35
Georgia	93.3	18	Oklahoma	65.9	44
Hawaii	80.1	25	Oregon	109.1	11
Idaho	200.5	1	Pennsylvania	63.3	45
Illinois	69.1	39	Rhode Island	71.2	34
Indiana	72.3	32	South Carolina	69.3	38
Iowa	90.3	19	South Dakota	194.7	2
Kansas	66.1	43	Tennessee	83.4	23
Kentucky	69.3	37	Texas	89.3	21
Louisiana	72.8	31	Utah	147.5	5
Maine	58.3	47	Vermont	163.0	3
Maryland	74.7	27	Virginia	73.1	30
Massachusetts	89.7	20	Washington	100.0	12
Michigan	66.7	42	West Virginia	54.5	48
Minnesota	131.1	7	Wisconsin	95.9	15
Mississippi	79.2	26	Wyoming	129.9	8

*Ranked from largest to smallest percentage change
Source: Selig Center for Economic Growth, Terry College of Business, University of Georgia, 1998

as a group are not the same as those of average U.S. consumers. The most recent Consumer Expenditure Survey carried out by the U.S. Bureau of Labor Statistics (based on data from 1995) indicates that African-American households spent only about 74 percent as much as average U.S. households and spent a higher proportion of their after-tax income on goods and services. The values are based on money income, which differs somewhat from total buying power, but nonetheless offers some insights into spending by African-American consumers.

- Despite their lower average income levels, African-American households spent more on apparel, telephone services, and natural gas than average U.S. households. African-Americans also spent a higher proportion of their after-tax income on housing, electricity, transportation, and food eaten at home. Yet they spent a lower percentage of their income on personal insurance and pensions, eating out, health care, and household furnishings.
- The Consumer Expenditure Survey indicates that 56 percent of African-American households are renters, compared to 36 percent of all households.
- African-Americans spend about the same proportion of their incomes as the overall population on many goods and services, including household operations, housekeeping supplies, alcoholic beverages, tobacco products, personal care products, and cash contributions. Combined with the relatively rapid growth of African-American buying power, such differences and similarities should provide many marketing opportunities to those targeting the African-American consumer.
- Among the diverse forces supporting the substantial and continued growth of African-American buying power, perhaps the most important is the increased number of jobs across the nation. Employment opportunities have improved for everyone, including African-Americans. The U.S. Census Bureau indicates that, in the past decade, the gap in high school completions between African-Americans and whites in the 25-to-29-year-old age group narrowed to the point where there was no statistical difference in 1997. The same report indicated that only about 13 percent of African-Americans are college graduates, compared to 25 percent for whites and 42 percent for Asian-Pacific-Americans.
- Advances in educational attainment will give African-Americans the credentials and skills needed to enter occupations and fill jobs where earnings are higher. At the same time, the increasing number of African-Americans who are successfully starting and expanding their own businesses also contributes to the gains in buying power. Favorable demographic

**Figure 3.1   Projected African-American Buying Power in the United
States, 1999 (percentage distribution)**

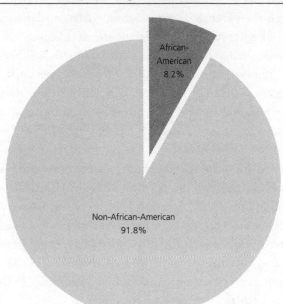

Source: Selig Center for Economic Growth, Terry College of Business, University of Georgia, 1998

trends are reinforcing these positive economic forces, as the
African-American population continues to grow more rapidly
than the total population.

- In 1999, the nation's share of total African-American buying
  power was 8.2 percent, up from 7.4 percent in 1990 (see Figure
  3.1). The group's year-to-year gains in buying power vary
  somewhat but remain substantial for each period. Annual gains
  ranged from 5.1 percent in 1991 to a peak of 8.3 percent in
  1995, and rose slightly in 1999 (6.1 percent) compared to 1998
  (5.7 percent). In each year, the percentage gain in African-
  American buying power has, or will, exceed the rate of growth
  in buying power for all consumers as a whole.
- Estimates of the absolute size and rate of growth of African-
  American markets are firm indications of market potential. In

1999, the ten states with the largest African-American markets, in order, were New York, California, Texas, Florida, Georgia, Illinois, Maryland, North Carolina, New Jersey, and Michigan. In order, the top ten states ranked by the rate of growth of African-American buying power during 1990–1999 were Idaho, South Dakota, Vermont, North Dakota, Utah, Nevada, Minnesota, Wyoming, Arizona, and New Mexico. All of these states have small but flourishing markets. No state appears on both top ten lists, but Florida and Georgia are among the nation's largest markets and, according to rates of growth, ranked fourteenth and eighteenth, respectively. The combination of size and growth rate makes these two states particularly attractive and dynamic markets.

- In order, the ten states (including the District of Columbia) with the largest shares of total African-American buying power are the District of Columbia, Mississippi, Maryland, Louisiana, South Carolina, Georgia, Alabama, North Carolina, Virginia, and Delaware (see Figure 3.2).
- Nationally, African-American consumers' share of the market increased from 7.4 percent in 1990 to 8.2 percent in 1999, a 0.8 percentage-point gain (see Table 3.4). Although the share of buying power controlled by African-American consumers will rise in every state, Maryland, Louisiana, Delaware, Georgia, Mississippi, Virginia, Florida, New York, New Jersey, and Alabama will experience the largest increases in market share.
- Measuring from the lowest rate, the ten states with the slowest growth of African-American buying power during 1990–1999 were the District of Columbia, Alaska, California, West Virginia, Maine, New York, Pennsylvania, Oklahoma, Kansas, and Michigan. The list is not surprising, since total buying power also is growing slowly in many of these states.
- The ten states with the smallest African-American markets, basically a result of their small African-American populations, are Montana, Vermont, North Dakota, Wyoming, Maine, South Dakota, Idaho, New Hampshire, Utah, and Alaska. The spending power of African-American consumers nevertheless is

**Figure 3.2   Ten States with the Highest Percentage of Total Buying
Power That Is African-American, 1999**

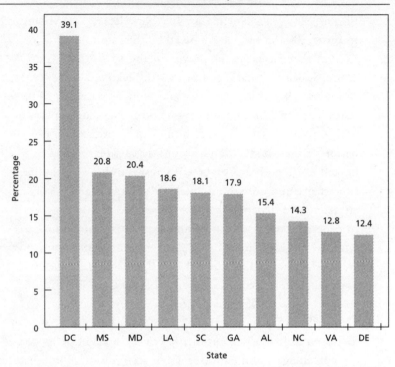

Source: Selig Center for Economic Growth, Terry College of Business, University of Georgia, 1998

blossoming in six of these markets: Idaho, South Dakota,
Vermont, North Dakota, Utah, and Wyoming.

Learning the Rules

Those are remarkable figures about the massive economic clout of
African-American consumers and, by extension, their viability as eager
consumers and participants in the American Dream.

However, one important point must be kept in mind. Marketing
to the African-American audience differs significantly from marketing
to a general, mainstream audience. Marketers who ignore this crucial
reality do so at their own risk.

Table 3.4 African-American Share of Total Buying Power for United States and States, 1990 and 1999 (percent)

Area	1990	1999	Area	1990	1999
United States	7.4	8.2	Missouri	7.1	7.8
Alabama	14.2	15.4	Montana	0.2	0.2
Alaska	3.0	3.0	Nebraska	2.3	2.7
Arizona	2.2	2.6	Nevada	4.0	4.8
Arkansas	8.7	9.1	New Hampshire	0.5	0.6
California	5.0	5.0	New Jersey	8.4	9.5
Colorado	2.9	3.3	New Mexico	1.5	2.0
Connecticut	4.9	5.7	New York	10.6	11.8
Delaware	10.4	12.4	North Carolina	13.6	14.3
District of Columbia	41.7	39.1	North Dakota	0.4	0.6
Florida	7.0	8.4	Ohio	6.9	7.8
Georgia	15.8	17.9	Oklahoma	4.6	5.2
Hawaii	1.7	2.1	Oregon	1.0	1.2
Idaho	0.3	0.5	Pennsylvania	6.0	6.7
Illinois	8.6	9.3	Rhode Island	2.6	3.2
Indiana	5.2	5.7	South Carolina	17.1	18.1
Iowa	1.1	1.3	South Dakota	0.4	0.6
Kansas	3.7	4.0	Tennessee	9.7	10.5
Kentucky	4.8	5.1	Texas	7.1	7.7
Louisiana	16.5	18.6	Utah	0.5	0.7
Maine	0.3	0.4	Vermont	0.2	0.4
Maryland	17.4	20.4	Virginia	11.3	12.8
Massachusetts	3.4	4.3	Washington	2.2	2.5
Michigan	9.1	9.8	West Virginia	2.2	2.3
Minnesota	1.3	2.0	Wisconsin	2.7	3.3
Mississippi	19.1	20.8	Wyoming	0.6	0.9

Source: Selig Center for Economic Growth, Terry College of Business, University of Georgia, 1998

Advertising to an African-American audience requires new thinking and new approaches. Mainly because of the language similarities, mainstream marketers seem to think that slipping African-American or other ethnic faces into what are otherwise traditional ad campaigns will do the trick and court African-American consumers. Such advertisers may be in for a rude awakening.

Marketing messages targeted to African-Americans require an elevated level of cultural awareness, otherwise the messages risk reinforcing ethnic stereotypes and alienating the very consumers they are intended to persuade. Consider, for instance, a traditional ad execution for a personal deodorant showing a young man running late for work, or an ad for a household cleaner featuring a housewife battling a messy kitchen.

As another example, a broadcast execution and print version that features a group of black women who are all plus sizes or who are all light skinned can inadvertently turn off a target audience that resists being generalized. Ads that overlook the diversity of shades and sizes within the African-American community can trigger responses such as, "You don't really understand African-Americans . . . you haven't taken the time to get to know me." Dropping in an African-American face could set off alarms about old racial stereotypes. It is a matter of plain common sense to realize that cultural orientation profoundly influences how certain messages are received.

African-Americans, after all, are a very media-savvy group. They are not only heavy consumers of broadcast media but discerning consumers as well. Media analysts have observed that, in contrast to more general audiences, African-Americans have a heightened sensitivity about whether the advertising messages aimed at them are authentic or not.

One certainty? It's important for African-Americans to see themselves in ads. Seventy percent of African-Americans say they're more likely to respond to an advertisement or an endorsement from an African-American actor or celebrity. But African-American faces alone are not enough. An execution that displays ignorance of cultural nuances or motivators can easily backfire.

This sense of awareness extends to media placement as well. Consider the top ten television programs watched by African-Americans versus those watched by all others. Only one show is common to both groups.

Building a solid relationship with African-American consumers requires a targeted media approach. Marketers must make commitments to broadcast and print media that offer a special relevance to the African-American community, rather than hoping to succeed by just throwing media weight at them or incorporating African-American consumers in broad-based media plans.

Hallmark's Mahogany brand is a good example. Hallmark launched its Mahogany line of greeting cards in 1987 with sixteen styles of cards. By 1997, they had sold over 800 card styles to an 80 percent African-American base. One reason for their success? Credibility. They've made it a point to hire African-American artists, editors, and authors, and they advertise their Mahogany brand in African-American media.

A Question of Respect

When confronted with such issues, some short-sighted marketers are apt to bristle. "African-Americans are too sensitive," they say. "Why should my marketing plan for African-Americans be so radically different from my other work? I don't need a separate plan for Italian-Americans or Irish-Americans. We're all Americans, aren't we?"

African-Americans *are* Americans—and by and large, they are proud of it. But they are also keenly protective of their cultural heritage and can be more suspicious of assimilation than other ethnic counterparts.

According to research conducted in 1996,

- Nearly 70 percent of African-Americans surveyed felt "the need to sustain ethnic traditions and symbols," as opposed to 46 percent of all other respondents.
- Seventy-eight percent of African-Americans believed "parents should pass on ethnic traditions," versus 62 percent of all others.
- Ninety percent of African-Americans agreed with the statement "I am proud of my ethnic heritage," compared to 78 percent of all others.

The key issue, however, can be summed up in one word, an attribute cherished by African-Americans: respect.

Respecting the consumer is a given in all marketing outreach, but it is even more vital when building a relationship with the African-American market. African-Americans have developed a finely tuned "radar" for media portrayals that lack an in-depth understanding of African-American culture, heritage, and institutions.

Doing Well by Doing Good

One of the best ways marketers can demonstrate their respect for the values of African-Americans is to support cause-related programs that help the communities where African-Americans reside—especially programs that honor or celebrate cultural heritage and pride of accomplishment.

Consider the success story of NationsBank. NationsBank has formed partnerships with key organizations, including the NAACP, 100 Black Men of America, Inc., and the United Negro College Fund, by supporting them with financial contributions. NationsBank regionally is considered number one among banks in the African-American community, building $100 million in new assets over the last three years.

African-Americans are highly responsive to organizations and efforts that give something back to the community, viewing such efforts as a gateway to mutual respect, rather than an attempt to exploit the market solely as a revenue opportunity.

It's not philanthropy but a simple economic formula: align with causes and events that strengthen the foundation of African-American communities. Do so in a manner that respects cultural heritage and values, and your company can gain the respect needed to forge the brand loyalty essential to long-term customer relationships. This is a win–win situation for all involved.

CASE STUDY: THE DIAHANN CARROLL LINE

At Stedman Graham & Partners, we were able to put all this theory into practice in 1997 when we helped introduce the Diahann Carroll brand of apparel for JCPenney. It was the first celebrity signature clothing line launched by and for an African-American woman.

It seemed natural to tie a new brand of women's clothing targeted to African-American women to Diahann Carroll, the first African-American woman to be the headliner on her own television show. With her elegance and celebrity, she was a good choice to be the first African-American woman to have her own line of women's clothing, too.

The objectives for the clothing line seemed to be a close match for Ms. Carroll's own style and image: elegant; dynamic, successful; making a statement; colorful, classy, high quality; and "effortless" style. To launch a new line of clothing as the Diahann Carroll brand—her own unique line of clothing, accessories, shoes, cosmetics, and even home furnishings—seemed a wonderful opportunity, positioning it as the brand of choice for African-American and other women aged 35–55, an expanding marketplace.

Ms. Carroll would be presented for what she really is, the height of African-American women's style and an example of success and leadership. In short, she is a woman who through her own sense of style, self-confidence, and talent was able to achieve and sustain a successful career. In her unique way, Ms. Carroll would serve to dignify and acknowledge the leadership role long assumed by women within African-American families and the community. According to the U.S. Census Bureau, many African-American households are headed by women. In fact, 48 percent of African-American households are headed by a woman, in contrast to 18 percent for the rest of the U.S. population.

Promotional elements of the product launch seemed to flow naturally from these concepts. Diahann Carroll "power" breakfasts were held near JCPenney stores in major African-American market areas. Local African-American organizations and targeted media became participants and cosponsors in these events. JCPenney customers participated in contests to win Diahann Carroll clothing.

Based on a "Style & Success" theme, people in different communities were invited to nominate women who were making a difference in their communities. These leaders were recognized in events surrounding the launch. Finally, the product launch was designed to be a natural and authentic extension of the concepts developed throughout the entire campaign: belief in African-American women, community involvement, and respect for the consumers we were trying to address.

Instead of renting out a lavish reception hall or launching the Diahann Carroll line in an established JCPenney store in the Midwest or in a suburb, we scheduled the line's gala debut at a newly opened JCPenney superstore in the Bronx, Diahann's hometown, located in a revitalized neighborhood that had long awaited the return of a major retail outlet to serve its growing needs. In essence, we took the event "home" and centered it in one of America's most established and revitalized African-American communities.

Although the event was attended by celebrities, we as organizers made certain to set aside time in the program to recognize members of the community—clergy, teachers, neighborhood leaders—whose contributions had made a significant difference in the lives of area residents.

The event was a celebration, not just an in-store promotion. With a sense of pride and participation, the community turned out to express its pride and enthusiasm for both itself and for its new store and its new product line. These actions helped elevate the event from just another glitzy party to a source of civic pride. JCPenney management termed this product launch the "best ever" in-store event in its history. The Carroll line quickly became the number one bestseller at key JCPenney urban locations, with millions in sales in 1999.

The right kind of activity, directed at the quickly expanding African-American market segment, is not only smart marketing but visionary marketing, too. It's an opportunity waiting to be tapped by any company looking toward the future.

Four

MARKETING TO HISPANIC-AMERICANS

In 1999, the immense buying power of 31 million Hispanic-Americans will energize the U.S. consumer market as never before. This major group, which comprises 11.4 percent of the country's population, will spend an estimated $383 billion on goods and services . . . Over the past nine years, the nation's Hispanic buying power has increased 84.4 percent (from $208 billion in 1990)—a percentage gain that is substantially greater than the 56.7 percent gain projected for total buying power . . .

> —Dr. Jeffrey M. Humphreys, University of
> Georgia's Terry College of Business, writing
> in *Georgia Business and Economic Conditions*,
> November–December 1998

Hispanic-Americans are a most familiar ethnic constituency; they have long been part of America's multiethnic fabric. Yet curiously, they may be the constituency that is least understood by mainstream corporate America. Coming to grips with this powerful market segment represents a clear mandate for American businesses that wish to succeed.

The Hispanic Country Within America

There were 37 million Hispanic-Americans in 1998, a population roughly equal to that of Canada. The U.S. Census Bureau projects a 25 percent growth rate for Hispanic-Americans over the next ten years.

That's in marked contrast to the growth rate for white Americans, which is projected to be *negative* 14.6 percent.

The population of Hispanic America is vast, and indeed it's expanding quickly. In fact, if all Hispanic-Americans resided in a single country, that country would be the *third-largest Spanish-speaking country in the world*.

Consider the following statistics:

Spanish-Speaking 1998 Populations (in millions)
Mexico, 99.1
Spain, 40.5
United States, 37.0
Colombia, 36.7
Argentina, 35.8
Peru, 25.3
Venezuela, 22.7
Chile, 14.9
Ecuador, 12.1
Cuba, 11.2

With 37 million constituents, ignoring the Hispanic-American market would be the rough equivalent of

- ignoring Austria, Switzerland, Belgium, and Portugal—35.2 million
- ignoring Poland—38.4 million
- ignoring Australia—18.4 million—twice

So the message is clear for alert businesses. The third-largest Spanish-speaking country in the world resides right here within our own boundaries. We understand this country better than other Spanish-speaking countries because *it is us*. We can sell to its citizens without dealing with foreign currencies or companies, distribution networks, tariffs, or customs concerns. And if we are involved in most categories of business—everything from packaged goods to apparel to retailing—the citizens of this "other country" are already our customers. Distribution channels and delivery systems to them are already in place and functional.

It would be difficult to think of another opportunity of this magnitude. Surely if we were to describe a country with the preceding characteristics—the size, accessibility, and so on—almost every business in America would jump at the opportunity to establish a presence there.

If your company isn't jumping at the chance to sell to that country, too, you are missing out on an opportunity of staggering potential.

An Opportunity for Advertisers

Of all our minority populations, and in contrast to African-Americans and Asian-Pacific-Americans, our Hispanic-American population is the easiest to access, embodying the potential for the greatest immediate return on investment, for several important reasons:

- Hispanic-Americans are already eager consumers, participating fully in the American lifestyle.
- Hispanic-Americans have larger households (with an average of 3.6 persons) than non-Hispanic-Americans (with an average of 2.6). So when you cement the loyalty of a Hispanic-American household, you establish more market share than you would by cementing the loyalty of other demographic segments.
- In addition, typical Hispanic-American heads of household are younger than those of white Americans and other segments. This means that Hispanic-American heads of household simply have more years to consume goods and services than their white, African-American, and Asian-Pacific-American counterparts. Establishing brand loyalty within this segment pays rich returns.
- Hispanic-Americans are younger on average than non-Hispanic-Americans. The average age of a Hispanic-American is 26. The average age of all Americans is 33. The message is, again, that brand loyalty of a Hispanic-American can translate into greater long-term profits. On average, that consumer will simply be on the scene longer to consume what you have to sell.
- Hispanic-Americans have chosen to live in certain highly specific cities and states (see Table 4.1). Smart businesses can direct their efforts in those regions, with a high degree of targeting.

Table 4.1 Hispanic-Americans Are Concentrated in Major U.S. Markets

Market	Hispanic-American Population	Percent Hispanic-American
Los Angeles	6,325,900	38.7
New York	3,645,100	18.1
Miami	1,422,600	38.1
San Francisco	1,243,000	18.4
Chicago	1,198,300	12.7
Houston	1,141,000	24.2
San Antonio	1,064,700	51.6
McAllen–Brownsville	823,700	89.5
Dallas–Fort Worth	786,900	14.9
San Diego	706,400	25.3

Sources: Market Statistics, Inc.; U.S. Census Bureau

- Hispanic–American media is a vibrant, established presence. From the Telemundo and Univision networks to Spanish-language radio to regional and national magazines and newspapers, abundant advertising vehicles can carry an advertising message to the heart of the Hispanic–American communities.

Few population segments represent a more viable market.

The promotional materials created by SiboneyUSA, a Hispanic-American advertising agency, state that Hispanic-Americans are the biggest, fastest-growing, most-concentrated, efficiently reached, advertising-friendly, consumer segment of all. That statement sums up the viability of the Hispanic–American consumer.

An In-Depth Look at Hispanic-Americans

Who are our Hispanic–American neighbors? Just like Americans of every heritage, they are made up of a varied and complex mosaic of people from many places. Statistically speaking, 63 percent of Hispanic-Americans have roots in Mexico, 15 percent in Central and South America, 11 percent in Puerto Rico, 5 percent in Cuba, and 6 percent in other Hispanic countries (see Figure 4.1). Each subgroup has its own distinct traits and profile that change every day as our Hispanic-American constituency grows both larger and more diverse.

Figure 4.1   Country of Origin of Hispanic-American Population, 1998

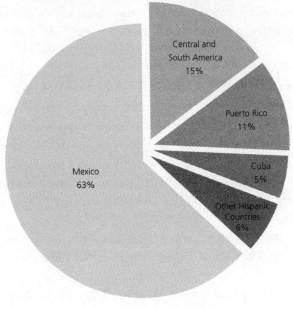

Source: U.S. Census Bureau

Here—with apologies for omissions—are some of the most notable members of our rich Hispanic-American tapestry.

Mexican-Americans for the most part can hardly be said to have "come here" at all. The reality is they "were here." As recently as 150 years ago, Mexico controlled the entire western region of our continent. Mexican-Americans are themselves a highly diverse constituency—both in terms of cultural background (ranging from Spanish aristocrats to native or "Indian" backgrounds) and socioeconomic power.

Puerto Ricans, our other group of Latino "elder statesmen," came to our mainland (to New York City, principally) during the 1950s and 1960s. Now entrenched in American society, many Puerto Ricans have already claimed their share of the American Dream, owning businesses, moving from inner cities into more upscale suburbs, and wielding considerable political influence. Our Puerto Rican neighbors are cobeneficiaries of life in an affluent America.

Cuban-Americans can largely be divided into two segments: those who arrived here during the 1950s, shortly after Fidel Castro came to power, and those who have come here more recently. The former group—characterized by success in business enterprises, patriotism to America, and political conservatism—is now an entrenched part of our cultural landscape. In contrast, more recent Cuban arrivals to our shores—ranging from Cubans who have been allowed to emigrate to the much-publicized boat people—tend to be more disadvantaged and have yet to establish a strong economic base on our shores. But given the ambition and stunning record of success established by their Cuban predecessors, their eventual success seems sure to follow, and more quickly than most of us might suspect.

Advantage-seeking Latinos from Central and South America (from countries as diverse as Peru, Panama, and Uruguay), motivated by political unrest and economic hardship, have been arriving on our shores, especially in the last few decades. This trend is likely to continue and increase with the stable state of the American economy.

As is the case with white Americans (encompassing many small subgroupings, such as Danes, Swiss, White Russians, and the rest), there is a varied but rich grouping of other Spanish-speaking constituencies—ranging from Spaniards to Argentinians whose families emigrated to America many years ago. This catchall grouping of "other" Latinos contains many fascinating gradations and subgradations. Many people of Polish heritage are in Argentina, for instance, as well as many people of Italian heritage. As immigrants to the United States, this last group of Hispanic-Americans considerably adds to the diversity of the Hispanic-American cultural and ethnic landscape.

Consider that these cities, whose names seem as American as apple pie, were named by Spanish settlers:

- Los Angeles
- San Diego
- San Francisco
- Santa Barbara

- San Antonio
- El Paso
- Amarillo

Hispanic-American Buying Power

Not only are Hispanic-Americans apt to be more long-term, stable consumers, but their economic power is increasing at a staggering pace. Hispanic-American affluence is spreading at a much quicker pace than that of white Americans. The growth of the Hispanic-American middle and upper classes is expanding quickly. Capturing the loyalty of a population that is rapidly accessing the means to affluence clearly is more potentially profitable than capturing that of a declining segment. Forty percent of Hispanic-Americans now earn over $35,000 a year. Hispanic-Americans currently spend much more of their disposable income than white Americans. Over 750,000 Hispanic-Americans currently own businesses.

Interestingly, Hispanic-Americans out-index non-Hispanic-Americans significantly in many key product areas, including groceries, where Hispanic-American consumers out-index non-Hispanic-Americans by 21 percent; children's clothes, by 42 percent; telephone use, by 14 percent; and footwear, by 22 percent (U.S. Bureau of Labor Statistics Consumer Expenditure Survey, 1995). Their spending is nothing short of astonishing. In the mid-1990s, Hispanic-American consumers' annual spending fell along these lines:

- $40.9 billion on transportation
- $26.9 billion on food for the home
- $18.8 billion on dwellings they owned
- $13.8 billion on apparel
- $10.5 billion on restaurant meals
- $8.5 billion on entertainment
- $8.4 billion on health care
- $7.9 billion on household furnishings and equipment
- $4.0 billion on telephone use
- $3.0 billion on personal care products and services

Demographic Outline and Economic Power: Findings from the University of Georgia's Terry College of Business

Dr. Jeffrey M. Humphreys's study, "Hispanic Buying Power by Place of Residence: 1990–1999," defined Hispanic-American buying power as the total personal income of Hispanic-American residents that is available after taxes for spending on goods and services. Unfortunately, as the report stated, "there were no geographically precise surveys of annual expenditure and income of Hispanic-Americans, and even estimates of Hispanic-American buying power are hard to find, especially for individual states."

Yet the University of Georgia study approaches the problem by providing estimates of Hispanic-American buying power during the 1990s for the United States, the individual states, and the District of Columbia. The estimates were reported in then-current dollars (unadjusted for inflation), as indications of

- the economic power of the Hispanic-American community
- the relative vitality of geographic markets
- the opportunity for new businesses or the expansion of existing ones
- a gauge of a business's annual sales growth against potential market increases
- an indication of the market potential of new and existing products

Because there were no direct measures of Hispanic-American buying power, the estimates reported were calculated using national and regional econometric models, univariate forecasting techniques, and data from various U.S. government sources. In general, the estimation process has two parts: estimating disposable personal income and allocating that estimate by race or ethnicity.

The study revealed the following:

- "Hispanic" refers to a person of Mexican, Puerto Rican, Cuban, Central or South American, or other Spanish culture or origin, and is considered an ethnic category, rather than a racial group. Persons of Hispanic origin therefore may be of any race, and since their culture varies with the country of origin, the Spanish language often is the uniting factor.

- Between the years 1990 and 1999, the nation's Hispanic-American buying power increased 84.4 percent (from $208 billion in 1990)—a percentage gain that is substantially greater than the 56.7 percent gain projected for total buying power and that exceeds the 72.9 percent gain projected for African-American buying power (see Tables 4.2 and 4.3).

- During the years 1990–1999, the Terry College of Business projected that the nine-year, 84.4 percent gain in the nation's Hispanic-American buying power would outstrip both the 56.7 percent increase projected for total buying power, the 55.3 percent increase projected for nominal gross domestic product, and the 37.4 percent increase projected in the Hispanic-American population. The U.S. Consumer Price Index increased 28.7 percent during this same period, but Hispanic-American buying power grew nearly three times as fast as inflation, which demonstrated the growing importance of Hispanic-American consumers.

- Because of differences in per capita income, wealth, demographics, and culture, the spending habits of Hispanic-Americans as a group are not the same as those of average U.S. consumers. The most recent Consumer Expenditure Survey conducted by the U.S. Bureau of Labor Statistics (based on data from 1995) indicated that Hispanic-American consumers spent in total only about 81 percent as much as average non-Hispanic-American households.

- The Hispanic-American population is growing more rapidly than the total population, a trend that is projected to continue. A relatively young Hispanic-American population, with most adults in their early career stages, also argues for additional gains in buying power.

- In 1999, Hispanic-Americans accounted for 5.9 percent of all U.S. buying power, up from 5 percent in 1990 (see Table 4.4). The group's year-to-year gains in buying power vary somewhat,

Table 4.2 Hispanic-American Buying Power by Place of Residence for United States and States, 1990 and 1995–1999 (millions of dollars)

Area	1990	1995	1996	1997	1998	1999
United States	207,915	289,368	304,359	327,734	353,985	383,306
Alabama	283	461	512	545	581	623
Alaska	220	294	301	318	335	360
Arizona	5,314	8,023	8,576	9,310	10,096	10,990
Arkansas	169	360	438	472	509	551
California	68,177	89,675	93,513	100,819	108,968	118,102
Colorado	3,900	5,663	5,988	6,370	6,755	7,183
Connecticut	2,331	3,023	3,146	3,425	3,706	4,030
Delaware	187	294	322	353	390	428
District of Columbia	461	601	614	650	689	734
Florida	19,315	27,516	29,314	31,822	34,733	37,874
Georgia	1,366	2,558	2,893	3,162	3,406	3,684
Hawaii	939	1,210	1,219	1,245	1,296	1,361
Idaho	391	671	716	770	825	889
Illinois	8,616	12,351	13,039	14,053	15,170	16,485
Indiana	1,042	1,564	1,680	1,794	1,920	2,062
Iowa	311	533	599	641	688	747
Kansas	882	1,315	1,413	1,518	1,637	1,776
Kentucky	238	349	385	415	448	487
Louisiana	1,192	1,717	1,777	1,889	2,000	2,130
Maine	79	103	115	127	140	155
Maryland	1,798	2,679	2,831	3,074	3,328	3,619
Massachusetts	2,573	3,463	3,620	3,989	4,382	4,800
Michigan	2,164	3,067	3,225	3,412	3,621	3,880
Minnesota	500	778	861	934	1,023	1,126
Mississippi	166	251	273	287	303	321
Missouri	754	1,069	1,157	1,253	1,356	1,479
Montana	86	124	124	132	143	155
Nebraska	334	616	698	757	817	889
Nevada	1,347	2,572	2,884	3,205	3,569	3,956
New Hampshire	154	241	259	282	307	337
New Jersey	9,079	12,494	13,021	13,968	15,078	16,275
New Mexico	4,797	6,613	6,838	7,144	7,539	8,039
New York	22,901	29,593	30,634	32,723	35,074	37,772
North Carolina	836	1,589	1,816	1,970	2,128	2,319
North Dakota	33	50	58	64	73	83
Ohio	1,523	2,125	2,227	2,366	2,529	2,727
Oklahoma	705	1,040	1,114	1,198	1,278	1,366
Oregon	892	1,551	1,692	1,863	2,057	2,282
Pennsylvania	2,095	2,943	3,126	3,372	3,657	3,962
Rhode Island	401	579	604	658	718	785
South Carolina	379	577	615	662	712	768
South Dakota	47	75	85	90	95	102
Tennessee	406	743	820	890	966	1,054
Texas	32,455	46,764	48,942	52,495	56,666	61,111

Area	1990	1995	1996	1997	1998	1999
Utah	706	1,164	1,301	1,425	1,551	1,683
Vermont	48	85	92	103	115	131
Virginia	2,182	3,310	3,586	3,906	4,225	4,640
Washington	2,025	3,328	3,617	4,004	4,427	4,877
West Virginia	101	139	144	154	168	183
Wisconsin	761	1,150	1,215	1,309	1,418	1,539
Wyoming	253	318	319	345	370	396

Source: Selig Center for Economic Growth, Terry College of Business, University of Georgia, 1998

Table 4.3 Percentage Change in Hispanic-American Buying Power and Rank of Percentage Change, 1990–1999, by State

Area	Rank	Percentage Change in Total Buying Power 1990–99	Area	Rank	Percentage Change in Total Buying Power 1990–99
United States	—	84.4	Missouri	27	96.2
Alabama	16	120.2	Montana	39	80.2
Alaska	48	64.0	Nebraska	6	166.1
Arizona	20	106.8	Nevada	2	193.7
Arkansas	1	226.3	New Hampshire	17	119.7
California	44	73.2	New Jersey	41	79.2
Colorado	37	84.2	New Mexico	46	67.6
Connecticut	45	72.9	New York	47	64.9
Delaware	13	128.9	North Carolina	3	177.4
District of Columbia	49	59.3	North Dakota	9	149.4
Florida	28	96.1	Ohio	42	79.0
Georgia	5	169.6	Oklahoma	31	93.7
Hawaii	51	45.0	Oregon	8	155.8
Idaho	14	127.1	Pennsylvania	34	89.1
Illinois	33	91.3	Rhode Island	29	95.6
Indiana	26	97.9	South Carolina	22	102.7
Iowa	11	140.0	South Dakota	18	114.9
Kansas	24	101.4	Tennessee	7	159.5
Kentucky	21	104.5	Texas	35	88.3
Louisiana	43	78.7	Utah	12	138.3
Maine	30	94.5	Vermont	4	170.5
Maryland	25	101.3	Virginia	19	112.6
Massachusetts	36	86.5	Washington	10	140.8
Michigan	40	79.3	West Virginia	38	81.8
Minnesota	15	125.5	Wisconsin	23	102.4
Mississippi	32	92.9	Wyoming	50	56.8

Source: Selig Center for Economic Growth, Terry College of Business, University of Georgia, 1998

Table 4.4 Hispanic-American Share of Total Buying Power for United States and States, 1990 and 1999 (percent)

Area	1990	1999	Area	1990	1999
United States	5.0	5.9	Missouri	1.0	1.2
Alabama	0.5	0.7	Montana	0.8	0.9
Alaska	2.2	2.6	Nebraska	1.4	2.3
Arizona	9.9	10.9	Nevada	6.3	8.9
Arkansas	0.6	1.1	New Hampshire	0.7	1.1
California	12.4	14.4	New Jersey	5.4	6.6
Colorado	7.0	7.4	New Mexico	24.4	24.1
Connecticut	3.1	3.8	New York	6.5	7.3
Delaware	1.5	2.1	North Carolina	0.9	1.4
District of Columbia	3.5	4.2	North Dakota	0.4	0.6
Florida	8.7	10.4	Ohio	0.9	1.1
Georgia	1.4	2.2	Oklahoma	1.6	2.1
Hawaii	4.6	4.7	Oregon	2.1	3.0
Idaho	2.9	3.8	Pennsylvania	1.0	1.3
Illinois	4.2	5.2	Rhode Island	2.3	3.3
Indiana	1.3	1.6	South Carolina	0.8	1.0
Iowa	0.8	1.2	South Dakota	0.5	0.6
Kansas	2.3	3.0	Tennessee	0.6	0.9
Kentucky	0.5	0.6	Texas	12.4	13.4
Louisiana	2.1	2.5	Utah	3.3	4.1
Maine	0.4	0.6	Vermont	0.6	1.0
Maryland	2.0	2.6	Virginia	2.0	2.8
Massachusetts	2.2	2.7	Washington	2.4	3.3
Michigan	1.4	1.7	West Virginia	0.4	0.5
Minnesota	0.7	1.0	Wisconsin	1.0	1.3
Mississippi	0.6	0.7	Wyoming	3.7	3.9

Source: Selig Center for Economic Growth, Terry College of Business, University of Georgia, 1998

but in each year the percentage gain in their buying power exceeded the rate of growth in buying power for all of the nation's consumers.

- Despite their lower average-income levels, Hispanic-American households spent more than non-Hispanic-Americans on food consumed at home, telephone services, and apparel. They also spent a higher proportion of their after-tax income on housing, personal care products, and services. Substantially less money was devoted to reading material, education, tobacco, health care, and entertainment.

- Hispanic-Americans spend about the same proportion of their incomes as non-Hispanic-American households on many goods and services, including food consumed away from home, transportation, electricity, alcoholic beverages, and housekeeping supplies.

- Fifty-four percent of Hispanic-American households are renters, compared to 35 percent of non-Hispanic-American households.

- Of the many forces supporting the substantial and continued growth of Hispanic-American buying power, perhaps the most important is better employment opportunities.

- The increasing number of Hispanic-Americans who are successfully starting and expanding their own businesses also helps to increase buying power. Favorable demographic trends also reinforce these positive economic forces.

- Estimates of the absolute size and rate of growth of Hispanic-American markets are firm indications of market potential, even though this market is much more focused on a few states than are the total and African-American consumer markets. The five states with the largest Hispanic-American markets account for 71 percent of Hispanic-American buying power. In contrast, the five states with the largest total consumer markets account for only 38 percent of total buying power. (Similarly, the five states with the largest African-American consumer markets account for just 37 percent of African-American buying power.)

- In 1999, the ten states with the largest Hispanic-American markets, in order, were California, Texas, Florida, New York, Illinois, New Jersey, Arizona, New Mexico, Colorado, and Washington (see Table 4.5).

- The top ten states, as ranked by the rate of growth of Hispanic-American buying power over 1990–1999, were Arkansas (the highest), Nevada, North Carolina, Vermont, Georgia, Nebraska, Tennessee, Oregon, North Dakota, and Washington. Most of these states have relatively small but flourishing markets.

- A third ranking, the market share claimed by Hispanic-American consumers, is important for very practical reasons; the higher their market share, the lower the average cost of reaching a potential buyer in the group. Targeting

Table 4.5 Estimates of the Total Population and Hispanic-American
Population of the United States and States, 1990 and 1999

Area	Total Population in 1990	Total Hispanic-American Population in 1990	Total Population in 1999	Total Hispanic-American Population in 1999
United States	249,397,990	22,557,638	272,423,443	30,988,807
Alabama	4,048,317	24,802	4,391,822	39,121
Alaska	553,102	17,986	633,763	25,436
Arizona	3,679,370	695,687	4,784,307	1,068,003
Arkansas	2,354,301	19,994	2,596,749	46,079
California	29,901,421	7,764,126	32,435,218	10,508,205
Colorado	3,304,004	428,622	4,075,261	589,338
Connecticut	3,288,975	214,321	3,279,105	277,016
Delaware	669,071	15,984	756,190	26,850
District of Columbia	603,792	32,743	522,624	39,511
Florida	13,018,496	1,595,378	15,045,138	2,281,158
Georgia	6,506,509	110,132	7,758,907	215,265
Hawaii	1,112,646	81,412	1,223,955	96,957
Idaho	1,011,904	53,501	1,297,421	96,232
Illinois	11,446,801	909,885	11,977,943	1,243,644
Indiana	5,555,019	99,372	5,985,033	142,518
Iowa	2,779,652	32,833	2,885,631	54,901
Kansas	2,480,630	94,241	2,633,180	140,006
Kentucky	3,692,529	22,132	3,964,108	31,606
Louisiana	4,217,362	93,669	4,398,995	118,545
Maine	1,231,284	6,866	1,253,513	10,037
Maryland	4,797,676	126,415	5,210,222	193,871
Massachusetts	6,018,305	289,067	6,167,126	394,418
Michigan	9,310,677	202,985	9,671,908	259,189
Minnesota	4,387,209	54,313	4,791,064	89,065
Mississippi	2,577,213	16,085	2,786,922	21,396
Missouri	5,126,241	62,172	5,488,053	86,320
Montana	799,826	12,236	926,357	16,634
Nebraska	1,580,648	37,212	1,693,860	71,315
Nevada	1,218,702	127,429	1,810,356	281,638
New Hampshire	1,111,861	11,404	1,208,179	18,620
New Jersey	7,739,502	745,384	8,125,939	1,008,471
New Mexico	1,520,039	583,620	1,819,483	725,095
New York	18,002,719	2,228,868	18,194,553	2,692,648
North Carolina	6,657,040	77,547	7,674,793	150,667
North Dakota	637,369	4,643	657,282	8,110
Ohio	10,861,875	140,506	11,271,070	181,512
Oklahoma	3,147,095	86,661	3,358,324	127,603
Oregon	2,858,757	114,171	3,359,612	207,449
Pennsylvania	11,895,491	233,804	12,133,727	325,344
Rhode Island	1,004,665	46,075	993,984	68,538
South Carolina	3,498,970	30,765	3,808,829	44,722

Area	Total Population in 1990	Total Hispanic-American Population in 1990	Total Population in 1999	Total Hispanic-American Population in 1999
South Dakota	696,636	5,263	760,896	7,872
Tennessee	4,890,621	33,028	5,560,645	60,272
Texas	17,046,399	4,376,932	19,974,760	5,940,023
Utah	1,729,784	85,329	2,152,892	139,371
Vermont	564,489	3,686	608,011	7,275
Virginia	6,213,684	162,169	6,902,643	260,422
Washington	4,901,289	217,830	5,788,516	370,869
West Virginia	1,792,429	8,529	1,833,457	11,158
Wisconsin	4,902,197	93,960	5,282,728	136,317
Wyoming	453,397	25,864	508,392	32,175

Sources: Estimates for 1990 were obtained from the U.S. Census Bureau (Internet release date: December 18, 1997). Estimates for 1999 were prepared by the Selig Center for Economic Growth, Terry College of Business, University of Georgia, 1998.

Hispanic-American consumers in diffuse markets is more expensive, although selective media or zip code mailings can lower the cost per individual. In order, the ten states with the largest shares of total Hispanic-American buying power in 1999 were New Mexico, California, Texas, Arizona, Florida, Nevada, Colorado, New York, New Jersey, and Illinois.

• Nationally, Hispanic-American consumers' share of the market increased from 5 percent in 1990 to 5.9 percent in 1999, or by almost one percentage point. Except for New Mexico, the share of buying power controlled by Hispanic-American consumers rose in every state, although Nevada, California, Florida, New Jersey, Arizona, Texas, Rhode Island, Nebraska, Illinois, and Oregon saw the largest increases in the group's market share.

• The ten states (including the District of Columbia) with the slowest growth of Hispanic-American buying power over 1990–1999 were Hawaii (the slowest), Wyoming, the District of Columbia, Alaska, New York, New Mexico, Connecticut, California, Louisiana, and Ohio. The list is not surprising since total buying power also is growing slowly in many of these states. The ten states with the smallest markets, basically a result

of their small Hispanic-American populations, are North
Dakota, South Dakota, Vermont, Maine, Montana, West
Virginia, Mississippi, New Hampshire, Alaska, and Wyoming. Of
this latter group, four states—Vermont, North Dakota, New
Hampshire, and South Dakota—have very vigorous growth in
Hispanic-American spending power.

Where Do Hispanic-Americans Live?

As Hispanic-Americans continue to become increasingly well-to-do
and successful, the answer to that question is becoming more and more,
"anywhere they want."

Yet the fact remains that, as of this writing, America's Hispanic-
American population is concentrated in some very specific areas that
by logical extension are highly accessible to marketers.

Consider this basic breakdown of where Hispanic-Americans live:

- Fifty-five percent of Hispanic-Americans live in just two states:
  California and New York.
- Seventy-five percent live in four states: California, New York,
  Texas, and Florida.
- Thirty-two percent live in just two cities: Los Angeles and New
  York.
- Sixty percent live in only ten cities:
  —in California: Los Angeles, San Francisco, and San Diego
  —in Texas: Dallas, San Antonio, Houston, and McAllen-
      Brownsville
  —in Florida: Miami
  —in Illinois: Chicago
  —in New York: New York City

Understanding and Transcending
the "Language Barrier"

The 1990 census (at this writing, still the most definitive source)
showed that more than 75 percent of Hispanic-Americans spoke English

"very well." And a 1996 poll conducted by the Center for Equal Opportunity found that for over half of all Hispanic-American parents, learning to read and speak English well was their first priority for their children's education.

Yet we also know that certain realities are not reflected by those statistics, just as they will not be reflected by the new census. The fact that Hispanic-Americans are learning English rapidly does not necessarily mean that they are bound to become completely assimilated into mainstream, white American culture.

We know that Hispanic-Americans, by and large, retain a keen sense of ethnic identity. Many acculturate to life in America, accessing the American Dream through education, entrepreneurship, acquisition of material wealth, and the rest. Yet Hispanic-Americans have not—and are unlikely to ever—become fully assimilated. Their distinct identity is too strong, as is their sense of cultural pride.

Even when the overwhelming majority of Hispanic-Americans can speak English like white native-born Americans, most will continue to speak Spanish. Even those who don't speak Spanish in their homes will retain a strong sense of Hispanic identity, much as members of other assimilating groups have retained a strong sense of heritage.

In the words of an executive from SiboneyUSA, a leading Hispanic-American advertising agency, "They acculturate by picking the best from both of their worlds . . . their old ways from home plus new ways from their new home." In practical terms for marketers, this means that our Hispanic-American neighbors, even those fluent in English, generally cannot be reached as effectively through mainstream marketing as they can through advertising channels that "speak to them" by respecting and reflecting elements of their own culture.

CASE STUDY: WELLS FARGO LENDS $184 MILLION TO HISPANIC-AMERICAN BUSINESS OWNERS

As we have shown in this chapter, Hispanic-Americans are eager participants in the American Dream. Most notably, they are at the forefront of American entrepreneurship. What better way, then, to gain acceptance and credibility in the Hispanic-American community than to provide a springboard for Hispanic-American businesses?

In an especially wise program, in October 1997, Wells Fargo announced a partnership with the United States Hispanic Chamber of Commerce (USHCC) to launch a Latino Loan Program to fund the growth of Hispanic-American businesses across the United States. Under the program, Wells Fargo committed to lend $1 billion over the next six years.

In 1997, Wells Fargo Bank lent $184 million through some 8,900 loans to Hispanic-American small-business owners nationwide, exceeding program goals by 10 percent in the first year of its $1 billion program.

"We are tremendously pleased with the success of this program," Tim Rios, vice president of corporate community development at Wells Fargo, stated to the USHCC at the time. "We are on track—even ahead of schedule—to meet our $1 billion commitment. This is a great success for us and a positive move to reduce historical barriers for the Latino community to secure business credit."

The Latino Loan Program was created as a result of findings from a 1997 Wells Fargo–sponsored study, "Latino-Owned Businesses: Access to Capital," that showed Hispanic-American business owners are far less likely than non-Hispanic-American business owners to have the business capital they need to fund their small businesses.

To qualify for a loan under the program, small-business owners must have been in business for at least three years, have a satisfactory personal and business credit history, be profitable, have an established business bank account, and not have declared bankruptcy in the past ten years. Loans from $5,000 to $100,000 are available nationally, and loans over $100,000 are available in the twenty-one states where Wells Fargo and Norwest have banking locations.

USHCC president and CEO George Herrera recently wrote, "Through our alliance with Wells Fargo, we are helping Hispanic business owners obtain access to credit. These loans are clearly having a positive effect and are fueling the growth of Latino small businesses across the country."

Clearly, the incentives represent a win–win proposition for both the bank and Hispanic-American entrepreneurs. This program represents forward-thinking initiatives and demonstrates the kind of leadership role that can be taken by forward-thinking institutions in our quickly changing American landscape.

CHAPTER Five

MARKETING TO ASIAN-PACIFIC-AMERICANS

The Asian-Pacific-American community has enriched our nation with its diverse culture, industrious spirit, and many talented individuals who have helped to build and strengthen our nation. The contributions of this community reach far and wide in our history and society, from laying the foundation of our railroad system in the last century to building today's technology industry. The influence of Asian-Pacific-Americans and Pacific Islanders in our arts, education, sports, media, business, and government is seen and experienced in our everyday lives. . . .

In such a diverse community that traces its ancestry to hundreds of countries, ethnic groups, and cultures, the challenges and needs of this population varies greatly. Sometimes these needs are masked by the overall success of the Asian-Pacific-American community, but we know the challenges are still there, such as language barriers for new immigrants, lack of education opportunity, no access to health care, or discrimination in employment.

> —from Vice President Al Gore's statement initiating Asian-Pacific-American Heritage Month, May 5, 2000

When we speak of marketing to Asian-Pacific-Americans, which has become the most inclusive and acceptable term of choice, we are not talking about one group of Americans but a mosaic comprised of many distinct components.

It makes little sense to lump all these people into one group. After all, Koreans and Pakistanis have little more in common than do Italians and Swedes, who are also part of our national fabric. Similarly, Americans who can trace their roots to immigrants who arrived here from China in the 1800s have comparatively little in common with immigrants who arrive from China today.

Yet marketing assumptions and studies of our Asian-Pacific-American neighbors have by now become normalized around the concept that Asian-Pacific-Americans are a group. Hence, we will remain with the concept of this particular grouping for this chapter.

What is the most effective and cogent way to understand just who is part of this diverse group? I am grateful to Bill Imada, a preeminent expert on marketing to the Asian-Pacific-American markets and president of Imada Wong Communications Group in Los Angeles, (New America Strategies Group division) for his help in codifying just who belongs to this diverse group.

Imada outlines the principal groups, subgroups, and constituencies within the Asian-Pacific-American communities. First, the Asian-Pacific-American market is made up of about 11 million consumers overall, representing between 3.5 and 4 percent of the American population. Second, the largest subgroups within the Asian-Pacific-American matrix are Chinese and Filipinos, and which group is larger is being debated. The most recent information says

- Chinese-Americans have the edge, representing close to 24 percent of the Asian-Pacific-American population.
- Filipinos are somewhere around the 21–22 percent range.
- Japanese-Americans run a distant third, representing about 13 percent of the Asian-Pacific-American population.
- Asian-Indians represent 11–12 percent of the Asian-Pacific-American population.
- Korean-Americans make up 11–12 percent of the Asian-Pacific-American population.
- Vietnamese follow, with about 9 percent of the Asian-Pacific-American population.

Where Is the Growth?

Again, Bill Imada is a source of insight here, as a keen trend watcher.

Interestingly, you're going to see the Japanese and Korean communities fall lower in ranking in the portion of the part of the Asian-Pacific "pie" they represent. Consider, for example, the fact that the Japanese-American population is experiencing very little growth. In fact, I think we are below zero percent growth, due to several factors. There's a high rate of interracial marriage among Japanese-Americans, exceeding 50 percent of all marriages involving Japanese-Americans. Also, a low birth rate. I'm willing to predict that sooner than we might think, the Japanese population will slip out of third place and fall to sixth place, or lower. I'm not sure what the new census will reveal, but I'm going to predict that they will probably fall out of third place easily, and probably fall into sixth or seventh place. We should see some surprising figures in that direction as soon as the next census.

In contrast, the Asian-Indian population and the Vietnamese-American population will probably surge, due to immigration, improving relationships between the United States and Vietnam, and other factors. The Chinese and Filipino populations will continue to outpace the rest of the Asian-American population in terms of growth, with larger-than-average household sizes, larger-than-average birth rates, and higher-than-average immigration rates. In the Chinese community, most of the growth will probably come from immigrants from main-land China and the PRC [People's Republic of China].

We are also going to see a tremendous growth in the South-Asian populations and Southeast-Asian populations, particularly people who are coming from Pakistan, the Indian subcontinent, Indonesia, Thailand, and probably more immigration from Cambodia.

All these figures, in sum, spell growth. The overall Asian-Pacific-American population is expected to exceed the 35 million mark by the year 2050. "I predict it will be higher than that," Imada says, "but the census is predicting about 35 million people by 2050."

The U.S. Census figures from the 1960s reveal that, during those years, the largest growth rate for the Asian-Pacific-American community came from American births.

In the 1960s and 1970s, that switched. Most of the growth rate became attributable to immigration. That pattern is continuing to this day. Most of the growth of the Asian-Pacific-American communities comes from immigration.

Who Arrived Here When?

Like most people who are not members of the Asian-Pacific-American group, we wrongly assumed that the first Asians to arrive in America were Chinese immigrants in the nineteenth century.

The "Pioneers"

The first Asians to arrive on mainland American shores were actually Filipinos in the late 1800s. They arrived here with French merchant trading groups who were active throughout the Pacific. A large Filipino group came with the French, and they set up colonies in what is now Louisiana. But they were probably the first group of Asians to arrive here in sizable numbers. A second group of Filipinos also settled in Hawaii to work on the farms and plantations there.

The largest Asian immigration, of course, started with Chinese coming here to work on the railroads and farms. Imada refers to these groups, quite rightfully, as the pioneers of Asian immigration. He explains, "They tended to be conservative, very traditional, uneducated or undereducated people who came from rural parts of China and the poorer parts of the Philippines. Yet despite their lack of education, these people were risk takers, willing to give up everything to establish livelihoods here. Many had no intention of staying in the United States for any extended time; they just wanted to earn money here and send as much of that money to their families back home as they could and ultimately go back to their homelands a little wealthier than they were before. In most cases that didn't happen, and these immigrants remained here." These pioneers represent the largest first wave of immigration from Asia to America.

The "Second Wave"

The second large wave of Asian-Pacific-American immigration took place from about 1918 through the early 1930s, and mostly was made up of Japanese, Chinese, and Filipino immigrants. While this is a diverse group, Imada summarizes that "these folks had traditional values overall and may have been a little more 'American' than their parents. In contrast to other immigrant groups that have placed a very high value on retaining their Asian cultures, many wanted to distance themselves somewhat from their parents, while still remaining multicultural."

Asian-Pacific-American Baby Boomers

"Asian baby boomers have followed largely the same path as American baby boomers," Imada summarizes. Most of their growth happened right after World War II, with high birth and growth rates from the late 1940s until about 1960. "These are primarily English-dominant people who are now reading the *New York Times* and the *Wall Street Journal*," Imada states, "and consuming general-market television. Overall, many are highly educated, white-collar professionals. And they are a very sizable group."

Other Constituents in the Asian-Pacific-American Population

In the last few decades, other varied groups have arrived here, and they too must be understood. Within these groups, significant subgroups and divisions exist.

A Varied Constituency of Southeast Asians from Vietnam, Cambodia, and Laos

In the years immediately surrounding the end of the Vietnam War, many immigrants arrived from these countries. Most were highly educated, many with strong connections to the U.S. government. A significant number from Vietnam were Catholics, and many had a tremendous amount of political influence at home and were able to escape before the collapse of their government. They were primarily white- and gray-collar workers in Vietnam. A large and significant group of people, they settled primarily in prosperous areas, including Texas, Silicon Valley, and Orange County. This group is primarily conservative with traditional values and, overall, highly educated and very smart.

"High-Tech" Asians

This may be something of a misnomer but useful in understanding this significant segment. Most members of this group come from Taiwan, Hong Kong, and Korea, along with a significant number of highly educated arrivals from India and Pakistan. Arriving primarily during the 1970s and early 1980s, many are highly educated professionals who hold advanced degrees. Many are multilingual entrepreneurs who move from country to country with ease. The most accomplished members of this subgroup are highly entrepreneurial and enjoy high discretionary income.

The "Second Wave" of Southeast Asian Arrivals

After the fall of Vietnam, in the late 1970s through the late 1980s, a large and significant second wave of immigrants arrived from Southeast Asia. They were a very large group, made up of well over one million people. Most visible among them were the boat people and other relatively poor refugees.

In many ways, this group is most similar to the pioneers that Bill Imada described, the very first Filipino and Chinese immigrants to arrive in America. Like those early first Asian-Pacific-Americans, this second-wave group was largely undereducated and were predominantly risk takers who arrived on our shores to escape poverty and for socioeconomic reasons. Many held traditional values, having come from agrarian backgrounds. Perhaps the most publicized and newsworthy members of this group have been the many hardworking Vietnamese who settled in Texas and other southern areas to work in the fishing industries.

Asian-Indian Americans and Pakistani-Americans

A diverse group to be sure, its constituents include many members who have resided in America for a very long time. Many belong to the high-tech Asian cohort. Many are highly educated professionals who have rapidly established themselves as successful professionals. A large number who possess advanced degrees have moved into the Silicon Valley and other high-tech areas across the country.

And Still More Categories of Asian-Pacific-Americans

In addition to the many groups and subgroups described so far, Bill Imada counsels us to be aware of several other significant subgroups of Asian-Pacific-Americans, too.

"Extenders"

Though the label is a generalization, it is true that many immigrants from Asian countries have a very strong sense of family. And their sense of family may be somewhat more "extended" than traditional Americans might expect. In addition to parents and grandparents, an extended Asian-Pacific-American family might include cousins, uncles, and aunts—even friends from back home or neighbors from a town or village.

With greater frequency than many other immigrant groups, Asian-Pacific immigrants to the United States—most especially, recent immigrants—invite members of such extended families to visit them in the United States. Often, the intention is for these family members to navigate their way through to green-carded, working status in the United States, or even beyond to eventual citizenship. Clearly, these extenders, who may be in the United States only briefly or for longer periods, are likely to be consumers of in-language media.

It might be tempting to assume that all such extenders have little economic clout. However, such assumptions can be faulty. Within the high-tech Asian and Asian-Indian communities, extenders can be trained professionals, scientists, and other well-educated individuals, who are trying to establish residency or citizen status in America.

Asian-Pacific-American Generation Xers and Generation Yers

These are, of course, the X- and Y-generation offspring of our Asian-Pacific-American baby boomers. Since they are often the offspring of well-to-do boomers, they are apt to have high discretionary income and engage in spending patterns that closely resemble those of other well-heeled youths within the Hispanic-American, African-American, and mainstream white communities.

Well-Heeled Members of the International Asian Business Community

A comparatively small number of extremely affluent international businesspeople represent an economic force that should not be lightly dismissed. Some are executives from Asian- and Pacific Rim–based corporations who live and work within the United States. Still others are international businesspeople who travel to the United States or own homes here. Primarily consumers of in-language media, they represent an attractive target market for upscale products such as jewelry, as well as food, furnishings, and automobiles.

Demographic Outline and Economic Power Findings from the University of Georgia's Terry College of Business

Turning again to Dr. Jeffrey M. Humphreys's buying power studies, we'll review some findings and predictions from his study entitled "Asian-American Buying Power by Place of Residence: 1990–1999."

- With close to $230 billion in spending power, Asian-Pacific-Americans are a powerful force in the U.S. consumer market (see Table 5.1). In 1999, 10.9 million Americans—4 percent of the country's population—claimed Asian ancestry (see Table 5.2). Clearly, their share of the market will attract increasingly more attention from producers and retailers alike.

Table 5.1 Asian-Pacific-American Buying Power for United States and States, by Place of Residence, 1990 and 1995–1999 (millions of dollars)

Area	1990	1995	1996	1997	1998	1999
United States	113,066	167,240	179,260	193,670	209,994	228,567
Alabama	284	437	463	498	536	581
Alaska	276	391	408	456	509	578
Arizona	718	1,238	1,372	1,514	1,669	1,846

Area	1990	1995	1996	1997	1998	1999
Arkansas	151	247	268	291	316	344
California	42,314	58,560	62,394	67,568	73,355	79,858
Colorado	747	1,243	1,355	1,475	1,601	1,743
Connecticut	1,057	1,677	1,799	1,970	2,144	2,344
Delaware	177	300	327	356	388	422
District of Columbia	216	365	375	382	388	397
Florida	2,279	3,985	4,406	4,785	5,224	5,699
Georgia	1,109	2,149	2,418	2,646	2,854	3,090
Hawaii	11,875	15,055	15,190	15,477	16,054	16,815
Idaho	111	174	186	199	213	228
Illinois	4,956	7,494	8,075	8,731	9,456	10,309
Indiana	700	1,108	1,208	1,306	1,414	1,537
Iowa	259	415	450	489	533	588
Kansas	403	608	655	704	761	827
Kentucky	295	475	524	568	615	671
Louisiana	465	739	783	837	892	956
Maine	82	116	123	132	140	150
Maryland	2,513	3,775	4,043	4,363	4,693	5,072
Massachusetts	2,124	3,351	3,624	4,034	4,476	4,953
Michigan	1,843	2,940	3,199	3,451	3,735	4,081
Minnesota	736	1,228	1,349	1,467	1,610	1,774
Mississippi	130	216	235	251	268	289
Missouri	637	994	1,082	1,162	1,247	1,349
Montana	43	62	65	71	79	87
Nebraska	136	244	277	307	338	375
Nevada	547	1,039	1,174	1,296	1,433	1,577
New Hampshire	152	232	258	279	302	330
New Jersey	5,679	9,144	9,872	10,780	11,845	13,015
New Mexico	178	319	344	375	413	459
New York	11,774	17,610	18,970	20,556	22,350	24,416
North Carolina	677	1,257	1,417	1,559	1,707	1,886
North Dakota	40	68	80	89	100	114
Ohio	1,822	2,761	2,975	3,208	3,481	3,810
Oklahoma	416	583	623	672	720	772
Oregon	856	1,363	1,496	1,638	1,797	1,982
Pennsylvania	2,238	3,430	3,735	4,048	4,410	4,799
Rhode Island	204	270	282	308	336	368
South Carolina	301	460	504	540	578	621
South Dakota	29	48	56	60	65	71
Tennessee	465	836	906	988	1,077	1,180
Texas	4,512	7,822	8,605	9,399	10,331	11,345
Utah	320	541	595	662	730	804
Vermont	36	70	76	84	94	107
Virginia	2,526	3,958	4,291	4,654	5,012	5,481
Washington	2,901	4,662	5,081	5,603	6,171	6,771
West Virginia	216	302	316	338	369	401
Wisconsin	512	836	900	997	1,110	1,239
Wyoming	29	43	46	50	54	58

Source: Selig Center for Economic Growth, Terry College of Business, University of Georgia, 1998

Table 5.2 Estimates of the Total Population and Asian-Pacific-American Population of the United States and States, 1990 and 1999 (number)

Area	Total Population in 1990	Total Asian-Pacific-American Population in 1990	Total Population in 1999	Total Asian-Pacific-American Population in 1999
United States	249,397,990	7,553,589	272,423,443	10,888,314
Alabama	4,048,317	22,198	4,391,822	31,220
Alaska	553,102	20,518	633,763	35,140
Arizona	3,679,370	59,133	4,784,307	106,048
Arkansas	2,354,301	12,811	2,596,749	19,608
California	29,901,421	2,983,951	32,435,218	4,104,573
Colorado	3,304,004	62,476	4,075,261	102,611
Connecticut	3,288,975	52,351	3,279,105	81,045
Delaware	669,071	9,277	756,190	15,426
District of Columbia	603,792	11,669	522,624	14,885
Florida	13,018,496	159,179	15,045,138	277,045
Georgia	6,506,509	77,981	7,758,907	150,714
Hawaii	1,112,646	701,232	1,223,955	769,765
Idaho	1,011,904	9,749	1,297,421	14,986
Illinois	11,446,801	295,954	11,977,943	413,124
Indiana	5,555,019	38,589	5,985,033	58,733
Iowa	2,779,652	25,986	2,885,631	39,182
Kansas	2,480,630	32,786	2,633,180	46,980
Kentucky	3,692,529	18,228	3,964,108	27,819
Louisiana	4,217,362	41,850	4,398,995	58,592
Maine	1,231,284	6,785	1,253,513	8,928
Maryland	4,797,676	143,355	5,210,222	210,553
Massachusetts	6,018,305	147,547	6,167,126	234,362
Michigan	9,310,677	107,473	9,671,908	161,286
Minnesota	4,387,209	79,540	4,791,064	131,636
Mississippi	2,577,213	13,219	2,786,922	19,427
Missouri	5,126,241	42,293	5,488,053	60,807
Montana	799,826	4,337	926,357	6,289
Nebraska	1,580,648	12,765	1,693,860	24,016
Nevada	1,218,702	40,418	1,810,356	83,095
New Hampshire	1,111,861	9,484	1,208,179	14,630
New Jersey	7,739,502	280,055	8,125,939	456,902
New Mexico	1,520,039	15,291	1,819,483	27,830
New York	18,002,719	717,042	18,194,553	1,021,001
North Carolina	6,657,040	53,865	7,674,793	100,350
North Dakota	637,369	3,533	657,282	6,622
Ohio	10,861,875	93,071	11,271,070	134,013
Oklahoma	3,147,095	34,968	3,358,324	46,700
Oregon	2,858,757	71,419	3,359,612	110,493
Pennsylvania	11,895,491	141,608	12,133,727	210,296
Rhode Island	1,004,665	19,092	993,984	24,649

Area	Total Population in 1990	Total Asian-Pacific-American Population in 1990	Total Population in 1999	Total Asian-Pacific-American Population in 1999
South Carolina	3,498,970	22,989	3,808,829	32,670
South Dakota	696,636	3,190	760,896	5,128
Tennessee	4,890,621	32,521	5,560,645	55,780
Texas	17,046,399	335,539	19,974,760	567,842
Utah	1,729,784	34,532	2,152,892	56,732
Vermont	564,489	3,263	608,011	6,831
Virginia	6,213,684	163,581	6,902,643	256,679
Washington	4,901,289	219,504	5,788,516	341,473
West Virginia	1,792,429	7,570	1,833,457	9,808
Wisconsin	4,902,197	54,886	5,282,728	89,556
Wyoming	453,397	2,936	508,392	4,434

Sources: Estimates for 1990 were obtained from the U.S. Census Bureau (Internet release date: December 18, 1997). Estimates for 1999 were prepared by the Selig Center for Economic Growth, Terry College of Business, University of Georgia, 1998.

- For the purposes of the study, the term *Asian* refers to a person of Chinese, Japanese, Hawaiian, Filipino, or other Asian or Pacific Islander ancestry, and is considered a racial group, rather than an ethnic category. Simply defined, Asian-Pacific-American buying power is the total personal income of Asian-Pacific-American residents that is available after taxes for spending on goods and services—the disposable personal income of the Asian-Pacific-American residents of a specified geographic area. Unfortunately, there are no geographically precise surveys of annual expenditures and income of Asian-Pacific-Americans. Even estimates of Asian-Pacific-American buying power are hard to find, especially for individual states.
- The Terry College of Business estimates that the nation's Asian-Pacific-American buying power rose from $113 billion in 1990 to $229 billion in 1999, an increase of 102 percent in nine years, or a compound annual rate of growth of 8.1 percent. The percentage gain is substantially greater than the increases in buying power projected for the United States as a whole (57 percent) and for other groups: 73 percent for African-Americans and 84 percent for Hispanic-Americans.

- Over the same period, total U.S. buying power increased by 57 percent, nominal gross domestic product by 55 percent, and the national Asian-Pacific-American population by 44 percent. Since the U.S. Consumer Price Index will increase 29 percent during this same period, Asian-Pacific-American buying power will grow more than three and a half times as fast as inflation.
- The increasing importance of Asian-Pacific-American consumers can and should create great opportunities for businesses that pay attention to Asian-Pacific-American needs. Because the group includes consumers of so many national ancestries and such diverse cultures, firms that target specific subgroups may find niche markets particularly rewarding. Indeed, many entrepreneurs may first begin with goods or services aimed at a specific national group—for example, Chinese or Filipino—and then branch out to the Asian-Pacific-American market in general.
- Many forces support the substantial and continued growth of Asian-Pacific-American buying power, but perhaps the most important is better employment opportunities for all Americans, including Asian-Pacific-Americans. Asian-Pacific-Americans also are better educated than average Americans, therefore a large proportion of them hold top-level jobs in management or professional specialities. The increasing number of successful Asian-Pacific-American entrepreneurs also helps increase the group's buying power. Favorable demographic trends reinforce these positive economic forces. The Asian-Pacific-American population is growing more rapidly than the total population, mostly because of strong immigration, which is a trend that is expected to continue. A relatively young Asian-Pacific-American population, with most adults in their early career stages, also argues for additional gains in buying power.
- In 1999, Asian-Pacific-Americans accounted for 3.5 percent of all U.S. buying power, up from 2.7 percent in 1990 (see Table 5.3). In each intervening year, Asian-Pacific-American buying power has grown or will grow faster than total U.S. buying power, thus a review of the decade reveals a pattern of substantial but varying annual growth: 7.6 percent in 1991, 9.9 percent

Table 5.3 Asian-Pacific-American Share of Total Buying Power for United States and States, 1990 and 1999 (percent)

Area	1990	1999	Area	1990	1999
United States	2.7	3.5	Missouri	0.8	1.1
Alabama	0.5	0.7	Montana	0.4	0.5
Alaska	2.8	4.1	Nebraska	0.6	1.0
Arizona	1.3	1.8	Nevada	2.6	3.6
Arkansas	0.5	0.7	New Hampshire	0.7	1.1
California	7.7	9.8	New Jersey	3.4	5.3
Colorado	1.3	1.8	New Mexico	0.9	1.4
Connecticut	1.4	2.2	New York	3.3	4.7
Delaware	1.4	2.1	North Carolina	0.7	1.1
District of Columbia	1.6	2.2	North Dakota	0.5	0.9
Florida	1.0	1.6	Ohio	1.1	1.5
Georgia	1.1	1.8	Oklahoma	1.0	1.2
Hawaii	58.1	58.0	Oregon	2.0	2.6
Idaho	0.8	1.0	Pennsylvania	1.1	1.6
Illinois	2.4	3.3	Rhode Island	1.2	1.5
Indiana	0.8	1.2	South Carolina	0.6	0.8
Iowa	0.6	0.9	South Dakota	0.3	0.4
Kansas	1.0	1.4	Tennessee	0.6	1.0
Kentucky	0.6	0.9	Texas	1.7	2.5
Louisiana	0.8	1.1	Utah	1.5	2.0
Maine	0.4	0.6	Vermont	0.4	0.8
Maryland	2.7	3.7	Virginia	2.3	3.3
Massachusetts	1.8	2.8	Washington	3.4	4.5
Michigan	1.2	1.7	West Virginia	0.9	1.2
Minnesota	1.0	1.5	Wisconsin	0.7	1.0
Mississippi	0.4	0.6	Wyoming	0.4	0.6

Source: Selig Center for Economic Growth, Terry College of Business, University of Georgia, 1998

in 1992, 7.4 percent in 1993, 6.7 percent in 1994, 9.1 percent in 1995, 7.2 percent in 1996, 8 percent in 1997, 8.4 percent in 1998, and 8.8 percent in 1999. During 1990–1999, the compound annual rate of growth in Asian-Pacific-American buying power was 8.1 percent, well above the 5.1 percent compound annual rate for the buying power of all U.S. consumers.

• Estimates of the absolute size and rate of growth of Asian-Pacific-American buying power are firm indications of market potential in specific areas. This market is much more focused on a few states than are the principal African-American consumer markets, but less so than the Hispanic-American market. The

five states with the largest Asian-Pacific-American markets
account for 64 percent of the group's buying power. In contrast,
the five states with the largest total consumer markets provide
only 38 percent of total national buying power. The five states
with the largest African-American consumer markets account
for just 37 percent of African-American buying power.
Hispanic-American consumers are even more concentrated
than Asian-Pacific-Americans; the five states with the largest
Hispanic-American consumer markets make up 71 percent of
Hispanic-American buying power.

- In 1999, the ten states with the largest Asian-Pacific-American
  markets, in order, were California, New York, Hawaii, New
  Jersey, Texas, Illinois, Washington, Florida, Virginia, and
  Maryland. Ranked by the rate of growth of Asian-Pacific-
  American buying power during 1990–1999, the top ten states
  were Vermont, Nevada, North Dakota, North Carolina,
  Georgia, Nebraska, New Mexico, Arizona, Tennessee, and
  Texas. Most of these states have relatively small but flourishing
  markets. The large majority of the Asian-Indian population
  resides on the East Coast of America—many of them in
  New York and its environs. In contrast, Chinese-, Japanese-,
  Filipino-, Vietnamese-, Korean- and other Asian-Pacific-
  Americans reside principally on the West Coast. Consider:
  Forty percent of the entire U.S. Asian-Pacific-American popu-
  lation resides in California.

- A third ranking, the market share claimed by Asian-Pacific-
  American consumers, is important for very practical reasons: the
  higher their market share, the lower the average cost of reaching
  a potential buyer in the group. Targeting Asian-Pacific-
  American consumers in diffuse markets is more expensive,
  although selective media or zip code mailings can lower the cost
  per individual. In order, the ten states with the largest shares of
  total Asian-Pacific-American buying power in 1999 were
  Hawaii (where Asian-Pacific-Americans account for 58 percent
  of the state's buying power), California, New Jersey, New York,
  Washington, Alaska, Maryland, Nevada, Virginia, and Illinois.

- Nationally, Asian-Pacific-American consumers' share of the market increased from 2.7 percent in 1990 to 3.5 percent in 1999, or by almost one percentage point. Except in Hawaii, the share of buying power controlled by Asian-Pacific-American consumers will rise in every state. California, New Jersey, New York, Alaska, Washington, Nevada, Massachusetts, Maryland, Virginia, and Illinois saw the largest increases in the group's market share.
- The ten states (including the District of Columbia) with the slowest growth of Asian-Pacific-American buying power during 1990–1999 were Hawaii, Rhode Island, Maine, the District of Columbia, Oklahoma, West Virginia, California, Wyoming, Maryland, and Montana (see Table 5.4). Total buying power also is growing slowly in many of these states. The ten states with the smallest markets, largely because of their small Asian-Pacific-American populations, are Wyoming, South Dakota, Montana, Vermont, North Dakota, Maine, Idaho, Mississippi, New Hampshire, and Arkansas. Despite their small populations, the spending power of Asian-Pacific-American consumers is growing very quickly in several of these markets, including Vermont, North Dakota, and South Dakota.

Reaching the Asian-Pacific-American Market

Recall the short disclaimer in Chapter 2 on marketing to African-, Hispanic-, and Asian-Pacific-Americans. Please bear in mind that some of the following statements are generalities that do not reflect the views or outlooks of many Asian-Pacific-Americans.

Many Asian-Pacific-Americans respond favorably to in-language messages. The descriptions of the various groups earlier should have made it clear that this statement holds more true for certain Asian-Pacific-Americans than for others. When marketing to acculturated, entrenched Asian-Pacific-American baby boomers, Generation Xers and Yers, for example, the power of delivering marketing messages in-language can be nearly negligible; however, when marketing to members of other groups, it becomes far more critical. For members of many

Table 5.4 Percentage Change in Asian-Pacific-Amerian Buying Power and Rank of Percentage Change, 1990–1999, by State

Area	Rank	Percentage Change in Total Buying Power 1990–99	Area	Rank	Percentage Change in Total Buying Power 1990–99
United States	–	102.2	Missouri	32	111.6
Alabama	41	104.8	Montana	42	104.0
Alaska	33	109.1	Nebraska	6	175.7
Arizona	8	157.2	Nevada	2	188.2
Arkansas	22	127.8	New Hampshire	30	116.5
California	45	88.7	New Jersey	21	129.2
Colorado	18	133.2	New Mexico	7	158.6
Connecticut	26	121.7	New York	36	107.4
Delaware	16	138.9	North Carolina	4	178.6
District of Columbia	48	83.6	North Dakota	3	184.3
Florida	12	150.1	Ohio	34	109.0
Georgia	5	178.5	Oklahoma	47	85.7
Hawaii	51	41.6	Oregon	20	131.5
Idaho	39	105.5	Pennsylvania	31	114.5
Illinois	35	108.0	Rhode Island	50	80.8
Indiana	28	119.7	South Carolina	37	106.3
Iowa	24	127.1	South Dakota	13	142.8
Kansas	40	104.9	Tennessee	9	153.8
Kentucky	23	127.2	Texas	10	151.4
Louisiana	38	105.5	Utah	11	151.1
Maine	49	82.2	Vermont	1	197.5
Maryland	43	101.9	Virginia	29	117.0
Massachusetts	19	133.2	Washington	17	133.4
Michigan	27	121.5	West Virginia	46	86.0
Minnesota	15	140.9	Wisconsin	14	141.8
Mississippi	25	122.6	Wyoming	44	99.9

Source: Selig Center for Economic Growth, Terry College of Business, University of Georgia, 1998

groups, from extenders visiting America short term to members of New York's vibrant Korean community to Vietnamese residents of Texas, in-language presentation is obviously more critical.

About 80 percent of the Asian-American households are now on existing mailing lists and databases, and there are some good ones. There are credit bureau lists and databases, response lists—including catalogs, subscribers and mail-order buyers—and there are compiled lists and data-

bases. Almost all can be segmented by nationality, and some can identify in-language households, including two dialects of Chinese—
Mandarin and Cantonese.

> —"Targeting Asian Americans, the Fastest
> Growing Ethnic Group" by Rick Blume, *DM*
> *News*, September 4, 1998

When a mailing is done in-language, the response rate is often
much higher than for whites.

Addressing people in the language they speak and via their preferred and established media promises much greater return on investment (ROI) for your marketing investment than delivering your
messages in a language your target audience does not understand.

According to a poll conducted by Gallup and SRI in 1995, Asian-
Pacific-Americans said they prefer to see in-language ads:

76 percent of Vietnamese
73 percent of Koreans
61 percent of Chinese
60 percent of Filipinos

Although more entrenched and established Asian-Pacific-
American consumers—the Asian-Pacific-American baby boomers and
others who have resided here for several generations—may not respond
so favorably to in-language promotions, even they respond well to the
presence of Asian-Pacific-Americans in the ads you use to reach them.

Family is vitally important to members of the Asian-Pacific-
American communities. As in Hispanic-American communities, Asian-
Pacific-American households tend to be multigenerational and large.
Again, this is more true within groups who have been here less long
than with more entrenched Asian-Pacific-American baby boomers and
their offspring. For this reason, establishing customer loyalty within
many Asian-Pacific-American households promises more ROI than
establishing loyalty within the traditional white American constituency.

Community involvements offer a viable, vibrant link to Asian-
Pacific-American communities. Immigrant groups have always tended
to reside within tight, geographically distinct communities. So it is with
many Asian-Pacific-Americans, as was discussed in Chapter 1 and in

the preceding sections from Dr. Humphreys's buying power study. Sponsorship of events and institutions that have meaning within these distinct communities offers a highly effective way to reach this market segment.

Specialized delivery systems work especially well in reaching many Asian-Pacific-American consumers. To quote Bill Imada, "Many Asian-Americans are people who respond well to actually seeing products. It is a generalization, but it seems that for many members of these communities and among the more recently arrived individuals and families, actually being able to see and touch products and try them out carries much more weight than reading about products. Often, it seems, buying decisions are made on this basis, and displaying your products or services where they can be tried—in a booth at a festival, perhaps, or in a retail location frequented by Asian-Pacific-Americans—can result in more market share than running ads in broadcast or print media."

Word of mouth is vitally important. This holds true more within communities and subgroups that are newly arrived in the United States. When one member of a community recommends your product or service to another member of his or her community, you have gained credibility and presence that would be hard to match by any ad or other marketing activity.

How can you get word of mouth to work for you? One of the most powerful ways is to retain frontline people who can talk to Asian-Pacific-American consumers in their own languages. This ties closely to the issue of diversity, which we will explore in depth in Chapter 7. Having telemarketers who can make the sale in the language of your consumers is of critical importance. But to succeed in the long term, more than just a sale is required.

Success can follow when word of mouth conveys the message that your company is language-friendly to members of the community you are trying to reach. Even more important, the presence in your organization of salespeople or service representatives who come from the community is of vital importance. One or two salespeople who speak the language of your target group can go very far indeed to help your penetration of the communities in question.

Stay tuned to Asian-Pacific-American media developments. Asian-Pacific-American media is growing exponentially every year. As recently as ten years ago there were about 100 Asian-Pacific-American media sources within the United States. There are now at least 600 sources in many categories—print and broadcast.

Not long ago, many cable stations ran only one hour a day of Korean- or Chinese-language broadcasts a day. Now that is changing and some real sophistication has developed in Korean and Chinese communities and the programming they watch. Within the Korean communities, for example, the number of twenty-four-hour radio stations is growing—two of them in Los Angeles alone. In San Francisco, Cantonese News has higher listenership figures than several of the general-market radio stations. When over 90 percent of a given community sees the ad you've run on a cable station or heard it on radio, you're receiving impressive penetration for your marketing dollar.

Asian-Pacific-American print media are far more diverse than the print media of the African-American communities. Unlike the African-American communities, which have a number of widely read African-American publications—*Black Enterprise*, *Vibe*, *Ebony*, and so on—the Asian-Pacific-American communities don't have such vehicles. Even an established publication such as *AsianWeek* lacks the strength, reach, and circulation of such publications as *Ebony*.

Mass-marketing media are far more scant within Asian-Pacific-American communities than within the African- or Hispanic-American communities. Getting to the hearts and loyalties of Asian-Pacific-Americans requires a more in-depth marketing approach. That may seem rather labor intensive and expensive, but in the end the benefits of establishing a marketing link to the members of the Asian-Pacific-American community far outweigh the downside and difficulty of doing so.

And there are vehicles that do that. The *Korea Times*, for example, has one of the highest circulations in North America, with seventeen bureaus in the United States and Canada.

Remember the entrepreneurial link. Many members of the Asian-Pacific-American communities are business owners, thus a highly entrepreneurial population. Consider that within the Korean community, many individuals are entrepreneurs and small-business owners. In fact, the percentage of Korean-Americans who own businesses is over 50 percent higher than the national percentile of the population that owns businesses.

Similarly, many Asian-Pacific-Americans see business ownership and entrepreneurship as the most effective way to gain permanency and establish success on American soil. This is one reason why programs and outreach to the business communities within your target segment can be very effective ways to leverage your success and presence within Asian-Pacific-American communities.

CASE STUDY: THREE SPONSORS TEAM UP FOR THE CHINESE NEW YEAR CELEBRATIONS IN SAN FRANCISCO AND LOS ANGELES

"Almost all successful marketers to the Asian community are involved in one event or two," says Bill Imada.

In accord with the principle outlined earlier—Asian-Pacific Americans are often responsive to seeing and testing products first-hand—Chinese New Year celebrations in San Francisco and Los Angeles are a logical place to sponsor booths, floats, parades, and VIP receptions, as well as to run full-page ads and execute direct promotions specifically to those communities.

For such efforts in these major California cities, AT&T, Bank of America, and United Airlines teamed up for a joint one-year marketing effort. Even though they don't have the same product, they were trying to market to the same population.

Objectives were simple. AT&T wanted to sell more long-distance accounts and get people to switch to AT&T if they were with another carrier. Bank of America had an equally simple objective: to get members of the Chinese-American community to open new checking accounts. United Airlines wanted to build its image within the Chinese-American community and, obviously, to sell airline seats. So these marketing giants teamed up and created a joint promotion, the components of which included the following:

- Holders of newly opened Bank of America checking accounts received six months' free checking and free checks that could be ordered in special Chinese and Vietnamese motifs (because Chinese New Year events were expected to attract members of the Vietnamese community as well).
- As an additional incentive, new account holders received a gift from AT&T: a prepaid calling card that let account holders make a preset number of hours' worth of calls anywhere in the United States or Asia.
- From its end of the equation, new AT&T customers and customers who returned to AT&T received free checks and six months' free checking at Bank of America.
- United's promotion was simple. Any new Bank of America customer received a coupon good for a discount on a future flight.

It was a relatively straightforward and simple program, yet its results greatly exceeded expectations. Some highlights:

- Although only 13 of the 200 Bank of America branches in California participated in the promotion, 22,000 new accounts were opened within the Chinese-American community. (Their goal for the promotion had been to open only 1,500 new accounts.)
- AT&T met its first-quarter goals for new accounts and switchbacks within one month of instituting the promotion.

This is a telling example of the power of event marketing and cooperative promotions within the Asian-Pacific-American communities. At bottom, it was simplicity itself. The sponsors simply gave people the opportunity to stop by a booth, talk to someone who spoke their language, see the checks and the calling cards, and sign up.

Six

WRITING THE MARKETING PLAN

Many marketers invest a lot of time and effort to understand everything they can about their consumers. Research is important, of course. But sometimes they miss a far more important question: Are they talking to their customers at all? Or are they ignoring them?

All the research in the world won't get people to buy what you are offering. You need a road map for how you will reach them. And in practical terms, that means writing a plan.

—Jeff Symon, president, Alternative & Innovative
Marketing, Escondido, California, in an interview with Barry Lenson, January 1999

Having read the preceding chapters, perhaps you are already beginning to develop some ideas about how to market your product or service to any or all of the ethnic communities. Certain marketing approaches may have looked promising for your business, and certain communities—African-, Hispanic-, and Asian-Pacific-American—may seem to offer promising markets for what you have to sell. So what should your next steps be?

In brief, develop a marketing strategy, create a plan that supports that strategy, and then get started with its execution. As an experienced marketer you may think, "Well, I know just how to do that. I've been around the block already more than a few times when it comes to creating marketing plans and putting them into motion." But if your next campaign is your initial approach to one or more of the ethnic markets that comprise the new America, spend a little time with this chapter before you begin to spend those all-too-scarce advertising dollars. Because unlike traditional marketing, certain pitfalls and "extra" considerations come into play with ethnic markets.

Don't assume the general view of your product is shared by the ethnic market you are pursuing. This is a prime pitfall for first-time ethnic marketers, who think, "The mainstream Anglo market has known about and bought our product for decades already. So it follows that we enjoy the same level of acceptance and recognition among these ethnic consumers. After all, they are Americans, too."

But such thinking can cost dollars. Many times over, research has shown that brand loyalties and brand awareness become fragmented across racial and ethnic divides, such as in the following two ways:

1. Brand loyalty does not always transfer intact across racial or ethnic lines. Mainstream white consumers, for example, are much more likely to feel strong brand loyalty toward products offered by major corporations than are African-Americans or Hispanic-Americans. The major brands of household products that are widely recognized and respected by mainstream white consumers, for example, often do not enjoy the same level of recognition and acceptance with emerging minority consumers. They are likely to ask, "What has this company done for me lately . . . what efforts have they made to win my business?"

2. Buying decisions are based on different criteria among the various ethnic and racial groups. A brand of laundry detergent, for example, that sells well among lower-income white consumers may not sell nearly as well among lower-income African-Americans. Similarly, the buying patterns for upscale luxury cars that sell well among upscale white Americans and upscale African-Americans are different. In almost all cases, your experience with white consumers will not translate once you've crossed the line and begun marketing to ethnic consumers.

At the base of these two considerations is the necessity of avoiding dustbin thinking, which assumes that ethnic consumers will be swept along in mainstream marketing campaigns or that carrying over a marketing effort that was successful with white consumers will work equally well in the ethnic markets.

The key in writing any marketing plan is to understand that African-, Hispanic-, and Asian-Pacific-Americans distinctly differ from the general market and must be targeted appropriately. You need to fully understand the cultural imperatives of each of these groups. For example, in recent surveys

- 61 percent of African-Americans say education is one of their most important concerns, compared with about 48 percent for the general population.
- 77 percent of African-Americans say that they feel the need to be more involved and active in their community, versus 61 percent for nonminorities.

Armed with such information—and it is increasingly possible to uncover it on the Internet and through other marketing resources—you empower yourself to create a marketing plan that will speak authentically to ethnic consumers' real concerns, right where they live. Once you've done the research to find out how they relate specifically to your products, then and only then are you in a position to write your plan.

Verse yourself in the culture of the customers you're trying to target and have a better understanding of how they feel and behave before you even begin to think about strategies.

"Hot Buttons" for Ethnic Consumers

While we are about to engage in some sweeping generalities, here is a short list of "hot buttons," or key points, to consider while addressing the new, emerging minorities. These hot buttons are not to be used blindly without further research into the communities you are addressing and the way they relate to your products and company. They are, however, very useful.

The key ethnic hot buttons follow.

- **Respect**
  Communicate in culturally relevant terms that show your respect for your customers. Otherwise you engage in mono-lithic thinking as described earlier in this book, where you rep-resent members of your target audience in terms of stereotypes instead of individual concerns.

- **Family**
  This is the "tie that binds" that cuts across all the ethnic con-sumer bases we explore in this book. African-Americans, by and large, have an intense and deep belief in their families. So do Hispanic-Americans and Asian-Pacific-Americans, for whom the family unit is sometimes large and multigenera-tional. Other key concepts logically emerge from the family concept, such as belief in education, in good health care, or the importance of community.

- **Community**
  All immigrant groups since the founding of America have bonded together into communities that offer support systems and resources. When you align your company with these com-munities, in their economic progress, businesses, organizations, and so on, you speak to ethnic consumers with a compelling and believable voice.

How Do Your Consumers Relate to Your Product?

The next vital question to be answered is, how do your target con-sumers relate to your product?

This step involves research. In other words, you need to under-stand what the operative indexes are regarding how well your type of product or service sells within the community you are addressing. As an example, let's consider a major purchase most Americans make—a car—and see how buying patterns differ among various groups.

In 1997, 43 percent of all Americans who bought cars purchased new vehicles. However, there are surprises. In fact, 63 percent of

Asian-Pacific-Americans bought new cars, along with 59 percent of African-Americans, but only 27 percent of Hispanic-Americans bought new cars.

The buying patterns established within one group do not carry over intact to another. Still more important for our purposes is the fact that minority consumers buy many items in higher quantities than white consumers; in marketing parlance, they "overindex" in those product categories.

Consider the statistics in Table 6.1, compiled by *Target Market News*, a leading trend watcher.

Tables 6.2 and 6.3 offer an alternative presentation of information on the spending patterns of African- and Hispanic-Americans. Unfortunately, as of the writing of this book, similar data are not available for Asian-Pacific-American consumer groups in the United States.

The data in the tables show examples of the kind of data you should be looking for to find how your product fits into buying patterns. Such data can be obtained from academic sources, consultants, industry associations, or more often these days, from a variety of sources on the Internet.

But while this information is vital in obtaining an overview of how consumers relate to your product, it is necessary to dig deeper by talking to members of your constituency about their attitudes, opinions, and patterns of consumption regarding what you have to offer to them in the marketplace.

Going into Focus Groups

Researching an ethnic marketing campaign requires using the standard research tools: media analysis, focus groups, etc. But it also requires specialized approaches and attitudes on the part of the marketer.

Dr. Andrew Erlich, a pioneer in ethnic market research and president of Erlich Transcultural Consultants in Woodland Hills, California, provides some insights.

> In any ethnic marketing effort, I'd counsel starting out by taking a somewhat unusual step and asking some questions that might not apply in other marketing efforts. I think the very first thing you have to do is

Table 6.1 Selected Product Categories in Which African-Americans Out-index (Buy More than) White Consumers

Note: In the following table, an index number of 145 means that African-American households' expenditures were equal to 145 percent of white households—in other words, 45 percent greater than white households.

Purchase	Index Number
Watches	134
Footwear	
Men's	106
Boys'	156
Women's	156
Girls'	315
Food	
Rice	171
Bacon	187
Pork chops	136
Ham	105
Sausage	170
Lamb	180
Fresh fish and shellfish	146
Poultry	129
Eggs	132
Oranges	125
Appliances	111
Nonalcoholic beverages	
Fresh fruit juices	126
Nonalcoholic beer	201
Vehicles	
New cars	108
New motorcycles	201
On-line services	265
Consumer electronics	
Sound components	104
Tape recorders	488
Taxi fares	263

Source: Excerpts from data compiled by *Target Market News* statistics, 1997

look for the internal commitment that your organization is going to have to the ethnic campaign you are about to launch. Because often, ethnic marketing is an afterthought.

Time and again, I have observed that the organization is simply unwilling to apply the same diligence to the research efforts behind a marketing effort targeting Latinos, or Asians, or African-Americans that it would devote to marketing to a more mainstream, white audience.

Table 6.2 Average Annual Expenditures by Item As a Percentage of After-Tax Money Income for African-American Consumers and All Consumers, 1996

Expenditures As a Percentage of After-Tax Income

Item	African-Americans (percent)	All Consumers (percent)
Food—at home	10.1	8.3
Food—away from home	4.1	5.0
Alcoholic beverages	0.6	0
Shelter	18.5	17.5
Natural gas	1.3	0.8
Electricity	3.5	2.6
Fuel oil and other fuels	0.2	0.3
Telephone	3.2	2.1
Water and other public services	0.9	0.8
Household operations	1.3	1.5
Housekeeping services	1.0	1.3
Household furnishings and equipment	3.5	4.1
Apparel	7.3	5.0
Transportation	18.5	17.8
Health care	4.4	5.1
Entertainment	3.8	4.8
Personal care products and services	1.5	1.2
Reading	0.3	0.5
Education	1.1	1.4
Tobacco and smoking supplies	0.7	0.8
Miscellaneous	1.9	2.3
Cash contributions	2.3	2.7
Personal insurance and pensions	7.6	8.8
Average after-tax money income ($)	24,297	33,864

Source: Percentages were calculated by the Selig Center for Economic Growth, Terry College of Business, University of Georgia, based on data obtained from the Consumer Expenditure Survey by the U.S. Bureau of Labor Statistics.

Let me give some examples. Often, an attempt to market to ethnic consumers is something of an afterthought. A corporation might be conducting ten, fifteen, or twenty focus groups for the general market, so they think, "Oh, yes, we'd also like to include some Hispanics or African-Americans, so why don't we just pick them up as part of our larger, umbrella campaign."

They will assume that African-American or Hispanic product consumption needs and behaviors are the same as for the general, white population. Or they are unwilling to really consider conducting research in sufficient depth.

Table 6.3 Average Annual Expenditures by Item As a Percentage of After-Tax Money Income for Hispanic-American Consumer Units and Non-Hispanic-American Consumer Units, 1996

Expenditures As a Percentage of After-Tax Income

Item	Hispanic-American (percent)	Non-Hispanic-American (percent)
Food—at home	12.3	8.0
Food—away from home	5.4	5.2
Alcoholic beverages	0.9	0
Shelter	20.1	17.2
Natural gas	0.8	0.8
Electricity	2.6	2.6
Fuel oil and other fuels	0.2	0.3
Telephone	3.2	2.1
Water and other public services	0.9	0.8
Household operations	1.2	1.5
Housekeeping supplies	1.4	1.3
Household furnishings and equipment	3.2	3.9
Apparel	7.0	4.9
Transportation	19.5	18.2
Health care	3.8	5.2
Entertainment	4.0	5.3
Personal care products and services	1.8	1.4
Reading	0.3	0.5
Education	1.0	1.5
Tobacco and smoking supplies	0.5	0.7
Miscellaneous	2.4	2.5
Cash contributions	1.3	2.8
Personal insurance and pensions	8.0	8.8
Average after-tax money income ($)	27,449	35,585

Source: Percentages were calculated by the Selig Center for Economic Growth, Terry College of Business, University of Georgia, based on data obtained from the Consumer Expenditure Survey by the U.S. Bureau of Labor Statistics.

I remember that one client said to me, "Let's research some Asians." And I said, "What Asians?" After all, there are many different Asian populations that have distinct cultures, distinct languages.

What was this client looking for?

As Dr. Erlich's words suggest, there are many levels of complexity to consider. If you are targeting Asian-Pacific-Americans, for example, even within a state or region where you know many Asian-Pacific-Americans reside, are you going after Filipinos, Japanese, Pakistanis, or another group? Even within any one group—for example, Chinese-Americans or Japanese-Americans—there is considerable complexity.

- What language do they use at home? What percentage of the group you are targeting speaks English in the home?
- Where and how do they shop?
- How completely are they acculturated and assimilated?
- Are they still very much in touch with their culture of origin?
- How much in-language media do they consume?
- How do they identify themselves in terms of where they fit in their community and in American society as a whole?

Often, because the questions that need answers are complex, marketers oversimplify the problem as a way of dealing with the complexity. Some even say, "Let's not do any research at all. Let's just hire an ethnic consultant whose expertise will show us what we ought to be doing."

Of course, some consultants know what they are doing. But just as often, the consultant also brings a limited perspective and will not ask or answer the questions that need to be addressed in focus-group settings and other forms of research. Companies need to apply to their ethnic consumers the same level of research and sophistication that they use for the general market.

Getting Ethnic Research Right

We are grateful to Dr. Erlich for the preceding insights, which sketch the process of ethnic research with appropriate complexity. We are also indebted to him for laying out the sensible structure for ethnic research that follows in this chapter.

First, define your goals. Before you even begin to step out and start your focus groups, it is important to define your goals and purposes clearly. Would you like to increase sales of calling cards by 30 percent among the 500,000 Hispanic-Americans who reside in a particular city? Or, as an investment and brokerage business, is your goal to attract Korean-American consumers within New York City—perhaps to catch up to a competitor who has already won the accounts of several thousand Korean-American investors?

As Dr. Erlich stresses, it's important to look at your internal systems and commitment before starting. If your goal is to attract Korean-American consumers, for instance, would that effort be supported by your internal sales force? If you would like to attract more African-Americans to your retail locations, what kind of greeting will they find when they arrive there? Does your sales force look like the market you want to reach? Are the appropriate systems in place to support your efforts? Is your organization really behind your efforts and willing to go the distance for the consumers you are targeting in the years to come?

The next step (again, before hosting focus groups) is to assess the population via secondary sources to find out as much as you can about the consumers you are targeting. In other words, conduct some quantitative secondary research to try to define the size and characteristics of the marketplace, answering such questions as

- How many of your target consumers are there?
- What do they earn?
- What is their average level of education?
- What are their jobs and professions?
- What are their principal subgroups?
- What is the size of the typical household?

Some steps might include:

- conducting a quick review of the ethnic media consumed by the group you are targeting, including radio, television, magazines, and newspapers
- reviewing census data on the size and makeup of the consumer group you are targeting, centering on regions or cities where you are making your effort
- going on-line and to the library to find academic studies, university abstracts, and articles regarding the constituencies you are trying to reach
- performing a competitive analysis of other marketing campaigns—their methodologies, successes, or failures in reaching the market you are targeting

Focus-Group Research

In the next phase, which Dr. Erlich calls qualitative research, you will no longer be looking for the rough parameters of your marketplace but for in-depth information about the consumers you are trying to reach—how they relate specifically to your brand, product, or service.

You will conduct in-depth interviews with focus groups (classic diadic/triadic interviews). You will recruit a limited number of respondents who match the profile of consumers you are trying to reach, and you will talk to them in detail about such things as the following:

- Their patterns of consumption of both your product and competing offerings in the marketplace.
- Their knowledge of your company and product.
- Their reaction and receptiveness to the concept that you have, the marketing communication that you are planning, and the positioning you're trying to establish with them.
- If you are planning an event or other sponsorship, the names of appropriate events, organizations, or entities to sponsor.
- Packaging is one prime area that needs to be addressed. How do the members of your focus group feel about the "look" of your product? How do they feel it might be changed or improved to be more appealing (perhaps through photographs of members of their own group instead of whites, for instance, or through the inclusion of other, more subtle cues)? Again, it is vital *not* to assume that a package that plays well with mainstream consumers will appeal equally well to consumers within the niche you are trying to address.
- Different brands play differently to different consumers. Several years ago, True North Communications conducted a study for a major personal care products and pharmaceuticals business that was the most "trusted" name in the general marketplace. African-Americans said they had heard of the company, but they didn't have any particular leaning toward it nor any particularly positive impressions. Such findings are not unusual when conducting focus-group research with ethnic consumers. The general perception is often not the same from group to group.

- Perceptions of price and value do not necessarily transfer intact across racial or ethnic lines. Research has shown, for example, that African-Americans respond favorably to the pricing of upscale automobiles, while traditional white consumers may make less of an association between price and implied value. Similarly, it has been shown that affluent Asian-Pacific-Americans may be somewhat more skeptical about spending money on high-priced brands of consumer goods, even though they can clearly afford these products as easily as can mainstream consumers. Unless you ask the right questions about the product or service you are trying to market specifically, your research findings may be misleading or skewed.
- Creative concepts and approaches. If you have marketing materials or ads, you will want to present them to your focus group for reactions and evaluation. You may even show them ideas that you have been using in the general market to see how well these materials will play with these consumers.

Problems of Recruitment

Recruitment (the selection of people to participate in your focus-group research) is the first complex task that must be handled well in a successful research effort.

In the interest of attracting focus-group participants quickly and easily, the most natural first thought often is to use a list. At this stage, it is wise to remember the basic rule that in conducting ethnic research *lists are notoriously poor.* In cultures highly driven by interpersonal relationships, as is often the case in ethnic groups, face-to-face recruiting is often necessary to allay any concerns or distrustful feelings people may have. So your success often hinges on exercising extreme care about who will do the recruiting for you.

Dr. Erlich offers this example of a recruitment campaign that required extreme tact and care: "Effective recruiting of participants often requires great resourcefulness. For example, my organization was about to conduct a study of people with Type II diabetes in minority populations. To attract suitable participants, we went out into the communities where our ideal participants lived. We put up signs; we distributed flyers; we spoke to pharmacists, physicians, and local community organizations in an attempt to get people who might otherwise not have responded. Such one-on-one recruitment is often the key. And it takes work. So it is critically important to not just hire a research company and rely on them to do the recruiting but have them explain their recruitment process to you well enough to assure you that they will handle recruiting with sufficient imagination, resourcefulness, and diligence. I'd strongly suggest retaining a company that can explain to you how they have handled a similar recruitment process capably in the past."

Referrals and resourcefulness are usually required because without the right respondents you run a very high risk of spending money to obtain misleading or inconclusive results.

Handling the Focus-Group Setting

The next critical step is making sure that the focus groups themselves will be handled capably. And again, working with ethnic populations requires special skills, outlooks, and systems on the part of your market-research firm.

The people who will conduct the focus sessions must be chosen with care. It would be difficult to overemphasize the importance of having the right leaders for your sessions. If language is an issue, will the leaders be completely fluent and credible to the participants? Even more important, will the session leaders be cross-cultural enough to help you, as the marketer, understand the themes and subthemes that emerge as part of the interviewing process? More than language is at issue here. A group leader or interviewer may be fluent in Spanish or Mandarin, for example, but does he or she possess a true understanding of the focus-group participants—the nuances and subissues that are part of their lives? Or a group leader might be African-American, but does he or she have an intimate knowledge of the concerns and interest of the *specific* group of African-Americans you are researching: upscale consumers, urban youth, or whomever?

Review the quality and appropriateness of the materials that will be used. It is very important to remember that more than language is involved in the construction and administering of questionnaires and forms. "Often, organizations will trip over dollars to save pennies in this area," Dr. Erlich observes. For example, a company will have an employee in house with a Hispanic surname and who seems to have a grasp of the language, and it will take the easy way out and have that person do the translations or write the materials that will be used. That can be an immense mistake because translation is an art and a science. Providing suitable in-language materials requires tremendous care, caution, and a keen knowledge of both the consumers who are being addressed and the many subtleties that are the stock in trade of effective market research. Remember, you are not simply translating a language. Ideally, you are translating a culture.

Be aware of information flow and feedback. This aspect of the focus-group process falls into two separate processes. First, as you are observing the focus group at work, how will you receive information from it? If translation is part of the picture, will the facility provide you with a simultaneous translation of what is being said? Will you be able to listen to the group's activities in progress? These might seem like fairly straightforward considerations. But as any marketer who has spent money on research knows, monitoring focus-group activity can become a highly charged experience. Questions intrude such as, Why is the group leader zeroing in on that question? or Why didn't the leader dig for more information in that critical area? When cultural or linguistic barriers are also part of the activity, possibly separating the marketer from the leader and the group, frictions and misunderstandings are even more likely to occur.

Second, how will you receive the follow-up reports and findings on your research? Clearly, the market-research company you choose should be able to provide reports that are not only translated but that convey some of the subtleties, complexities, and nuances that were uncovered during the research.

Selecting a Market-Research Company and Facility

Clearly, in view of the preceding considerations, it is vital to select a competent market-research company to handle your research activities. Selecting a company with expertise in these markets requires some probing and direct questioning. Before signing on for market research with any company, even with a well-known one, be sure to ask some pointed questions:

- What studies have they conducted in ethnic markets over the last year, the last two years? Understandably, they may not want to share client names. But they should be able to describe in general terms what they have done.
- Do they have specific, applicable experience dealing with products or services in the same categories as yours?
- Who on their staff will be used to plan and conduct your research—from the high-end planning down to nuts-and-bolts operations? What experience have they had in the past?
- In light of the needs of your specific study, how do they plan to handle the critical recruitment of focus-group members?

Results and Evaluation

Armed with the results of focus-group activity, you should be able to plan your marketing campaign in some detail and with fairly predictable, quantifiable expectations.

You might project based on research that lending your sponsorship to a well-established local event with banners, product giveaways, and other event-specific activities will expose your brand to 25 percent of a city's Japanese-American market. Or you might project that running in-language advertising on a local Hispanic-American radio station will boost brand awareness by 20 percent.

Obviously, the next major research phase occurs after you have run your ads, sponsored your event, or implemented the marketing campaign based on the research just described.

The Bad News/Good News Aspect of Multicultural Research

After conducting focus-group research, you may feel somewhat discouraged. Perhaps the people you polled had not heard of your company, or had negative impressions of it, or were not heavy consumers of what you have to sell.

Well, that's the bad news. But it is also the good news because those same negative messages can spell opportunity for you. You may have arrived at just the right time, possibly at a time when your competitors have not recognized or addressed the market segment you are trying to reach.

Many multicultural Americans are highly brand loyal. Now that you're under way, you have a chance to establish and build that kind of equity. And if you get started now, your lead is going to be harder to match. If you can come in first, those other companies may well be in a "me too" position after you in the marketplace. That is opportunity waiting to happen.

After the Focus Groups Comes the Plan

Once you have discovered through research what people perceive as the key benefits about your product and which product in your product line is most appealing to them, it is time to formalize and write the plan.

For your reference, you will find several such plans (with the names of the companies disguised) in the Appendix at the end of this book. By reviewing them you will see the kind of program planning that must be put in place before the program is launched.

Let's take an in-depth look at one such program for a client we will call Take-Home Food Market. Take-Home was a restaurant chain expanding into the take-out food market at the time. As we know, restaurants offering good-quality take-out foods for home dining have become increasingly successful over the last ten years. As time-pressured baby boomers have entered and passed through their prime child-rearing years, the need for good-quality, immediately available foods for home consumption has made them very much in demand.

Recognizing that time pressures due to career and family translate across racial and ethnic lines, Take-Home was interested in capturing a larger share of the African-American market.

The Situation

For seven years, Take-Home Food Market had been experiencing sales declines, particularly in southern locations in the continental United States. Fortunately, Take-Home's management had the intelligence and foresight to ask the right questions about why those sales declines were taking place. And instead of simply pouring more dollars into mainstream advertising, they were willing to entertain some innovative, intelligent ideas about adapting to the changing face of their consumer market.

They came to our organization for help because they realized that the very markets in which their sales were declining sharply were the ones with significant African-American population figures. So in conjunction with Take-Home's management, we began to research the possibility of mounting an integrated marketing program within the African-American sectors in key southern markets.

- We conducted focus groups in key cities to determine the specific Take-Home products (versus their entire product line) that appealed most strongly to the African-American target market.
- We fully investigated the psychographics of the primary markets being considered: young, professional African-American consumers, often with children at home, who were pressed for time. In short, young professionals in need of convenience and service.
- We conducted a competitive analysis to determine the position of Take-Home versus similar restaurants. We evaluated quality of service, food offerings, frequency-of-purchase figures from consumers, and other data.

Bringing the Client Up to Speed

Since Take-Home was relatively new to making a concerted marketing effort directed at African-Americans, we pointed out the following operative principles to Take-Home's management within the context of their marketing plan:

- African-American consumers respond favorably to targeted messages. Yet at the same time, simply placing ads in African-American media is not enough to ensure their buying behavior. What is communicated and how it is communicated are what will win brand loyalty.
- The majority of African-Americans prefer African-American role models to be represented in advertising campaigns. We

urged Take-Home to know that 70 percent of African-
Americans have reported that they're more likely to buy a
product when African-Americans are featured in advertising
and marketing messages. We also reported to Take-Home that
African-Americans are responsive to product endorsements
made by African-Americans.

• We stressed that a successful marketing campaign targeted to
African-Americans would require a closely targeted media
approach. Simply featuring African-Americans in mainstream
television advertising or presenting product endorsements by
prominent African-Americans in mainstream television commercials, would in all likelihood not result in sufficient return
on investment (ROI) for Take-Home's marketing dollar.

Consider the fact that, while African-Americans watch a great
deal of television (73.5 hours per week versus 48.5 for all other people
living in the United States nationally), African-Americans are not
watching the same shows as other Americans. In fact, if you compare
the top ten most-watched shows named by African-Americans with the
top ten most-watched shows named by all other Americans, there is
only one show in common. We also suggested to Take-Home that radio
is a medium of choice for African-Americans.

Results of Our Research

Point-of-sale and other market statistics we gathered demonstrated that,
in most major southern markets where sales were declining, the drop-
off in sales could be correlated directly to lack of support and acceptance within the African-American consumer markets, the dominant
population group.

We also found, based on our focus groups, that African-American
consumers expressed a marked preference for certain menu items offered
by Take-Home over other items. Key elements turned out to be

• Food content: beef and heartier entrées were preferred by
African-Americans over lighter entrées and selections.
• Portion size was another factor uncovered in focus-group ses-
sions. If portions were found to be too small, African-American

consumers were unlikely to return to Take-Home locations a
second time or to become repeat customers on a consistent basis.

• Quality of service: focus-group activities also determined,
interestingly, that African-Americans found the level of service
at Take-Home locations to be very disappointing. This issue
tied closely to concerns of respect and perceived value. Unless
Take-Home could do something to address that question
among African-American constituents—and in a way that was
consistent with the rest of their marketing initiatives—results
would surely fall short of expectations.

Strategy

Based on the research, psychographic analysis, and market considerations just outlined, we were able to develop a targeted communications
program for Take-Home. The goal was nothing less than repositioning
the chain in the perception of the African-American consumer market.

The initiatives we recommended focused on three key criteria:

1. Food selection. To win a larger share of the African-American
   market, Take-Home would need to examine its menus and
   include more of the heartier (meat-oriented), appetite-
   satisfying foods identified in our focus-group sessions.
2. Perceived value. To win a larger market share, Take-Home
   would do well to consider placing a new emphasis on the pricing and sizing of menu portions.
3. To establish a culturally relevant position for Take-Home
   within the key market areas would require specialized ads,
   media selection, sponsorships, and community involvement.

To these ends, we reviewed the positioning of Take-Home in
regard to existing promotions already in place nationwide. In particular, promotions centered on popular superheroes who were already
"speaking" to the children of the target demographic that Take-Home
intended to address.

We also determined that Take-Home's longtime affiliation with
a national community-based youth organization was something that
could be built on and would play effectively to the African-American

constituents. We suggested that one way to reinforce the knowledge of this longtime connection would be to create a special direct-mail coupon piece to be mailed to all African-American consumers within the demographic targeted areas.

Media

Because of the large African-American population within our target cities, there was an abundance of high-quality African-American media across print and broadcast outlets. We decided that radio and TV were the appropriate media, with an emphasis on young, urban radio programs that research showed were favored by our targets. We selected drive-time radio to reach our target at the end of the day—at the very time they were thinking, "What can I quickly put together for dinner?" At the same time, we also planned to implement some special advertising, stressing in-store promotions, in partnership with magazines that we knew were read by African-Americans in our target areas.

Results

Results were excellent. By asking the right questions and implementing appropriate and targeted strategies, we were able to help Take-Home post more than a 10 percent revenue increase in only one year among African-American consumers in targeted southern areas. And because Take-Home's management made a commitment to stay with their new consumers in the long term, the success has remained constant for over five years now, growing consistently from one year to the next.

Among Take-Home's ongoing initiatives have been

- development of new ads and other marketing initiatives to speak consistently to African-American consumers
- an ongoing review of menu and pricing to be sure that African-Americans will find appealing items in their locations
- a growing internal diversity program to integrate Take-Home into the markets it is trying to address
- stringent quality control over not only the food itself but the quality of service customers find upon arriving in Take-Home's locations (As we confirmed in focus groups and stressed to

Take-Home's management, unless African-American consumers felt welcome buying their foods at Take-Home, all the
other marketing initiatives would have been pointless.)

ROI Analysis—How Did You Do?

Once your campaign has been executed, or put in progress, how do you
evaluate success? Of course, you can monitor sales and see what hap-
pens. Or you can poll people and see how their attitude toward your
company or products has changed.

Fortunately, more sophisticated and useful new approaches have
evolved. Richard Mascolo, president of Skunkworks, offers these
observations.

> The ideal is to engage not just ROI analysis, but what we call a closed-
> loop process, meaning that at the end of a marketing effort we try to
> understand the effect of what we have done and then apply that knowl-
> edge to our next efforts on behalf of our client. When you understand
> the effect of the decisions you've made, you are able to arrive at a sta-
> tistical framework that allows you to go back to the front of the process
> and make better decisions the next time.
>
> So you are engaged in a process of back-end ROI analysis that loops
> back and becomes part of your front-end planning the next time
> around. Ideally, it should be a continuous learning process.

Making Optimal Use of New Information Sources

One of the things that marketers are doing with increasing sophistication is classic "mix modeling"—a statistical technique that has been used
in the marketing world, primarily by packaged-goods marketers, for
more than ten years. This technique monitors not just sales and other
basics but goes deeper and establishes statistical understanding of just
what each piece of the marketing mix produces for the marketer, and
furthermore, how all the parts of the mix coordinate statistically.

Because of computing power, new techniques, and a variety of
other factors including the sophistication of both suppliers and
clients, the mix-marketing approach has become more widespread and

pervasive in its application, Mascolo states. It provides a very sophisticated level of ROI modeling. Thanks to the growing sophistication of marketing data available, it has become increasingly possible to statistically isolate the tangible business contributions of the different elements of a marketing mix. The elements can be viewed either in terms of big pieces, such as advertising versus sales versus pricing, or data considered at very granular levels. For example, what is the difference in return between a fifteen-second television commercial and a thirty-second television commercial in terms of creating tangible results or sales? Now formulas can accurately describe the different contributions of the mix elements. With the new research tools, you can compare the efficacy of each dollar spent in the general market to what that dollar would return in the targeted ethnic marketing.

Establishing Baseline Criteria

We could go into many hows and whens of research, but perhaps it is time to posit a more fundamental and far simpler question: What would your position be in the marketplace—how much would you be selling—if you were undertaking no marketing activity at all?

This may not be as dumb a question as it sounds. Most brands and most companies, after all, coast along on momentum, be it from the sales generated at point of sale, from residual brand awareness, or even from momentum that remains from advertising and marketing efforts undertaken in the past. We do know that advertising has a residual value; sometimes, even years after a dollar has been spent on advertising, a company can continue to receive payback in increased sales and brand awareness.

How do you arrive at your baseline measurement? That is a complex issue, Richard Mascolo states. Obtaining data is more difficult than simply looking at point-of-sale data or reviewing profit-and-loss sheets. Understanding your baseline data requires a near-artistic sense of how some of these different factors impact on consumer activity regarding your product, including

- pricing
- the products and marketing activities of your competitors
- seasonality

- sales efforts
- local and regional economic conditions
- trade promotions
- weather
- advertising generated on behalf of your products by retailers

The goal in establishing a baseline is to understand the profits you generate as a fundamental point of measurement, separated from what you might normally obtain from advertising. In other words, your baseline should answer the question, How well would we be doing if we were conducting no advertising or marketing at all?

Once your baseline figures are established, and they can be for the general marketplace as well as for specific ethnic segments, you are in a position to evaluate the results and returns of your marketing efforts.

Measuring the Mix

What marketing statisticians and magicians like Richard Mascolo are able to do through measuring and analysis is answer questions that were not even askable only fifteen years ago. Questions like

- How much of your total sales is attributable to print advertising? To radio? To TV ads?
- If you have print and TV ads running at the same time, how much more effective is their combined contribution than the sum of just print plus TV?
- If you are running newspaper ads to support an event you are staging, what is their statistical contribution to event attendance and the bigger picture of generating sales?

Such complex and elusive information can be obtained today because of the many sources of data available: from Nielsen ratings to point-of-sale retail data to detailed information from radio stations on total listenership when your ad is played.

In sum, Mascolo's mix analysis can be a strategic tool for those marketers who desire to better understand the specific contributions of each element of their marketing program, and it might just be an excellent step as you begin to add ethnic marketing to your mix.

Unfortunately, that information could take up several books on its own. And doing it well really does require the expertise and knowledge of someone who understands the many variables at hand, the sources of information, as well as the many causalities at work in analyzing and understanding so much raw, interconnected data.

In summary, remarkable results can be achieved in multicultural campaigns when the right questions are asked and the right marketing plans and methodologies are put in place. Spend some time with the various marketing plans that are reproduced in the Appendix. By adapting the approaches and methodologies they reflect, you will greatly increase the chances of reaching success in your own multicultural marketing initiatives.

Chapter Seven

THE STRATEGIC VALUE OF DIVERSITY

The Diversity Imperative

Tony Watson grew up in the Cabrini Green projects in Chicago and attended the U.S. Naval Academy. During a distinguished thirty-one-year career in the U.S. Navy, Mr. Watson achieved the rank of rear admiral and commanded a fleet of nineteen nuclear submarines. Today, Mr. Watson is chief executive officer and cofounder of U.S. Alliance Group, a leading management search firm specializing in staffing solutions with nontraditional populations, including transitional and prior-service military personnel, women, and persons of color.

> It is a real opportunity to work in the world of diversity. It affords me a chance to open some doors for deserving people and to give something back.
>
> In part, my firm's purpose is to respond to companies when they say, "We'd like to hire appropriate minority executives, but they don't exist," or when they say, "We can't hire them because we can't find them quickly enough."
>
> I was brought up in the projects, and now I have the opportunity to knock on some doors and suggest to people that there is a real opportunity today to gain access to talent they might not have thought about before.
>
> I've always lived by the philosophy that smart is relative to the task at hand. When I graduated from the naval academy, my father pulled me

aside and said, "I want you to remember something, you may know more than I know, but you don't know what I know."

It took me some time to realize that he was giving me the strongest philosophy lesson that I could ever have. I realized later what he meant, that smart is relative to the task at hand. I remember an instance when I was commanding a submarine, deep underwater, and a young 18-year-old mechanic went to the head mechanic and said, "Something is wrong with one of the motors that operates the seawater system. It sounds funny."

That comment led us to pull the motor and inspect it, repair it, and keep the system running and operational. Now, we could have just said, this guy is only a kid. So what if he thinks a motor sounds funny? We're in charge here!

But as I learned from my father, intelligence depends on the task at hand. And I think it's important for corporate America to recognize the strength that diversity brings to the table in so many ways. When a workforce is comprised of people from many different backgrounds—people of color, women, Hispanic-, and Asian-Americans—it represents a real operative strength.

So many corporations feel that diversity represents a lowering of standards. But I would argue just the opposite. Diversity means raising standards.

When you build a diverse workforce, you bring together a varied depth of experience. It's not a melting pot you're aiming for. It's a garden salad. You might put some salad dressing on it and polish up the skills of the people who are part of it, but a diverse workforce makes a very good combination.

Fundamentally, the purpose of business is to provide solutions to customers' needs at whatever level. Diversity does that. It means creating a workforce that understands your consumer base.

Let me tell you a story about my future son-in-law, who is Hispanic and just a terrific guy. He was a mess specialist in the navy, working in food services. He left the service and had a few jobs, including working for UPS. Then he met a man who runs an auto dealership in Reading, Pennsylvania, who offered him a job. Now, Reading is 55 percent

Hispanic, yet my future son-in-law was the first Latino and bilingual salesperson to join the sales staff of that dealership.

In his first three weeks, he sold nine cars. He became the top salesperson overnight. He has the kind of personality that people really like. Because he's from the military, he has the habit of saying "yes sir" and "yes ma'am." But the word is spreading through the Hispanic community that he is there, and customers are already referring new customers to him. Hispanic customers take their business to him because he's a very personable young man and he can also speak their language.

Consider that kind of input and outreach spread across a large company. Yes, there is appropriate outreach across the entire customer base. And when there is a diverse workforce in house, and those people are having meetings with the company leaders, well, then you have a situation where company leaders are keyed into more key market sectors. They aren't just looking at how the company is doing on the numbers, but how it is doing in the Hispanic community, the Asian-American community, the African-American community, with women, and with all other customer groups. It is a real operating strength.

When I look back at the disaster that happened at Texaco back in 1994, it's quite clear to me why it occurred. There simply were not any people in place whose presence would reorient what top management was thinking and doing, and whose presence would prevent that kind of disastrous thinking, talking, and acting from taking place. Unfortunately, too many companies today are still acting in ways that will result in just those kind of disasters.

In my mind, that is the real millennium bug that will bring down many businesses in the years to come. It's not a computer problem. It's a failure to recognize the imperative need for diversity—a failure that will cause disastrous problems for companies if they do not act soon to implement diversity initiatives. The companies that act decisively now will win the loyalty of the emerging groups of consumers in America today, who will grow in numbers and buying power in the coming years. The companies that don't act will fail to gain those loyalties in the marketplace. The disasters they incur will be the real millennium disaster, one that will run well beyond the so-called millennium computer bug, which will, at worst, cause some computer problems for a month or two after the dawn of the year 2000.

Tomorrow's most successful companies most likely will no longer even think of diversity. It will be such a part of the way they do business, of their inner fabric, that the whole concept of building a diverse workforce will become an archaic and antiquated relic from an earlier age when companies could afford to merely *market to* people instead of *becoming* them.

We need to concede, however, that we have not yet come that far. True, today's smaller, more market-driven and entrepreneurial companies are often diverse by their very nature. They have emerged from the marketplace in which they are doing business, and as a result, their inner constituency closely mirrors that of the market to which they want to appeal.

But in many larger corporations and smaller to midsize companies as well, the news that diversity must be part of the way a company does business has yet to hit home in its full impact. Too many companies feel that

- Real diversity is a matter of image building or public relations. If they place minority employees in visible positions, the job will be done. They need to be line versus staff positions, where they can truly impact the business and control the bottom line.
- Diversity is a human resources issue, a legal issue, or one related to the Equal Employment Opportunity Commission (EEOC).
- Diversity is a matter of being altruistic. Of course, hiring minority employees can often be the right thing to do. But unless it is seen as a vital mandate for business success—a success strategy rather than simple outreach—minority employees are unlikely to rise through the corporate ranks or have the needed transforming power over company initiatives and goals.
- Diversity is a matter of advertising. An African-American, Hispanic-American, or Asian-Pacific-American who appears in advertising will show minority people in the marketplace that the company understands them and has their interests at heart.

- Diversity is a rank-and-file situation; it needs to be represented at the middle- and senior-management ranks and at the board level. But to be effective, diversity requires a commitment from the top that is represented at all levels of the organization, especially at the senior manager levels where decisions are made.

Finally, two of the most limiting and damaging misconceptions of all:

- Diversity represents a lowering of standards for what is expected of employees. Quite the contrary: a company that resolves to hire, train, and retain a diverse workforce represents a raising of the standards bar. Through diversity, a company builds a human resource pool that will equip it to flexibly adapt to the demands of today's and tomorrow's America.
- Diversity is a matter of damage containment. An ongoing stream of news stories, it seems, reflects this view, which holds that companies need not concern themselves about diversity until something goes wrong. Perhaps a top executive makes an insensitive or biased comment to the press, or the company is charged in a bias suit that makes the news. At that point, it becomes essential for the company to make some kind of gesture to set things right. Consultants are hired, and a diversity campaign is mounted. Sometimes, something good results but usually only if the company has decided to make a real commitment to its diversity initiatives rather than merely try to contain an image problem.

The Mandate for Business

What can diversity do for you, as the employer? What it really does for you is present you as the employer of choice and a preferred brand for a larger, more diverse audience. That is the whole goal.

If you are a major corporation, your goal should be to become that employer of choice, a place that attracts the right kind of minority candidates to your door. You are a sought-after employer.

Why will most nondiverse companies become, increasingly, less and less competitive in the coming decades? There are many reasons—some obvious, some less so.

- Within the next few decades, nondiverse companies will become increasingly less appealing within most markets and submarkets in North America. In fact, the best and brightest professionals will also be diversity candidates. As the marketplace becomes increasingly diverse, "closed" and predominantly white companies will appear increasingly anachronistic in contrast to the more market-attuned organizations that surround them.

- Nondiverse companies will, more and more, cut themselves off from vital sources of intelligence about the market, the competition, and much more. Focus groups and research are fine and essential. But an organization's own internal ranks are the most important source of information about the concerns and perceptions of buyers. When a company internalizes much of that knowledge through diversity, it becomes more competitive and attuned to what is happening in the marketplace.

- Nondiverse organizations will limit their ability to grow. As noted earlier, diversity starts at the top through the recruitment and retention of executives who are either members of minority groups or who are well sensitized to the value of diversity. But as America diversifies in the coming decades, a company's ability to grow and prosper largely hinges on its ability to recruit and train younger and entry-level employees. When a company fails to meet this mandate, it limits its human resource pool severely and, over time, is more likely to lose its competitive edge.

What kind of thinking, in contrast, is likely to build diversity and greater success in the future? We would define it in the following way: To excel and succeed in the coming decades, it is not enough for a company to appeal to its consumers. A company must become its consumers. Nothing else will suffice if a company is committed to growth; and in the end, nothing else will succeed.

Putting Diversity in Place

As noted earlier, the key to achieving real diversity is real commitment. That kind of commitment plays out in many ways through the organization, from the top to the bottom.

While individual company strategies may vary, here are the main components to keep in mind that can lead to success.

A Real, Top-Down Commitment to Diversity

A successful diversity initiative is a new direction that requires ongoing participation and maintenance on the part of company leadership.

Examples are now common among our leading corporations:

- American Express has created a Diversity Council, made up of members of senior management, that meets every six or eight weeks to discuss the corporate diversity initiative.
- Hewlett-Packard's Diversity Leadership Council, also comprised of members of the top executive team, conducts an ongoing appraisal of diversity efforts in all company areas. Key to the effort is an ongoing policy of reminding all managers of the corporation's commitment to diversity in all areas of operations.
- DaimlerChrysler has undertaken similar initiatives and places emphasis on benchmarking against other companies in their diversity undertakings. Their commitment to being state of the art with regard to diversity issues might well reward the company with increased competitiveness in the coming decades.
- At Mobil, the move toward greater diversity was mandated by the diverse constituency of its consumer base, both domestically and abroad. Mobil's operations, after all, take place in more than 125 countries.

  Back in 1984, Lou Noto, Mobil's chair and CEO, began a new diversity initiative by establishing a Leadership Council to spearhead its Global Inclusion and Diversity initiative. The key working points for the program were culture and communication, leadership and accountability, recruitment and outreach,

The "Diversity Elite"

Each year, *Fortune* magazine and the Council on Economic Priorities, a nonprofit research organization, compile a list of what they term their "Diversity Elite"— the best companies for diversity in America. Among the criteria used to judge these companies are the number of minority members on boards of directors, the number of minority members among the top twenty-five paid employees, and the overall percentage of minority officials and managers.

Example: Union Bank of California, which tops the list with a number one rating, has the following statistics: seven out of seventeen board members are minority members, five of the twenty-five top-paid employees are also minority executives, and 53.7 percent of the overall workforce is made up of minorities.

Fortune's 1999 Diversity Elite in rank order:

1. Union Bank of California	26. American Express
2. Fannie Mae	27. Gannett
3. Public Service Co. of New Mexico	28. Bell Atlantic
	29. Applied Materials
4. Sempra Energy	30. Sun Microsystems
5. Toyota Motor Sales	31. Colgate-Palmolive
6. Advantica	32. Citigroup
7. SBC Communications	33. Consolidated Edison
8. Lucent Technologies	34. PG&E Corp.
9. Darden Restaurants	35. United Parcel Service
10. Wal-Mart Stores	36. Nordstrom
11. Allstate	37. Adolf Coors Brewing
12. Chase Manhattan Bank	38. Pitney Bowes
13. Marriott International	39. Shoney's
14. US West	40. Merck
15. Federal Express	41. Abbott Laboratories
16. Southern California Edison	42. S.C. Johnson & Son
17. Bank of America	43. DuPont de Nemours
18. Hyatt	44. Eli Lilly
19. TIAA-CREF	45. Computer Associates Intl.
20. Xerox	46. Schering-Plough
21. BellSouth	47. Avon Products
22. Knight Ridder	48. J. P. Morgan
23. AMR	49. Pepsico
24. Texas Instruments	50. Ryder System
25. Ameritech	

and retention. In an effort to make these priorities operative down through the ranks, Mobil included them among the list of "Score Card" traits used to evaluate each manager's performance.

- In the early 1990s, several important lawsuits were filed against the Denny's chain, alleging discrimination against African-American clients.

But by 1994, when the suits were settled, Denny's had already begun to demonstrate a strong commitment to diversity. Among other steps, Denny's instituted a special toll-free number where customers could report any instances of discrimination they had observed in Denny's establishments and set up an active program of diversity recruitment and training for all current managers.

Denny's not only talked about diversity, but it put money behind its words. In 1992, at the time of the discrimination suits, Denny's had no minority-owned vendors. By 1996, the company paid $80 million in contracts to vendors who were minority owned.

CEO Jim Adamson was a motive force in bringing about the transformation, and his efforts did not go unnoticed. In fact, he was awarded the NAACP's Corporate CEO Achievement Award in 1996.

In less than a decade, Denny's transformed its image in the marketplace through its diversity efforts.

Putting the Pieces in Place

What makes for a successful diversity initiative? Success hinges on recruitment, retention, and ongoing commitment.

Effective tools and strategies for reaching those goals are many and varied. Here are some that are being used effectively at many companies today.

- A full-time, committed diversity officer with the title Director of Diversity can be added to the human resources staff.
- A special diversity council, made up of top-ranking executives from major divisions and departments, can meet regularly to keep diversity efforts on track and plan new initiatives.

- Human resources, especially, needs to work with top management to frame and implement diversity hiring goals. Recruitment practices and plans should be part of this process.
- Mentoring programs have proven to be highly effective in assuring the long-term success and retention of a diverse workforce. In such programs, established and successful executives agree to mentor younger employees of their own ethnic backgrounds—whether African-American, Hispanic-American, or Asian-Pacific-American. Such programs go a long way toward teaching needed skills and attitudes to younger employees, as well as demonstrating, through the ranks, the company's top-down commitment to diversity.
- The company can encourage employees of similar ethnic or racial backgrounds to meet regularly for discussion, social events, or production of their own in-house publications. Such groups, often called affinity groups, should be seen as an asset rather than a threat.
- Public relations and media relations officers should be reminded that, alongside press releases regarding new products, acquisitions, and hiring of new executives, they should also send out press releases highlighting the company's initiatives in the diversity area.
- Diversity training can, and should, be part of ongoing training at the company. Note here that the thrust of such training is not to teach incoming employees about the company's diversity priorities and policies but to train and refresh the diversity orientation of all current employees. Such training activities are especially critical when a company newly directs its attention toward the issue of diversity. Without training "older" managers, who were in place before the diversity initiative, frictions and misunderstandings in implementing new diversity policies can often occur.
- To round out an effective diversity initiative, you also need vendor diversity. When your vendors and distribution channels are as diverse as your company internally, you position yourself to compete more effectively in the marketplace and strengthen your image as a company that is attuned to your consumers.

- Corporate communications. News of a company's diversity efforts need to be communicated through press releases, event sponsorships, advertising, and all other channels. Keep in mind that the purpose of a diversity initiative should not be to create an image of a diverse company. The real purpose should be to achieve an internal balance that closely mirrors the constituency of the company's customers.
- Regularly produced in-house newsletters (often monthly or quarterly) that deal exclusively with company diversity initiatives. Such publications can help keep managers and employees at every level attuned to diversity issues regarding recruitment, retention, success stories, etc.
- It should be stressed that good communications of company diversity initiatives, which express the efforts really being made, are an important component of diversity efforts. Through media and other outreach, the company lets consumers know of its commitment to diversity and builds position as "employer of choice" for its potential job candidates. Other benefits accrue as well. When Hispanic-, African-, and Asian-Pacific-Americans are aware of a company's strong efforts to promote diversity, they are more likely to keep that company "top of mind" when the time comes to think of potential employers. The result is a deeper and better qualified pool of applicants. Your goal is not to recruit but to become an employer of choice.
- Measurement and maintenance of the program. As in any corporate initiative, the implementation of diversity programs needs to be measurable. A variety of factors need to be watched and tracked, including minority recruitment, training initiatives, mentoring programs, retention statistics, and communication about the program to the marketplace.

Strategies for Recruiting a Diverse Workforce: Becoming Employer of Choice

Obviously, a varied mix of employees is required for a company to become diverse. Overall, this process can be broken down into two main components.

The first component is the recruitment of top executives. There is no one-size-fits-all advice to offer on this topic. What a company needs to do to achieve diversity in its top-management ranks depends on its existing top-executive mix.

It's true that an Asian-Pacific-American chief financial officer (CFO), or African- or Hispanic-American, is likely to possess the same skills set as another CFO. So he or she will be hired for abilities and skills that stand apart from any special knowledge of the marketplace or his or her ethnic outlook. Yet this kind of assumption has limitations. A marketing executive with a minority background, for example, likely possesses outlooks, attitudes, and abilities that will equip a company to market more effectively than before to members of that executive's constituency. Even in nonmarketing areas, where a particular nonmajority ethnic background may be perceived as a neutral benefit, that executive's outlook will often add a greater depth and level of corporate intelligence than what was present before. Having a CFO who is a minority sends a message to minority employees throughout the firm and to diverse candidates that that company has a top-level commitment to diversity.

Due to many socioeconomic and demographic factors, achieving a diverse workforce within a company is difficult if all a company does is run ads for employees before attempting to hire minorities from the applicant pool. The company will need a further and deeper commitment, especially if it is committed to the process of expanding its presence and efficacy in emerging new markets. That is one reason for recruitment from within, the second component.

Diversity Recruiting: A State-of-the-Art Approach

Wesley Brown & Bartle Company, a leader in diversity recruiting, has spent years developing and using a state-of-the-art system for diversity recruiting called Strategic Sourcing.

Strategic Sourcing entirely circumvents the traditional system of interviewing and recruiting suitable executive candidates. The hiring company no longer waits until a position becomes available before beginning the executive-search process.

Strategic Sourcing makes communicating directly with minority candidates an ongoing, organic part of company operations. Before a position is available, the company institutes the practice of meeting with minority executives from a number of different companies and disciplines. The company might call African-, Asian-Pacific-, or Hispanic-American candidates to say, "We don't have a job, and that's not why we are calling. We would just like to invite you in for a talk about our industry, about what we are doing, and about what you are up to." This way, the potential employer develops a wide-based series of contacts among successful executives, some of whom might one day be appropriate for positions that become available.

Strategic Sourcing is a very effective tool in diversity recruiting for many reasons. First, the candidate and company meet on "even ground"—in a low-pressured setting where they simply share ideas and information. The process takes place over time, no attempt is made to match a candidate to a job, and no decisions need to be made on either end. Both company and executive are simply getting to know one another and forming impressions. On the one side, the candidate has time to internalize information; think about the company's policies, activities, and priorities; and consider the company's appeal as an employer. From its side, the company can form impressions of executives who one day might make appropriate additions to the leadership ranks. Now when a position becomes available, the company has already encountered a number of executives, some of whom might be appropriate candidates for further discussions. This pool of potential job candidates is called a Diversity Tracking Model.

Strategic Sourcing works as an effective tool in diversity recruiting for another, more subtle reason. It has a unique ability to circumvent the "deselective behaviors" process through which minority candidates are eliminated from consideration. A deselective behavior is simply a mechanism that occurs when a hiring firm eliminates a candidate from consideration in a specific hiring decision.

Such cut-and-dry decisions are part of the landscape when a specific job needs to be filled. Candidates are eliminated for certain disqualifying factors, such as insufficient supervisory experience, lack of background in industry or field, and lack of expertise in one job component such as public relations experience, sales background, etc.

Through Strategic Sourcing such quick elimination of candidates is no longer part of the process, so more in-depth discussions between companies and possible hires may take place on a continuous, open-ended basis.

There is still another, more subtle reason why this approach is effective with diversity recruitment. It is simply that deselective factors are more likely to surface in companies where there is entrenched resistance to hiring minority candidates. Consciously or otherwise, non-minority decision makers are likely to deselect minority candidates early in the hiring process by deciding they are inappropriate for the position to be filled.

Not long ago, for example, I heard of a rather extreme case of this happening. When interviewing an African-American executive, a white representative of the hiring firm asked, "How many direct reports did you have in that job?" naming a previous position. The executive replied that he had twenty-two. Then the interviewing executive asked the African-American candidate to name them, and the candidate could only name nineteen of them. The white executive reported back to his management that "He claims to have supervised twenty-two people, but he can't name them." This is either overt or covert discrimination at work. In either case, the actions of the interviewing executive were highly deselective and likely curtailed further discussions with the executive in question.

Strategic Sourcing can circumvent such problems and at very little cost to the hiring firm.

Wesley Brown & Bartle Company's Twenty-Five Key Steps to Achieving Diversity

Wesley Brown & Bartle Company, an executive-search firm specializing in diversity recruitment, has been recognized by *Fortune* and many American corporations for its pioneering role in building diversity. Their "Twenty-Five Key Steps to Achieving Diversity," summarized here, offer an excellent guide for corporations eager to build genuine diversity through the ranks.

1. Establish a corporate diversity policy signed by the chief executive officer that endorses workforce diversity as a fundamental

core value of the company; distribute individually addressed copies of the policy to all employees.

2. Require all corporate officers, managers, and exempt supervisors to sign letters committing themselves to implementing the diversity policy.

3. Tie a meaningful percentage of the annual compensation of officers, managers, and exempt supervisors to the achievement of specific individual diversity goals that are an integral part of annual performance reviews.

4. Display the corporate diversity policy with state and federal equal employment opportunity (EEO) posters throughout the organization. Make achievement of EEO standards a significant part of the responsibilities of all company managerial personnel; publish EEO results regularly.

5. Formulate a diversity recruitment strategy that employs specialists in minority recruiting as a supplement to traditional recruiting sources; institute a separate corporate human resources budget to fund diversity recruitment on a company-wide basis.

6. Establish strong and regular contacts with colleges and universities with a high percentage of minority students to ensure access to high-potential minority graduates; establish relationships with minority professional organizations.

7. Establish diversity succession plans that designate managerial career opportunities for minority employees throughout the organization.

8. Appoint a director or vice president of corporate diversity reporting to the CEO or senior management who has a demonstrated operations success record. Delegate line authority and a budget for diversity initiatives. Put a company star in the post.

9. Endorse the use of Diversity Tracking Models[1] by functional areas that lack diverse representation to ensure an adequate pipeline of qualified, high-potential minority candidates.

---

1. Diversity Tracking Model is the external diversity succession planning system available from Wesley Brown & Bartle Company.

10. Mandate that all external recruitment sources include female and minority candidates in the final slates for all management-level searches; distribute the corporate diversity policy to all recruiters and require adherence to the policy by all vendors.

11. Monitor all screening, reference checking, testing, and hiring practices to ensure applicants are considered on the basis of their qualifications alone.

12. Conduct ongoing company-wide diversity training with participation by senior management to imbue diversity concepts in the corporate culture and ensure a sustainable cultural change.

13. Exercise caution in dealing with newly established diversity training firms; inexperienced firms claiming to be diversity experts may do more harm than good.

14. Incorporate a diversity section in all employee communications to publicize diversity successes and emphasize top-management support on a continuous basis.

15. Encourage the development of diversity newsletters at all levels of the company: corporate, business units, and individual departments.

16. Establish a corporate diversity council and encourage formation of diversity task forces and committees in each business unit; endorse diversity clubs or associations; provide company facilities for meetings of the council, clubs, and committees.

17. Endorse mentoring programs. Assign majority and minority mentors to advise and assist minority employees in functioning successfully with members of the traditional workforce; make successful mentoring a significant objective in performance appraisals.

18. Establish a substantive management development program designed for women and minority professionals; monitor progress frequently; assign responsibility for the program to a company executive who is considered a rising star.

19. Develop a meaningful company-wide feedback program so management can accurately gauge the success or failure of all diversity programs, and be prepared to take corrective action if required.

20. Circulate to all managers the Hudson Institute Report, Workforce 2020, which cites demographics on the growing importance of women and minorities in the workforce.

21. Acquaint senior management with the high cost of workforce bias and the significant direct and indirect costs of not retaining qualified minorities.

22. Obtain the commitment of senior management to a corporate diversity timetable for achieving realistic diversity objectives in a reasonable but accelerated time frame.

23. Establish a diversity retention program to enhance the company's ability to retain high-potential minority professionals; institute realistic diversity exit interviews that are focused on determining the actual reasons for resignations by minority professionals. Have a minority interviewer conduct post-exit interviews with former minority employees. Report results to senior executives.

24. Publish and circulate the company's progress on its diversity action plans. Publish a diversity annual report.

25. Imbue pride in company executives for their success in achieving performance-driven diversity objectives. Keep diversity objectives separate from affirmative action numbers–oriented goals; maintain focus on achievement by individual employees, not groups of employees.

And . . . realize that achieving true performance-driven workforce diversity is not as simple as incorporating the preceding twenty-five steps. Diversity, like core values of quality, must become the essence and culture of the organization, not a separate initiative.

CASE STUDY: TEXACO

As was the case with Denny's, Texaco's much-respected initiatives toward diversity began with an image problem in the marketplace. On November 4, 1996, newspapers and news programs across the United States reported that Texaco executives had been caught on tape making discriminatory comments about African-Americans. The result was a pending discrimination lawsuit and a firestorm of criticism directed at the company.

In the days following, Texaco tried its best to respond decisively, reaching out to employees, religious leaders, and shareholders, doing its best to assure them that discrimination was not part of the company culture at Texaco. In December, Texaco launched a plan for workforce diversity and for partnering with minority-owned businesses to improve Texaco's image in the marketplace.

At the time, Texaco chairman and CEO Peter Bijur issued the following statements to explain the company's purpose in making the new initiatives:

"First, and most important, because they are the right thing to do. They reflect the most fundamental value of our company, respect for the individual. Within Texaco we are totally committed to this core value, and it is the number one leadership standard for our management team. Respect means something else as well: zero tolerance for discrimination of any kind.

"Second, these initiatives make good business sense. A diverse workforce allows us to align closely with the marketplace—especially important given the increasing globalization of our industry—and to have an employee population with a wide range of ideas and perspectives."

Texaco's new Diversity and Economic Outreach Plan instituted programs in these main areas:

- Building the workforce: to create a diverse workforce through recruitment, hiring, retention, promotion, and career development.
- Increased involvement with suppliers: The goal was to increase overall purchasing activities with minority- and women-owned businesses from $135 million in 1996 to a cumulative total of more than $1 billion over the next five years; to increase financial activities with minority- and women-owned banks and money managers from $32 million to $200 million; and to increase insurance coverage from minority- and women-owned insurance firms from $25 million to $200 million.

- Texaco's five-year goals were to double the number of minority- and women-owned wholesale marketers and to triple the number of African-American-owned outlets.

Willie Stanfield, an African-American, was appointed assistant to the chairman with responsibility for the economic outreach programs.

Beyond mere damage control, these efforts at Texaco have already gone a long way toward not only repairing a tarnished corporate image but replacing it with a justifiable reputation for a real commitment to diversity.

CASE STUDY: HEWLETT-PACKARD

The Hewlett-Packard Company (HP) has emerged as a leader in diversity over the last few decades. Creating a diverse, inclusive work environment has been a mandate at HP, even before the EEO guidelines of the 1960s and 1970s and the affirmative action initiatives of the 1980s.

In the mid-1980s, HP intensified its diversity efforts by adding more strategic programs, spurred by an employee survey that showed many employees of color did not feel they had an equal opportunity to advance their careers at HP. Rather than running away from this feedback, management embraced it and reexamined its work environment, involving all employees in the process. HP's effort is impressive, to say the least.

Here are some excerpts from HP's document called *Our Competitive Advantage: Work Force Diversity*, a brochure distributed within HP as a guidebook to creating and maintaining diversity.

What Is Work Force Diversity?

Work force diversity is having a work force that is made up of many unique individuals at all levels of the organization—one that is rich with men and women that come from different cultures, experiences, lifestyles, backgrounds, perspectives, and skills. It is an environment where everyone is included and valued. It is the environment we are working to create at Hewlett-Packard.

The Dimensions of Diversity

Each of us brings individual differences, experiences, and perspectives to the work place. Our opportunity is to leverage the many dimensions of diversity throughout the world to meet our customers' changing needs. HP's competitive advantage in the marketplace is its people and its ability to make differences our strength.

Ethnicity	Religion
Age	Sexual Orientation
Culture	Gender
Physical Attributes	Language
Nationality	Race
Thinking Styles	Economic Status
Lifestyle	

Creating a diverse, inclusive work environment—making HP *the best place to work for everyone*—is a journey of continuous renewal. Each step in the process has an important significance to remember as we progress. Together the steps create a Diversity Value Chain that represents the foundation we're relying on to fulfill our Global Diversity Vision.

Our Global Diversity Vision

An inclusive environment that benefits from diversity at all levels, values individual differences, and enables all employees to develop and contribute to their full potential while meeting the work/life demands of the twenty-first century.

The Business Reasons
- Our customers, suppliers, and strategic partners are increasingly global and multi-cultural. We must be positioned to relate to them. Our customers are changing—their needs and expectations for products and services are diverse. We must be able to understand, interface, and respond.
- Our competitive advantage is to become the leader in innovation, creativity, problem-solving, and organizational flexi-

bility. We must have diverse perspectives, talents, and teams to meet this global challenge.

- The work force demographics are changing in most countries. The labor pool is shrinking; labor shortages are projected. The competition to attract and retain top talent is increasing. We must be the best place to work for everyone to ensure our business success.

To fulfill our diversity vision, we have created a proactive strategy. It is a dynamic strategy that honors the needs of our organizations throughout the world and it will change as we change. We believe each component of the strategy is essential for our success and that we, the people of HP, are the creators of making our company *the best place to work* in every location.

Management leadership: ensure management ownership and
    involvement
Diversity learnings: increase awareness and inspire action
Outreach & recruitment: expand candidate pools and increase
    access to opportunities
Development programs: increase development opportunities
    to retain top talent
Work/life programs: create a supportive and flexible work
    environment
Employee participation: create opportunities for dialogue
    and open communications

Our Diversity Journey: Key Elements

The following programs and initiatives represent key actions that support our Global Diversity Strategy and have contributed to our progress.

Management Leadership
- Company "People" Hoshin established *people* as one of the two breakthrough priorities for the company. Our "people" hoshin communicates our direction and plans for continued progress toward making HP *the best place to work* for every

employee—it includes diversity, work/life, and development
strategies.
- Diversity Leadership Council develops and drives key diversity initiatives worldwide. It is comprised of senior executives representing all of HP's businesses and related Corporate functions.
- Corporate Objectives were updated to reflect diversity and inclusion.
- Diversity Strategic Plan provides a guide for HP organizations in their own diversity journey. It defines where we are today as a company, where we're going, and how we plan to get there.
- Worldwide Dialogue with Senior Managers was held to assess diversity progress and needs. Over 300 senior managers were invited to participate in this global conversation. The results were used to define what ACCOUNTABILITY for diversity success would include at HP.
- Diversity Accountability Framework is a resource for managers describing our Global Diversity Goal, the fundamental behaviors/actions needed from every manager to accomplish it, and the measures that will reflect our success.

Diversity Learnings
- Diversity Education & Training Strategy establishes a consistent delivery of diversity education at HP. It describes the array of educational options that are available to HP organizations to meet their diversity training needs.
- Diversity Best Practices Forums provide opportunities for HP organizations to learn from others. *Best practices* sharing has been a highlighted feature of our management and diversity specialist forums, newsletters, and other communications.
- Diversity Home Page supports HP organizations throughout the world. It includes on-line tools, such as our diversity presentation materials, diversity education resources, and other diversity resource information.
- Diversity Resource Center is a diversity reference library. It includes books, periodicals, videos, and other diversity educa-

tion and training materials, which are available to HP organizations to support local diversity initiatives.

Outreach & Recruitment
- SEED/Targeted College Recruiting Programs were expanded to identify top candidates early and strengthen our on-campus relationships to increase diverse candidate pools.
- External Search Firms were identified and relationships developed with them to assist us in increasing diverse hiring resources.
- Diversity-Focused Ad Campaign was developed to enhance our ability to communicate and attract diverse candidates to HP.
- Internal Job Posting Levels were increased to broaden access to higher level opportunities for professional growth and advancement.
- K–12 Education Program invests in the future work force. Its three goals are (1) to ensure early learning readiness, (2) to improve proficiency in science and math, and (3) to increase the number of women and minorities in science/math disciplines for future candidate pools.

Development Programs
- Accelerated Development Program (ADP) is a year-long accelerated management development program for high potential mid-level managers. Its objective is to advance leadership skills, knowledge, and establish mentoring relationships. Its goal is to identify, develop, and increase the number of diverse candidates for senior management positions.
- Leadership Effectiveness And Development (LEAD) Program is a formalized leadership development opportunity for high potential/high performing employees. It is designed to develop leadership skills, knowledge, and mentoring relationships to enhance career development options and opportunities.
- Efficacy Seminars provide a series of workshops designed to promote personal responsibility and accountability for employee career development for women and people of color.

Work/Life Balance
- HP Work Options provide a broad range of alternate work options for work/life flexibility.
- Work/Life Education for Managers was conducted to educate managers on the broad range of offerings available to support work/life issues.
- On-Line Work Options Guide was added as an on-line tool. The guide outlines the purpose and guidelines for each option.
- American Business Collaboration for Quality Dependent Care (ABC) is a program to expand the supply and improve the quality of dependent care services where employees of member companies live and work. HP joined with 20 other major corporations in expanding this $100 million initiative.

Employee Participation
- Employee Network Groups that foster employee communication, professional development, and teamwork are supported throughout the world.
- Diversity Advisory Boards, Councils, and Task Forces are encouraged in every organization to establish priorities and actions to support local initiatives.

Summary: The HP Way & Corporate Objectives

Our global diversity vision, goals, strategy, and actions are based on the HP Way, the core beliefs, values, and principles that have contributed to HP's success. They are summarized as follows.

HP's values are a set of deeply held beliefs that govern and guide our behavior in meeting our objectives and in dealing with each other, our customers, shareholders, and others. We have trust and respect for individuals. We focus on a high level of achievement and contribution. We conduct our business with uncompromising integrity. We achieve our common objectives through teamwork. We encourage flexibility and innovation.

Corporate Objectives

HP's corporate objectives are guiding principles for all decision-making by HP people:

- Profit
- Customers
- Fields of interest
- Growth
- Our People
- Management
- Citizenship

Supporting Policies & Practices

As we have continued to grow and change as a company, we have responded by ensuring our policies and practices support our core beliefs and values, our guiding principles, and our goals to make HP the *best place to work for every employee.* Below is a summary of some of the policies and practices that support our diversity success.

Policies
- Electronic job posting
- Harassment-free work environment
- Domestic partner benefits
- Non-discrimination policy
- Employee network group guidelines
- Open Door Policy
- Education Assistance Program
- Employee Assistance Program (EAP)

Shared Practices
- Open communications
- Employment security based on performance
- Management-by-objective
- Share in company's success
- Provide development opportunities
- Value diversity

- Pay among leaders
- Flexible work hours
- Safe and pleasant work environment

CASE STUDY: NEW TIMES: THE FACE OF THE OLD GRAY LADY IS CHANGING, THANKS TO ARTHUR SULZBERGER JR.'S MINORITY HIRING PROGRAM

While the entire newspaper industry seems to have jumped on the diversity bandwagon, perhaps no daily has garnered as much praise and criticism for its commitment to multiculturalism as the *New York Times*. Everyone agrees the newspaper's new attitude began when Arthur Sulzberger Jr. inherited the publisher's title from his father, Arthur "Punch" Sulzberger, in 1992.

Arthur Jr. "prodded editors into broadening the paper's news coverage to an unprecedented degree in an effort to appeal to a younger, more diverse readership," Susan E. Tifft and Alex S. Jones write in their new book, *The Trust: The Private and Powerful Family Behind the New York Times*. Furthermore, they write, 47-year-old Sulzberger "radically changed the *Times'* corporate culture by encouraging the hiring of more minority employees."

"Arthur has been at the forefront of diversity," William E. Schmidt, *Times* associate managing editor, related. "This is a very important issue to him."

By 1998, the minority segment of the paper's "professional" news staff—including reporters, editors, and photographers, and excluding such positions as secretaries, clerks, and librarians—had grown to 15.6 percent, up from 13.7 percent five years ago. The figure puts the *Times* comfortably ahead of the industry's overall 11.5 percent minority representation, according to the American Society of Newspaper Editors' numbers.

Over the past few years, the *Times* has instituted a number of programs aimed at seeking out and retaining minority talent: a recruiting committee directed by deputy managing editor Gerald Boyd, the highest-ranking African-American in the *Times'* newsroom; minority internship and scholarship initiatives; and copyediting workshops at historically black colleges.

The *Times*, like other large newspapers, regularly sends a contingent of editors and recruiters to conventions of minority newspeople—including last summer's massive UNITY '99 gathering in Seattle. Schmidt calls the conventions "a big recruiting tool," noting that at UNITY, Sulzberger himself met privately with several minority newspeople the paper was trying to woo.

In addition to the copyediting workshops, the parent New York Times Company last spring began a minority copyediting program. Funded by the *Times* and the company's Regional Newspaper Group, the initiative provides for two trainee positions each year at *Times*-owned papers in Sarasota and Lakeland, Florida.

"The idea [with the minority programs] is you grow your own," Schmidt said. "You can't just go to the job fairs to get this stuff done—you've got to go out to find these people, get them excited, and show people you're willing to invest in them."

The *Times* has also strengthened its staff-development effort, naming Nancy Starkey, a former education reporter, to the newly created post of assistant managing editor/staff development. Her purpose: to give minority—and nonminority—news employees "constant feedback to help them through the sort of Byzantine, if not politics, then just sort of bureaucracy at the *Times*," Schmidt explained.

The editor admits that for years, the *Times* was a notoriously "sink-or-swim culture. There was a period as recent as the mid-90s where there were a lot of complaints, even from our own staff, that, you know, we go to all this trouble to recruit people . . . and then we're not equipped to help them deal with the kinds of cultural and professional barriers that anybody meets at the *Times*."

Schmidt, a white male, recalled that when he joined the paper from *Newsweek* in 1981, hardly anyone spoke to him his first few weeks. "You had to come in here and show your stuff," he said. "That's the way it worked."

A former *Times* staffer who did not want to be identified said, "Black people have always hated working at the *New York Times* because most *New York Times* employees in the past were treated like they were on a plantation. Black people were more sensitive to it, but in fact every-body was treated that way."

Another ex-employee related, "There are blacks at the *Times* who do not get the kind of attention and support their white counterparts get. You're put in a situation there where time and time again, you have to prove yourself, and it would have been nice if it were a situation where you're given the benefit of the doubt." Minorities, the former staffer charged, are too often passed over for the choicest assignments at the *Times*—heading up a new section of the paper, for example, or running a bureau. "It is rare, if ever, that black people are tapped for those things."

Indeed, a big question these days is who will succeed Joseph Lelyveld as *Times* executive editor three years from now, when he reaches the paper's mandatory retirement age. Editorial-page editor Howell Raines and managing editor William Keller, both white men, are widely considered front-runners for the job. But another question arises: Who will replace Raines or Keller should one of them move up? One former minority staffer thinks Boyd would be a natural for Keller's job, calling him the "heir apparent." When asked to speculate about the future, Boyd responded, with a laugh, "I do not play that game."

Other staffers see race as a virtual nonissue inside the *Times*. Archie Tse, who came to the *Times* as an intern in 1993 and now works as a graphics editor there, said that as an Asian-American he has experienced "very little prejudice" at the paper. "I don't really think about race that much in my relationships with my colleagues," he said, noting that the thirty-member graphics team is multiethnic and headed by an African-American. "I really feel that good work here is rewarded, and it doesn't matter what your race or ethnicity is." Tse conceded he would like to see more minorities in management posts at the *Times*, however.

No one expects that just because the *Times* has made strides, prob-lems don't remain. As Schmidt says, "I'm not saying if you went through the newsroom, you wouldn't find reporters who will complain and gripe [about issues related to diversity]. But I do think that com-munication is better."

Some critics contend that newsroom diversity efforts have taken political correctness too far—placing quotas above qualifications.

Hilton Kramer, who worked at the *Times* for seventeen years from the late 1960s to early 1980s, and until recently penned a regular column devoted to criticizing the paper for the *New York Post*, conceded that opening the doors to minorities provided some talented, budding journalists a chance they might not otherwise have had. The problem, he maintained, was that too many new hires at the *Times*, at least in his day, were not qualified.

"Working with minority recruits in the early 1970s was a nightmare," said Kramer, who was cultural news editor at the time. "Very few of them could write. They certainly couldn't revise anything. Anytime you told them a piece had to be edited or revised, they threatened to go to the Newspaper Guild [a union representing *Times* employees] . . . Everybody was tiptoeing around the fact that these new people were hired by people who didn't have to deal with them in the regular, daily process of gathering and publishing the news."

Kramer isn't surprised that diversity is a top priority of the *Times* under young Sulzberger. "It's part of the liberal agenda," he said, "and the *Times* is right out there, banging the drums for every liberal agenda."

Boyd, who has worked at the *Times* since 1983, called the perception that his paper and the industry as a whole operate under a quota system "a myth."

"Figures for the industry in general suggest that there certainly have not been quotas," he said.

Schmidt allows that in the past, hiring mistakes "were probably made. I think our determination now is to keep the bar high." He pointed out that certain individuals have "washed out" of the internship program. "There are people who have not made it here who are minority hires. We've tried to be as supportive as we could."

The setbacks and shortcomings have not tempered the editor's enthusiasm about fashioning a more diverse workforce and a more diverse product. "This city is changing every moment," he said. "In order for us to stay up on it, for us to be able to deal with the diversity of this community . . . we need people with a lot of talents, a lot of voices, a lot of languages, a lot of perspective. And to me, that's the bottom line."

Source: By Tony Case. ©1999 ASM Communications Inc. Used with permission.

CHAPTER Eight

ETHNIC SPONSORSHIPS AND EVENT MARKETING

When we started out using our business to do things that met the social needs of the community, all the business people—our accountants, lawyers, financial people—all told us that this was going to be our undoing, going to drive us down the tubes. It was not possible, they told Jerry and me, for a business to work to meet social needs and make a profit at the same time. That was bunk . . . as we devote more and more of our resources to improving the quality of life in the community, we're selling more ice cream and making more money.

—Ben Cohen of Ben & Jerry's, quoted in *Lifestyle and Event Marketing* by Alfred L. Schreiber, McGraw-Hill, 1994

There is no question that sponsorship of appropriate causes, events, and organizations is a marketing approach ideally suited to selling in emerging minority markets. By identifying and putting your corporate support behind community programs, meaningful performing festivals, and even schools and hospitals, you demonstrate strong corporate empathy for the people those entities serve.

Events "talk" directly to emerging consumer groups. Handled well, they can go a long way toward demonstrating your understanding and support for the very groups you are trying to reach.

The following excellent article by Lisa Skriloff, president of Multicultural Marketing Resources, Inc., a New York City–based public relations and marketing firm representing the nation's leading experts in targeting minorities and women and corporations that sell to these groups, provides an excellent object lesson on just how effective appropriate sponsorships can be within minority communities.

Ethnic Holidays: A Marketing Opportunity

Major cultural festivals and holidays represent unique opportunities for marketers to speak to consumers at culturally relevant events and community venues. Smart marketers would do well to review possible tie-ins with Hispanic, African American and Asian American holidays to show these important consumer groups that their business is important by acknowledging the holidays that are important to them.

I spoke with three experts in marketing to these groups to learn the whys as well as the dos and don'ts for ethnic holiday marketing. Our experts:

Saul Gitlin is Vice President of Strategic Marketing Services, Kang & Lee Advertising, the leading full-service advertising agency linking corporate America to the Asian-American marketplace.

Isabel Valdés is President, Cultural Axis Group of Axis Worldwide, a leading research division of this marketing services company.

Howard Buford is President, Prime Access, Inc., a multicultural marketing firm specializing in advertising and direct marketing to African-American, Gay & Lesbian and Latino consumers.

Marketers that want to establish a relationship with ethnic communities need to address these communities not only when they want to sell or promote services but to acknowledge the important cultural aspects of these communities said Saul Gitlin. Acknowledging cultural events and holidays is a way to build a bond, a way to show commitment and a way to recognize their diverse lifestyles.

In the Asian market, all the current advertisers never fail to put out important messages of greeting for the major holidays, he noted. Kang & Lee works with advertisers such as AT&T, Bank of America, the California State Lottery and Sears, all of which develop special community programs to greet consumers on these major holidays.

The important holidays in the Asian market include Asian Lunar New Year, which is celebrated by the Chinese, Korean and Vietnamese communities and the Moon festival, celebrated by Chinese and Koreans. During Lunar New Year, many marketers tie in to community venues such as the San Francisco Chinese Lunar New Year parade, which is the largest nighttime parade in the US and the largest celebration by Chinese outside mainland China.

Yet new marketers should be careful about using the holiday seasons as their first foray into the ethnic market. The holidays are good opportunities to greet consumers and offer special sales or promotions connected to the holidays, said Saul Gitlin. But because there is a lot of advertising greeting during these times, it might not be the ideal time to introduce new products, he said. Asian American consumers are sensitive to the recognition they get from major corporate marketers that they not only have money to spend but that their holidays are important to them, Gitlin noted.

Tying in to holidays is something that has worked very well, said Isabel Valdés, whose company has done research with retailers wishing to tap into the ethnic markets. Holidays touch you on an emotional level, she said. The industries that do this well are retail and financial services like banks, which have done campaigns during holiday week, she noted. How people feel about their holiday is very powerful and moving. The fact that a store displays ads in Spanish and celebrates the holiday is one of the most direct ways to tell a consumer, "We like you. We want your business." By doing it right, you are building a bond with the consumer.

Among the holidays celebrated by Hispanics, she cited the national holiday of each of the countries as one of the top rated in terms of forming a bond. Mother's Day is also important but is celebrated on different days depending on the country of origin.

The religious holidays are very powerful and unite all the Hispanic communities, such as Christmas and January 6, Los Tres Reyes, when we give gifts, Valdés said.

Cinco de Mayo is a holiday celebrated by US Hispanics, she added, noting that many US marketers use this opportunity for outreach.

What might retailers do? Use a flag in a decorative way, she suggested, play the music of that country, have checkout counter help wear a button, have an aisle displaying foods from that country, do a taste testing, etc. In short, use this as a marketing sales opportunity. Retailers should tell manufacturers about their plans and let them have a table and participate.

First, stores should find out what kind of audience they have, for example, a Cuban-American or Mexican-American population and then identify those days which are essential for those communities.

Howard Buford concurs that the January 3 Kings Day is significant for the Hispanic community and notes that his agency has worked on special ad executions for Eastman Kodak around this holiday. Hispanic Heritage month (held each year from September 15 to October 15) is big. There are lots of events you can sponsor—cultural events and social events. We have done events for Remy Martin, primarily in Miami and New York, at an art gallery showing or photo exhibits.

As far as African American holidays, he notes that Kwanzaa, the period between Christmas and New Years', is important in this market. Also, the period between Martin Luther King's birthday in January and then through February, Black History Month is a crucial time, known as the Freedom Window.

This is the time for marketers to show their appreciation of consumers and their embracing of their heritage, their contributions in history, said Buford. If, for example, a retailer is selling clothes, now is the time to bring out the prints with the African influence, he suggested. We have done Remy Martin–sponsored events at this time at B. Smith's (in NYC) and in Chicago at the DuSable Museum of African American History.

You know, all these consumers are members of out groups. You have to understand the out group mentality, he explained. It means not being included in mainstream advertising. So when a marketer does something clearly for them, that strengthens that relationship. It tells them you're thinking about them, that they're important. It's not just a matter of including them in ads. Understanding and celebrating their holidays is a way to underscore that.

> —Lisa Skriloff; reprinted with permission from
> the bi-monthly newsletter, *Multicultural
> Marketing News*[1]

---

1. Lisa Skriloff is president of Multicultural Marketing Resources, Inc., a public relations and marketing company representing experts in reaching the nation's Hispanic, African American, and Asian American consumer markets. MMR publishes *Multicultural Marketing News* and *The Source Book of Multicultural Experts* and operates The Multicultural Marketing Resource Library and Museum. Contact info: Multicultural Marketing Resources, Inc., 286 Spring St., Suite 201, NY NY 10013. Phone: 212-242-3351. Fax: 212-691-5969. E-mail: infobrokr1@aol.com. Website: www.inforesources.com.

Putting the Power of Sponsorship to Work

What is one of the most effective ways to demonstrate to your target customers that you share their values and concerns? Or even that you understand and participate in their lives?

One very effective way is sponsorship. With some thought and investigation, you can find opportunities here, in places where your targeted consumers are already involved:

- ethnic music or arts festivals
- amateur sports programs
- performing arts organizations, such as theater companies, concert series, dance companies
- local or regional professional sports teams
- hospitals
- disease foundations
- religious organizations
- service organizations
- zoos
- public schools
- museums and cultural institutions

Making the Right Choice

To make the best selection from among your available options, you have to do your homework, and that means really getting to know your consumers—their concerns, preferred involvements, interests, and problems.

It is vital to conduct interviews with representatives of your community, including some or all of the following:

- **Representatives from the Media**
  Every community or city has its local newspaper, magazine, radio station, and TV station. Talk with the editors, the program directors, and the commentators. They are the people with the most acute sense of what is taking place within the community. They know who the key influencers are and what type of activities they are involved with.

The Simplest Way to Reach Spanish-Speaking Hispanics Is to Address Us in Our Own Language

What a great language I have, a fine language we inherited from the fierce conquistadors. They took everything and left everything. They left us the words.

—Pablo Neruda

The power of language is undeniable. It defines our humanity. We use language to express our brightest hopes and darkest fears.

Yet language also has the power to separate and isolate us.

Today, there's an impassioned debate in some marketing circles regarding the role of language as it relates to media selection. There are those who believe that English should be the language of choice in this country. Others offer the opinion that there is room in this extraordinary republic for more than one language. As was seen most dramatically in California recently, arguments concerning bilingual education can reach such an emotional pitch, it's as if they appealed to some fundamental, almost visceral sense of right and wrong. The fiercest battles we take up seem to revolve around the most abstract notions of who we are and who we aren't. The line in the sand is a chasm.

But this is not meant to be a debate about politics. It's about driving sales. About how best to reach out to and communicate with the person who we want to notice our product or service. The reality is that the most efficient and effective way to reach any of us is to use media that honors and embraces diversity. Those who ignore this will be punished by history, the most unforgiving client of all. The simple and direct path to success is to address us in our own language.

This isn't a time to teach us a lesson about patriotism. Or a debate about who got here first. But it is time for a reality check. The bottom line is that we're not about to change, to give up our language, the language of our culture. We could not fathom asking anyone else to do that.

Language is what identifies us as a culture. We may be conversant in other languages, and there is certainly a stratum of our population that considers English its first tongue. But for the vast majority of us, Spanish is in the fiber of our souls. And the sooner this truth is accepted, the better off we'll all be.

At the end of the day, it seems that the issues are more about comfort levels in this democracy than race, color, or the shape of your vowels.

Because in most cases, the majority of media directors, marketing managers, media assistants, brand managers, associate media directors and product managers don't go home at night and relax reading Garcia Marquez or watching Univision.

This brave new world of "others" is as unknown to most of the good folks in media as the royal blood-soaked jungle floor was to Cortes. And probably as intimidating. Just substitute a few foreign words and improbable statistics for the odd butterfly and random jaguar, and you'll get the picture.

The view from the other side is just as compelling. With 31 million residents of the U.S. considered Hispanic, we are a critical mass that does not need acculturation the same way the Irish, Poles and Slavs did. No, this time it's different. Very different. With unprecedented numbers, we are already fully vested in the American dream. We have a language that will get us to work and home again, allow us to buy all of life's necessities and make a fair living without ever really having to take up the language of Chaucer, Blake or Updike.

So what are we left with? Two worlds living cheek by jowl in a parallel universe. What's wrong with this picture? How in the world could Howard Stern possibly be second to Spanish-language radio personalities neither he nor you has ever heard of in both New York and Los Angeles?

The problem is that it is not in accord with the fundamental premise of mass-media marketing. And that is to reach, affect, alter or sustain behavior through advertising, among other things.

We end up talking at each other and not to one another. Two monologues instead of one. Targeted media that misses the target.

In a word, what is keeping us apart is fear. And fear is the orphaned child of ignorance.

I believe that if we can continue to appreciate and respect something that is foreign, as this country always has, there is hope. Imagine for a moment taking your children around Halloween to visit their grandmother's grave. Of course, you'd take candy and food and toys and candles. A little different, you say. But it's actually the norm for those who observe Day of the Dead each year. Yes, we are different, but that doesn't mean we have to be strangers.

Because we actually have a lot in common.

To reach an individual, you have to speak to them in their own language, literally and figuratively. In the case of Hispanics, that means biting the bullet and stopping this shadow dancing by buying time on a Spanish-language network, space in a Spanish-language publication or impressions with Spanish-language out-of-home.

There's really no other way around it. We are here. We came here. We were born here. We live here. This is our home. And we are here to stay.

So what good comes of shaking up the routinized media buys that seem so comfortable? For one thing, the community is better served. You are putting money where people live. Nurturing the growth of local voices, which sound loud and clear to those in the neighborhood. It is an investment that is not forgotten or ignored. It is the opening of a dialogue.

Second, the race issue in America can be addressed, if obliquely, with a better understanding of each other's perspectives. It can make us less different to one another and more real.

Finally, it opens up the media universe as we know it to a discussion that's not so freighted with misunderstandings and misperceptions.

The real shame is missed opportunities. Money left on the table. Every day of every year. On the most basic level, we like looking at ourselves. Be it on television, in magazines and newspapers, or in direct mail. We may be interested in the dominant culture, but it's not always a reflection of who we are. And we like to hear ourselves talk and sing on the radio. We like the sound of our language in all of its vagaries. We even like the differences between the dialects of our countries (Cubano, Venezolano, Argentino) and our provinces (Oaxacan, Zapatecan, Michoacanian). It's only natural.

Let's look at it from another angle. What would your family do if you were suddenly transferred to China, and you are not Chinese and do not understand Mandarin? And the assignment was for the rest of your life. Would you immediately stop speaking English? Would you want your school-age children to speak English at home even if they were allowed to speak Mandarin in class? What about food? No meat loaf, only variations on sweet and sour. And wouldn't you be more likely to try a new Asian dish if it was marketed to you in English and you knew what was in it? And would you stop watching CNN and concentrate on the state-sponsored opera for entertainment?

Not to belabor the obvious, but these are the kinds of changes that are sometimes asked, if not demanded, of our immigrant population. Not to mention the second and third generations from lands south of Laredo, Nogales and Calexico.

The heart of the matter is a matter of the heart. It is the language that we think in, dream in, pray and sing in. It is our native tongue, central to our identity. It is literally how we understand the world and the products marketed to us in that world. Translation isn't enough. A straight translation is rarely without a few unfortunate twists and turns that can upend the most conscientious effort. Like poetry, there is a feeling beneath the surface of the words.

The same is true in Spanish. There is something ineffable about the invisible connective tissue of the words favored by Cervantes, Paz and Fuentes. There is another, more subtle read to all of this, as there is in any language. It is as often as not what is unspoken that is most vital. That is the indelible message that is heard, remembered and acted upon.

If we could just put our assumptions aside for a moment and take a fresh look at a dynamic market that yearns for recognition, I believe we would be much further ahead on every count. Collectively, we need a reality check. We need to talk the talk, which is Spanish. And walk the walk which is Spanish-language media.

Anything less points to a collective case of denial that hasn't been seen since the first Puritan ran home and breathlessly told his wife he had just emptied his musket into the last Pequot.

Source: By Anita Santiago. ©1999 ASM Communications Inc. Used with permission.

- **The Business Community**

  This includes representatives of prominent area businesses owned by your target segment. They might be from banking, manufacturing, aerospace, or publishing. It is important to speak with representatives of the industries that best represent the business makeup of the area you are trying to reach.

- **Government**

  Although it can be risky to become too involved in the political life of a region (a change of administration, after all, can result in your campaign going out the door, too), it is vital to understand the spheres of political influence within any community. If your plan is to create a sponsorship for Asian-Pacific-, African-, or Hispanic-Americans, and there is one of their number who is on the city council or in a prominent elected position, then it clearly behooves you to set up a meeting to discuss your plans and ask for suggestions.

- **Cultural Life and the Arts**

  Performing arts organizations, libraries, museums, zoos, and the like have major influence on life in many communities. Look beneath the surface at the people who are involved and at what type of programs are in place for community outreach.

  Some art museums, for example, are just art museums; others have many programs for schoolchildren or lecture series for senior citizens. Some symphony orchestras have children's programs or special outreach programs for Hispanic- or African-American children. Theater companies may offer plays for children or give special programs in hospitals or nursing homes. You have to ask questions to uncover opportunities for involvement. There is always more than what you see at first glance.

- **Nonprofits**
  It is well worth seeking out nonprofits that aid members of the constituency you are trying to reach with your sponsorship efforts.

- **Sports**
  This category includes all levels: amateur, school-related, and professional. It is vital to look at amateur sports organizations within any community—for example, the favorite local soccer league of the Caribbean or Latino segments—and at school-related athletics, especially high school sports. They, too, can provide excellent places to make an impact within your target community.

The following are questions to ask the key "influencers" in the target group you are investigating:

- Who do you feel are the most respected or influential individuals in your community? Why?
- What about organizations? Which do you feel are the most influential? Why are they important, and how are they structured, and how do they affect the community?
- What are the most influential local business organizations?
- Which religious institutions have the most influence in your community or group?
- Which civic organizations exert the most influence on people's lives? How about cultural, nonprofit, social organizations?
- What is the status of local colleges, universities, and private schools? What type of people attend, and what influences do these institutions exert on community life?
- What are the most influential political organizations within your community and group?

The overall goal to conducting these conversations with influential individuals is to discern the outlines of the power structure at work within the group you are targeting. Perhaps you'll see the same names on the boards of the Hispanic Chamber of Commerce, the Museo del Barrio, and a local hospital, too. Those are people you should get to know.

Through this process, you should gain a feel for the various forces within any community. You should have a better idea of where to get involved with things that shape the daily lives of community residents. You'll also see what they aspire to, what groups they belong to, and what groups they would like to belong to. The next step is to create a potential match between your company and opportunities for sponsorship, whoever and whatever they are.

Going through this process will uncover a number of possible involvements. Here are some that may come up along the way:

- A decade-old jazz festival is held each year in local parks. Run by the local urban music radio station, it seems a likely place to boost your credibility and acceptance with the city's African-American residents.
- The local zoo, situated in an area with many Latino citizens, presents classes for neighborhood children. You could provide funds to expand it and gain a lot of credibility with Hispanic-American consumers.
- A hospital could benefit from an infusion of funds into its programs for HIV and AIDS patients. Even if large-scale funding is beyond your means, creating an event to raise awareness and even provide testing could raise your company's visibility and profile as a good corporate citizen.

And so on. Virtually all cities offer many places for businesses to become involved. Deciding where to do so becomes a strategic process.

As you consider two or three places where you might become involved, more questions arise. How well does one program compare with others you might fund? Which of the programs you are investigating hits your target audience most squarely? Which is most in accord with your company image?

Any company considering sponsorship of an event or program needs an objective evaluation system. It is essential for selecting an optimally efficient program from among the many activities available. The system also must provide a yardstick for such factors as sponsor clutter, different brand positions, and competition. It is wise to evaluate the potential effectiveness of a sponsorship opportunity against five major criteria:

1. the positioning of your company or product
2. your company or product image
3. sales and performance objectives
4. marketing strategies
5. tactical effectiveness of the sponsorship, including the executional efficiency of the program

Judge each element under the preceding five major categories and assign them points. It is easiest to use a point system based on a scale from 1 to 10.

The sponsorship evaluation checklist will help you manage this evaluation process effectively, as well as help you evaluate and compare different sponsorships you are considering. Where ethnic and minority sponsorships are involved, the results can truly be a win-win proposition for everyone involved

CASE STUDY: DOUBLE DUTCH PLAN FOR SPONSORSHIP OF A MAJOR FAST-FOOD CHAIN

Let's take a close look at a very good sponsorship program plan developed to help a major fast-food chain demonstrate a commitment to African-American, inner-city youngsters. This excellent plan was never executed for reasons known only to the client, and the name of the company for which it was developed has been deleted. The program represents state-of-the-art thinking and should be an eye-opener to any businessperson seeking sponsorship opportunities with ethnic consumers.

Sponsorship Evaluation Checklist

Positioning and Image

☐ Has logical or believable brand link?

☐ Consistent with company image and personality?

Audience Reach and Appeal

☐ Reaches target market(s) with right demographics, psychographics?

☐ Appeals to values and lifestyles of target market(s) perceptually, attitudinally?

Marketing and Sales Objectives

☐ Generates awareness by making a durable impression?

☐ Stimulates trial or retrial by existing users, former users, nonusers?

☐ Encourages loyalty?

Marketing and Sales Strategies

☐ Consistent with current marketing messages?

☐ Creates news?

☐ Impact can be measured?

Tactical and Executional Effectiveness

☐ Can be easily and effectively extended with advertising, promotions, public relations, direct marketing, in-store materials, or activities?

☐ Can be effectively extended at retail?

☐ Managed by reputable, competent promoter?

☐ Legally acceptable, safe?

Desired Criteria

☐ Positions product or company as hero or leader?

☐ Consistent with your company's image, culture?

Audience Reach and Appeal

☐ Has high excitement for target market?

☐ Offers regional and local extensions?

Marketing and Sales Objectives

☐ Establishes new ground in product category?

☐ Helps promote and sell your other products?

☐ Builds or enhances equity in product name?

Program Overview: Double Dutch

The term *double dutch* refers to jumping rope—a sport highly popular with inner-city kids. Popular with girls and boys of all ages, jumping rope was a rare sport-related concept that played equally well with both boys and girls. Other aspects of rope jumping also made it an ideal vehicle. It is highly competitive and demanding. In addition, it has character-building power, demanding creativity, agility, lots of practice, sportsmanship, and above all, teamwork.

The fact that jumping rope is popular in all states across the country was another plus. If a program were rolled out nationally, with national finals, it could bring together rope-jumping teams from across the country.

Double Dutch Objective: Empower Kids

Ambitious in concept, the idea was to provide scholarships to kids whose teams demonstrated high skills, good sportsmanship, and creativity. The underlying objective was not to generate press coverage or build in-restaurant traffic (even though those pluses would result) but rather to generate a path to help worthy African-American inner-city kids move off the streets into institutions of higher learning. These kids might learn to live up to their potential if only the right door were held open to them—and this was the real objective of the Double Dutch program.

The mission of the program was "to reclaim our youth . . . to foster the behavior associated with becoming successful adults: relating to others with understanding and respect, developing decision-making skills, making a commitment to practice and self-improvement, and building pride and self-esteem."

Double Dutch Execution

Double Dutch competitions would be hosted at local parks and gymnasiums. Local winners would advance to compete in citywide championships. Sign-up packets and information would be available at all restaurant locations, which would both generate traffic and build awareness of the program through special displays and product-related promotions. A sign-up packet would include details of the program, registration forms, and possibly premiums such as T-shirts. The program would also invite the participation of restaurant employees. They could take part, group together to sponsor teams, etc.

The intention was to launch Double Dutch in early spring. Participants would have two months to form teams and train. Then about four months after initial participant sign-up, national finals would be held.

Individual teams would comprise three or four jumpers (singles and doubles teams). All team members would be in the same grade. Competitions would feature both freestyle and speed components. Teams would be judged in accordance with the official rules of the American Double Dutch League.

Initially, the Double Dutch program would be tested in Chicago, then rolled out nationally into every ethnic and racial market. With demonstrated success, the plan was to have Double Dutch become an annual event.

Promotion

A promotional campaign would be created using the fast-food chain's advertising agencies. Elements would include broadcast promotions, print ads, and in-store display and registration kit distribution.

Licensing and Merchandising

A number of products could be produced surrounding the program, including

Double Dutch T-shirts, shorts, water bottles, jump ropes, hats, etc.
a national catalog of merchandise
Double Dutch scholarships given to winners
a *How to Double Dutch* promotional videotape
a national television special could be produced, featuring
    competition footage and presenting human-interest stories
    on the participants

Benefits to the Sponsor

Beyond its immediate benefits of generating in-location traffic and sales, the program promised to enhance community relations and goodwill. It would build a database for future marketing efforts, generate publicity, and stimulate sales through licensed products.

More important, it would position the company as one that contributed to the community through the program—a good example of doing well by doing good.

Budget

In light of the many benefits promised by a successful execution of the Double Dutch program, the per-city cost was surprisingly low, as reflected by the itemization in Table 8.1 that reflects projected costs for each restaurant location:

Table 8.1

Item	Cost
Printed Collateral Material (entry forms, rules sheets, tournament welcome packages, certificate of participation, etc.)	$3,000
Competitor Equipment	
Shirts and shorts	$2,000
Jump ropes (#8 sash cord)	$350
Competition Equipment	
Mechanical counters	$250
Start/stop time clock	$50
Whistles/buzzers	$20
Stopwatches	$100
Calculators	$200
Note paper/pens	$100
Trophies/ribbons	$2,200
Scholarship awards	$7,000
Event insurance	$25
Marketing/PR support	$5,000
Total Cost Per Event	**$20,295**

CASE STUDY: THE NATIONAL BLACK FINE ARTS SHOW

The annual National Black Fine Arts Show in New York has become a cultural landmark. Started in 1997 by Josh Wainwright of Wainwright/Smith Associates, it served as something of a wake-up call for New York's more staid art lovers. Many of them, in fact, seemed somewhat surprised to discover, through the event, that there were so many upscale, well-informed, and affluent African-Americans who were ready and eager to invest sizable sums of money to acquire the works of such African-American artists as Romare Bearden, Elizabeth Catlett, Chester Higgins, and Charles White.

By the second event, in 1998, the National Black Fine Arts Show had already become a cultural landmark in the city. Spike Lee and other luminaries attended, and the celebrities were not only members of the African-American community. Enlightened sponsors were on hand to take advantage of this important opportunity to build ties to the African-American constituencies. As press materials for the show stated powerfully, "As we collect, we are strengthening our history." It was a great opportunity for forward-sighted businesses to establish their support for the interests and concerns of African-Americans.

Nine

TAPPING THE POWER OF ETHNIC MEDIA

Until recently, African-Americans, and other people of color, were disenfranchised from mass media employment and ownership. Black journalists, technicians, and media professionals were essentially shut out of one of the most powerful industries in this country. With the very notable exception of the print medium, minorities in America were forced to see themselves through the eyes and voices of others, with little opportunity to control those images.

In a very real sense, people of color in this society were living testaments to what W. E. B. DuBois spoke about in 1903 when he said: "It is a peculiar sensation, this double-consciousness, this sense of always looking at one's self through the eyes of others . . . one feels his twoness—an American, a Black; two souls, two thoughts, two unreconciled strivings; two warring ideals in one dark body, whose dogged strength alone keeps it from being torn asunder."

But we know that the images portrayed so predominantly in the media do not reflect reality. After all, most Americans, regardless of race, aspire to the same ideals. They want decent, good-paying jobs, a sound education for their children, safe communities, and an opportunity to live the American dream. Media images that distort this basic reality, particularly when they reinforce negative racial and ethnic stereotypes, do not serve the public and are offensive to all of us.

> —from "Mastering Opportunity," remarks of William
> E. Kennard, chairman, Federal Communications Commission, in his speech to the National
> Black Media Coalition, December 2, 1998

In 2000, *Mediaweek* and the New America Strategies Group (NASG—a multicultural communications and marketing group that I [Alfred Schreiber] cofounded with True North Communications) released a Multicultural Media Survey reporting that advertising expenditures for multicultural focused media equaled $3.6 billion in 1998, more than double 1993's spending of $1.7 billion. Within only five years, ethnic media spending grew more than in the previous fifty! Yet the bad news is the spending on ethnic media still lags behind. In fact, less than 2 percent of the overall media spending within America's overall pie of $200 billion is targeted at Asian-Pacific-, Hispanic- and African-American constituents.

However, many high-visibility ethnic media outlets are finally getting on the map with, for example, *Latina*; *People en Espanol*; and the birth of Radio Unica, one of the largest Hispanic radio networks. And in November 1999, two of America's largest corporations, CBS and Chase Manhattan, established The Prism Fund, a $1 billion fund to spur ownership of radio and TV stations by women and people of color. Hundreds of new media outlets are arriving on the scene.

We can also look to the vitality of the Internet, where new ventures such as the BlackVoices.com, Black Entertainment Network's new $30 million Internet site, and quepasa.com are beginning to chip away at the digital divide.

So although things have lagged, the opening salvos have been fired and things are changing. In this chapter, we'll look at trends and gain an understanding of how you can establish a presence in the expanding array of targeted ethnic media.

Multicultural Buying Surges: Results of the *Mediaweek*/NASG Study

A 1999 study, commissioned by *Mediaweek* and New America Strategies Group, sought to examine ad spending in media outlets primarily aimed at African-, Hispanic-, and Asian-Pacific-Americans. Part of the study's purpose was to better understand how much is spent by both national and local marketers on reaching ethnic consumers through "multiculturally focused media" (or MFM).

Radio Execs Have Been Preaching Diversity, but the Message Hasn't Made It Through the Ranks

From the top down, radio's executives say, having a diverse work force goes hand in hand with utilizing good business practices. Most have made it a top personal priority and say they encourage their managers to ensure minorities are recruited and developed in the company. Yet, even as radio expands program offerings to an audience that is growing in diversity, radio's public face is at odds with this philosophy.

Case in point: Doug Tracht, aka, The Greaseman. In February, Tracht expressed his dislike for a Lauryn Hill song by saying, "No wonder people drag them behind trucks," referring to the murder of a black man in Texas who was dragged to his death. Tracht was immediately fired from his job as morning man on Infinity-owned WARW-FM in Washington, D.C. He has repeatedly apologized but is being sued by the station for $100,000 in lost advertising dollars.

Not a soul in the radio business would publicly defend what Tracht said on the air. But privately, many radio execs lament such on-air racial slurs as a hazard of a business that puts individuals on the air for a long period of time without a net. Something needs to be done, and no one knows that better than radio's leaders.

"Miracles don't happen overnight," says Gary Fries, president, Radio Advertising Bureau. "There's continued attention and continued effort, but the bottom line is that the progress we've made hasn't raised the needle where we can all say we're proud."

They face a difficult challenge. At another D.C. Infinity station, WJFK-FM, syndicated afternoon personalities Don and Mike are busy apologizing for a comment in August some deemed anti-Hispanic. The pair called city hall in El Cenizo, Texas, and berated councilwoman Flora Barton for the town's decision to conduct meetings in Spanish.

Then there's the continuing scuttlebutt over a promotion on ABC–owned KLOS-FM in Los Angeles, where, more than a year ago, morning team Mark and Brian gave out small black gardening tools called "black hoes." The promotion went on for about five weeks, until the station's traffic manager, Judy Goodwin, who is African American, complained. When it was brought to his attention, Bill Sommers, the station's general manager, stopped the promotion and fired the program director. Two months ago, Goodwin and a black account executive, Carla Woodson, separately filed suit against ABC. It remains unsettled.

And who can forget the leaked Katz Radio memo a year ago in May that characterized the urban audience of a radio station as "suspects, not prospects"? The industry is still reeling from that one, prompting the FCC to study the effect of advertising practices known as "no urban dictates" and "no Hispanic dictates" in a study released in January entitled "When Being No. 1 is Not Enough."

Part of the problem with diversity in the radio industry is that no one knows the extent to which minorities are fairly represented in the nation's radio stations. Since the U.S. Court of Appeals struck down the 30-year-old equal employment opportunity rules in 1998, which required radio stations to demonstrate a commitment to recruiting minorities and keep records of minority employment, there's been a return to uncertainty about minorities in media.

FCC Chairman Bill Kennard wants to bring back the rules in some form. So does the National Association of Broadcasters.

With no EEO rules, the FCC has dismissed various complaints. Recently, the FCC threw out a $12,000 fine against Bakakel Communications' WKSI-FM and WPET-AM in Greensboro, N.C., and an $11,000 fine against Regent Communications' WCRZ-FM and WFNT-AM in Flint, Michigan.

So no one knows if the 12,000 radio stations in the U.S. have a more diverse work force than they did in 1997, the last year for which there are records. Here's what is known: Before the EEO rules were enacted, minority representation in broadcasting was poor. In 1971, three years after the old EEO rules were adopted, minorities made up only 9.1 percent of the broadcast work force; only 6.8 percent of upper-level broadcast positions were held by minorities.

In 1997, the last year the EEO rules were in force, the percentage of minorities in broadcasting was 20.2, up from 19.9 percent in 1996. Minorities in upper-level positions accounted for 18.2 percent, up from 17.8 percent, according to the FCC's 1997 broadcast employment report, which did not break out statistics separately for radio and TV.

"If you look at what's happened in our business over the past 20 years, some very talented minorities have moved up from just getting started in the business to positions as program directors, general managers and general sales managers," noted Bob Neil, president, Cox Radio.

There's also the growing number of urban and Hispanic stations—and their mounting success. "That has increased opportunities," says Richard Weening, executive chairman, Cumulus Media.

There are fewer minorities, however, in radio news departments: only 11 percent in 1998, a drop of 5 percent from the previous year, according to a recent Radio-Television News Directors Association study. Minority news directors followed the same trend, dropping from 11 to 8 percent.

More is known about minority ownership, an issue that has come into the spotlight as a byproduct of consolidation. From 1993 to 1998, minority radio owners increased from 293 to 305, while the total number of stations increased by 445, according to the National Telecommunications and Information

Administration. In 1998, minorities owned 189 out of 4,724 AMs and 116 out of 5,591 FMs.

"The Telecommunications Act was the death knell to minority ownership," said David Honig, executive director, Minority Media and Telecommunications Council, pointing to the local ownership rules that allow owners to have as many as eight stations in a market. "We lost one-quarter to one-third of minority owners."

Andrew Schwartzman, president/CEO of the Media Access Project, agrees that the Telecommunications Act turned small and medium-sized operators into buyers or sellers. "Most minorities didn't have access to capital, so they were sellers," he said.

Only a few minority-owned companies managed to survive and thrive, such as Radio One, the 16th-largest radio group overall in terms of revenue, according to BIA. But for the most part, minority owners face increasing difficulty both in securing capital and finding properties they can afford in a booming market where stations are trading for as much as 18 times cash flow.

"My biggest challenge has always been financing," said Ro Nita Hawes-Saunders, president and general manager of WROU-FM and WRNB-FM in Dayton, Ohio. It took Hawes-Saunders 10 years to secure the financing to buy her first station, WROU, in 1991. She said it was just as hard to buy her second station, WRNB, in 1996, the year the Telecommunications Act was passed.

"With my first station, it was because I hadn't run a station," she said. "The criteria for ownership worked against me because the financiers were individuals who have expertise in an area where there are few minorities. Now, it's because I'm small. I cannot and will not get into a bidding war."

Like recruitment and employment, minority ownership hit another regulatory hurdle: the end of minority tax certificates in 1995, stripping away what little incentive there was for group owners to sell stations to minorities. Even with FCC Chair Bill Kennard speaking out in favor of some form of minority tax incentives, few hold out much hope for an incentives bill proposed by Sen. John McCain (R-Ariz.) and Sen. Conrad Burns (R-Mont.).

Nevertheless, radio's group owners, led by CBS CEO Mel Karmazin and Clear Channel chairman/CEO Lowry Mays, are speaking with their wallets, deliberately spinning off stations to minority owners. Two years ago, CBS sold five stations to minorities to close its deal with Westinghouse. It's pledged to do the same thing when it spins off properties from the CBS–Viacom merger.

In November 1999, Karmazin and Mays announced the creation of a $1 billion minority investment fund, The Prism Fund, with the goal of increasing the number of minorities and women broadcast owners.

Now if these top leaders could only push their thinking down into radio organizations that are getting bigger and tougher to manage. Perhaps a more sensitive work force would have prevented a black hoe promotion or an employee from writing an offensive memo.

"The challenge is to communicate the policy down in the company. You have to make it an integral part of the culture," says Richard Weening, executive chairman, Cumulus Media. "You can write policies forever, but you have to have an informed human-relations function that is readily accessible so that if there are problems, we can deal with them."

Source: By Katy Bachman. ©1999 ASM Communications Inc. Used with permission.

In summary, the study found that

- Advertising expenditures in MFM were $3.6 billion in 1998—more than double 1993's expenditures of $1.7 billion. These encouraging results show a growing level of recognition that ethnic media works. The study found that larger MFM received two-thirds of national advertising, such as national magazines and the BET (cable) channel. The other third went to local media, primarily minority-aimed newspapers and radio outlets.
- The use of multicultural media in U.S. advertising has more than doubled in the last five years, to about $3.6 billion annually. But that's only 2 percent of overall U.S. advertising expenditures (estimated at more than $200 billion), leading many of the study's respondents to conclude that they do not receive their fair share of ad dollars.
- The number of minority-media outlets has grown quickly to about 1,600, "and the revenues are up also," said Laura Teller, president of Teller Group Consulting of Miami, which conducted the study. "But they should be higher." Many of the study's respondents apparently agreed. Only 12 percent said they were receiving their "fair share"; 88 percent said they were obtaining "less than their fair share" of the ad pie. None believed they were receiving more than their fair share.
- In-language communication is still lagging. The study also indicated that many minority consumers avoid being mainstreamed, wanting instead to "be spoken to in their own languages."

"People who focus on reaching these people in English are missing a significant portion of the population," Teller stated, pointing primarily to Hispanic- and Asian-Pacific-American consumers.

- African-Americans feel somewhat distanced from mainstream media. Teller said African-Americans prefer their own broadcast and print options because they offer "a different tone" than general market media.
- Among different types of ethnic media, television is growing fastest, followed by radio. Print media is not only smaller but has been growing more slowly than broadcast media.
- Advertising expenditures on Hispanic-focused media are highest. Hispanic-focused advertising spending has been growing faster than those of other groups.
- Expenditures in different types of media differ significantly by multicultural group. Hispanic-Americans are more heavily focused on TV; African-Americans concentrate mainly on radio; and Asian-Pacific-American expenditures center mostly on print.

Advertisers need to focus their pitch to tap the ethnic market. Such strong evidence shows the benefits of using ethnic media to reach African-, Hispanic-, and Asian-Pacific-American consumers. Ample evidence points to minorities' willingness to use much of their $1.1 trillion in annual spending power. Other data has ethnic media delivering significantly higher returns on investment for advertisers than general-market advertising. And studies have conclusively demonstrated that brand-loyal customers of color buy everything from cosmetics to cars and diapers to dishwashers in greater numbers than their white counterparts.

Yet minority-focused media continues to be overlooked by the ad community, citing the fraction of advertising budgets (about $3.6 billion in 1998) that was put into 1,700 ethnic-media outlets. While upscale, the minority marketplace is unquestionably ignored.

"People are looking for excuses about why they don't use ethnic media because they're leaving their comfort zone," contends Eliot Kang of New York–based Kang & Lee Advertising, an agency recently acquired by Young and Rubicam. He and others argue that minorities use different media, most of it in their native languages, than general-market audiences. "Ask any forty-plus Asian if he's ever watched *Seinfeld*," Kang said. "I'll bet you a big dinner he hasn't."

Getting the Most from Your Ethnic-Media Effort

Thus far in this chapter, we've looked at the macro picture of ethnic media in America. You may be asking yourself, "This is interesting, even revealing, but how can I put the power of targeted ethnic media to work for me?"

1. Codify and understand the relationship between your product and the marketplace. At this point, I would refer you to Chapter 6 ("Writing the Marketing Plan"), where you can find solid advice on understanding the relationship between what you are selling and the consumers you are trying to reach. If you hope to sell floor coverings to Hispanic-American consumers in Texas, Florida, and California, you might need to conduct surveys and focus-group sessions to find the answers to questions like these:
   - How do Hispanic-Americans feel about my company?
   - What is their consumption of products like mine? How do they index in my product category, as compared to members of other ethnic groups?
   - How much money does a Hispanic-American household spend on floor coverings annually? How much does the typical Hispanic-American family intend to spend in the coming year?
2. Identify likely media choices to reach your target market. Will it be via Korean-language cable TV in New York, on Spanish-language radio in Dallas, or on a website created for African-Americans? The choices are many.

   How can you find these media outlets? The quantity of information is staggeringly large, from lists of Spanish-language newspapers to directories of Asian-language radio stations to indexes of magazines read by urban youth.

Some sources of this information include the following.

Organizations

African-American Chamber of Commerce
Various branches in major cities from coast to coast, including
425 Sixth Avenue, Sixth Floor
Pittsburgh, PA 15219-1811
(412) 392-0610

The U.S. Hispanic Chamber of Commerce
1019 Nineteenth Street NW, Suite 200
Washington, DC 20036
(202) 842-1212
http://www.ushcc.com

Asian-American Chamber of Commerce
P.O. Box 12481
Shawnee Mission, KS 66282
Note: no phone number listed
http://www.asianamerican.org/as.html

Ujamaa.net (an Internet directory to African-
American-owned media and business)
Ujamaa.Net, Inc.
P.O. Box 11095
McLean, VA 22102-7995
(703) 798-1036
http://www.ujamaa.net/

Books

- *African-American Newspapers and Periodicals: A National Bibliography*, edited by James Philip Danky, Maureen E. Hady, and Henry Louis Gates, Jr.; Harvard University Press.
- *1999 National Hispanic Media Directory, Part One: U.S. Media Companies*, edited by Kirk Whisler and Octavio Nuiry; WPR Publications.
- *The Complete Directory to Prime Time Network and Cable TV Shows* by Tim Brooks and Earle Marsh; Ballantine Books.

This is obviously only a partial listing; thankfully, directories and organizations are not the only way of identifying media outlets for a target audience. You can also, in surveys and focus groups, ask members of your targeted constituency about the publications they read, the TV shows they watch, the radio they listen to, and much more. Another effective media-identifying approach is to meet with the "gatekeepers" for the community you are trying to reach—the head of a local Chinese-American civic association, the president of the local chapter of the African-American or Hispanic chamber of commerce—and simply ask about the media of choice in the region.

Yet another very basic step to take that is often overlooked is to expose yourself to the media you are thinking about buying. Listen to the radio. Buy the newspaper. Watch the cable show. Visit the Web page. And when you do, ask questions like these:

- What are the demographics of the media outlet? Do they match your product's demos?
- What is the editorial environment? Does its style match the one you are trying to project? How can you tailor your creative approach to be best received on this radio station, cable show, or whatever?
- Are our direct competitors already advertising on these media? If so, what are the competitive advantages and disadvantages of beginning to advertise now? If not, what is the opportunity for getting on board now?

3. Codify your goals. The only way you plan your use of media—and gauge how much to spend, your creative, etc.—is to know just what you are trying to accomplish. Is your goal to sell a certain quantity of product? To build brand awareness? To promote awareness of an event you are sponsoring? How much media you will buy, when you will use it, and how you will assess the results will all flow logically from the answers to these very basic questions.

4. Meet with representatives of the media outlets you are considering. Describe your agenda and goals, and assess how effectively the media outlets will help you reach them. Has the cable TV show that interests you advertised products similar to yours

in the past? If so, how good were the results? How many people in your target group—urban youth, for example, or upscale African-American suburbanites—tune in to that radio station during particular time periods? What is the circulation of that Filipino newspaper, or that Korean lifestyle magazine, among the people you are trying to reach? Asking such questions will help you assess whether the return you would receive for your advertising dollars will be large or small.

5. Find appropriate creative and other expertise. Whether you are selling bankcard services to Chinese-Americans in New York or San Francisco or time-shares to Latinos in Texas, you need someone with proven expertise and a wealth of ideas to help you meet your specific goals.

   As mentioned earlier in this book, avoid the tendency of believing that all you need to get this job done is "someone who speaks their language" or someone who is of the same ethnic background as the group you are targeting. A Spanish-speaking person may know more about the Latino mind-set than a non-Latino. An African-American-owned ad agency may seem to know the "lay of the land" among the African-American consumers in the targeted locality. Yet as a savvy marketer with accountability for dollars spent, you owe it to yourself and your company to ask extensive questions about the agency's experiences and successes with your targeted consumers.

6. Go into focus groups to test the relationship between your creative and your target audience. This is a critical step. If you are contemplating creating a commercial spot for an automobile-maker, for example, and your goal is to sell cars to Hispanic-Americans, be sure to bring those concepts before Hispanic-American consumers in extensive focus groups. Or if you are creating a series of print ads to attract more African-Americans to your fast-food outlets in the Midwest, be sure to meet in focus groups of African-Americans from the Midwest to get feedback and evaluation of those ads.

   Above all, avoid any leaps of faith where ethnic or multicultural marketing is involved because everyone in the business could point out instances where well-thought-out, seemingly appropriate advertising efforts failed to make an impact on the targeted consumers. Many could cite cases where inappropriate ads even offended consumers.

The bottom line is ask before you overspend.

7. Engage in a program of continuous learning. Evaluate the results of your advertising and marketing against your goals. How good were the results? Where were those results disappointing? On the flip side, where did results exceed your expectations? Above all, *why*?

When you begin your next media effort targeted at Korean-, Filipino-, Hispanic-American heads of household, or African-American entrepreneurs, how will you build on what you have done well in your past use of media? How will you understand things that did not go well and avoid the crippling mistakes of the past? The only way you can build your expertise and success is to start asking questions. And then go on to ask and ask some more.

A Crippling Error: Leaving Ethnic Americans out of Your Plan

It isn't standard practice for agencies to propose ethnic buys as routine parts of media plans, suggests Heide Gardner, the American Advertising Federation's (AAF) vice president for diversity and strategic programs. Gardner, part of an AAF task force seeking to increase minority-owned and targeted media's piece of the ad pie, blames a fundamental "lack of understanding of how cultural cues and trust in minority-formatted media" can impact an advertiser's bottom line.

Others are more blunt. "It's segregation," argues Kofi Ofori, who recently authored a major study on ethnic media for the Federal Communications Commission (FCC). According to him, shrinking market share awaits advertisers who don't board the ethnic bandwagon soon. "Even when people stand to make more money, it's another issue to employ people of color and to get out of old habits." This year Ofori's Washington-based firm authored an FCC study that found widespread ad discrimination in radio. Every dollar per listener earned by a general-market station garnered just 78 cents per listener in minority stations, the study says. For example, consider soft-drink consumption and personal care purchases among Hispanic-Americans. While Hispanic-Americans comprise 11 percent of the U.S. population, says Christy Haubegger, founding publisher of *Latina* magazine, they buy 22 percent of Coca-Cola Classic. "We're using 16 percent of the lip liner, but there's not a cosmetic company yet that has directed 16 percent of their budget to this audience," she told the *Mediaweek* researchers.

Yet minorities assign considerable value to advertising messages based not only on the ad's content but also on its context, be it between a magazine's covers or interspersed in a station's programming. "An invitation to purchase feels a lot different when it's on my nightstand," Haubegger summarized.

Certainly, some major advertisers have sustained, even grown, market share by using minority-focused media. Frequently cited kingpins were telecommunications companies such as AT&T, MCI, and Sprint; automakers; and packaged-goods firms such as Phillip Morris' Kraft. But many other advertisers continue to resist dealing with ethnic media.

Roadblocks

Many experts agree that being in a presentation with media buyers can be a daunting task for those who advocate using in-language media, particularly media for Hispanic- or Asian-Pacific-American audiences.

Correcting such imbalances starts with realizing that minorities and their media represent a critical mass with the very real potential to increase an advertiser's market share. Other pro-ethnic advocates contend that the difficulty is considerably more complex, but most focus on getting rid of decades-old stereotypes about minority consumers, their buying habits, and the media they use. It's an attitude that may be slowly changing on Madison Avenue as more research becomes available.

Asian-Pacific-Americans and the Media: Mainstream Media Must Take Our Differences into Account in Order to Cross Over Successfully

Do you think of America as the great melting pot, the place that would "like to teach the world to sing, in perfect harmony"? Do you believe that sooner or later, through successive generations, we will all become one people, of one mind, together forever in pursuit of a vaunted enlightenment that will put us all at the service of one another for the common good? Better think again. The '60s have been over for some time now. Just look around. The reality now is diversity. And in order to have diversity, you must first have differences in culture and the attitudes, opinions and beliefs that shape it. And so, while the world still could sing in perfect harmony, the lyrics would surely be a cacophony.

It is important for marketers and planners to understand that the success of mass advertising now depends on the ability to identify, study and reach multi-segmented groups and/or multi-ethnic groups. Yes, we are a diverse population, but those individuals and classes of people who control mainstream media outlets continue to gear their editorial product toward young, white America. This has reinforced the "disconnect" between ethnic populations and mainstream media. The disconnect is evident in declining circulation at newspapers, ratings in broadcast television and household penetration among magazines.

Advertisers and planners need to realize that the no. 1-rated show on TV may not reach the majority of Hispanic, African and Asian consumers because these audiences can rarely relate to, or identify with, any of the characters or jokes on the show. Even worse is the lack of understanding of a specific culture or ethnicity. Certain programs are often downright stereotypical and offensive to minority viewers.

There has been some attempt by mainstream broadcast networks such as the WB [Warner Brothers] and UPN (and Fox in the early '90s) to extend their reach into minority communities, particularly among African-Americans. But those efforts are often short-lived and conceived primarily to skew a network's total demographic more toward young, urban viewers. There have been similar efforts to add reach in the Hispanic community, but they presuppose that Hispanic viewers will adopt a show that speaks to them in English. With the exception of ABC's *All-American Girl*, which starred Margaret Cho, nobody has tried to take a mainstream TV show into the Asian community, but if it were tried, it would not likely be successful. Of all ethnicities, Asians have the highest in-language dependency. This strongly reflects on their mainstream and in-language media consumption. For example, among Chinese audiences, where two-thirds of the population prefers to speak in-language at home, the media-consumption ratio is 2:3 (in-language to mainstream TV) and 1:1 for radio.

For print, where it is necessary to have a strong command of the English language, 55 percent of the readers prefer in-language newspapers to mainstream newspapers, according to the 1993 *Yankelovich-Asian Monitor*.

Most ethnic consumers, regardless of the speed at which they are able to adapt to mainstream culture, want to be informed of developments from their country of origin. This thirst for ethnically relevant knowledge or information cannot be obtained through mainstream news media. The Filipino and South Asian market, for example, have a stronger command of the English language, compared to other non-English-speaking immigrant groups, yet they continue to keep track and inform themselves of overseas developments through in-language media. For these multicultural groups, it is extremely important to be aware and informed of the news in both cultures because of their daily involvement in both societies.

To satisfy this demand, in-language media has emerged, offering an immediate solution to the need among ethnic audiences for cultural identification among news, information and entertainment programming produced locally and overseas. The establishment and availability of ethnic media varies for each ethnic group, but most do share similar characteristics. In the early stages of most ethnic media, print is the primary medium due to the support from parent companies overseas, low printing and distribution costs, and a high literacy rate among new immigrants. Broadcast media is slower to emerge because of difficulties in distribution, with the exception of Hispanic media. With the emergence of cable and satellite TV, in-language media has overcome early-stage obstacles and could feasibly surpass in-language print media within a few years.

To date, the Hispanic media, which is being viewed as the pioneer of ethnic media, has begun to receive some recognition and consideration from major advertisers. But surprisingly, Asian media is still ignored when it comes to mass advertising. They are being excluded because the marketers and planners are not willing to invest the time to educate themselves about the opportunities and challenges of Asian media. They are ignoring an Asian market that, while it accounts for only 4 percent of the overall U.S. population, commands an astounding $229 billion in buying power.

Most advertisers need to realize that the "disconnect" between ethnic consumers and mainstream media has provided an opportunity that should be explored rather than ignored. Reaching these consumers in their own languages as part of their overall marketing strategy will create a perfect mass-reach, well-rounded media plan for any advertiser. The relationship advertisers will establish by answering the call for ethnically targeted media and culturally sensitive marketing will set them far beyond others in the industry.

Many multicultural media executives say they are optimistic about their future advertising revenues. Eighty percent told the *Mediaweek* and New America Strategies Group researchers that they were expecting increases to grow through 2001, even though the prevailing opinion was that they weren't receiving their fair share of ad revenue. Most also stated their belief, however, that minority-focused media is still generally considered a "fringe buy" by mainstream marketers.

Fighting the Afterthought Mentality

As mentioned in earlier chapters, Hispanic-, African-, and Asian-Pacific-American populations are growing at seven times the rate of the general market. They represent nearly 30 percent of the U.S. population; by 2040, they will account for more than half of all Americans. And the 2000 Census should be another wake-up call to Madison Avenue.

Recent examples show that some advertisers have come to recognize the importance of ethnic growth markets:

- JCPenney noted a dramatic payback in targeted marketing with its "white suit" campaign. It featured African-American women in tailored white attire, reflecting the long-standing tradition among blacks of wearing white to church on the fifth Sunday of the month. The ad campaign ran in African-American women's magazines and quickly helped sell out white-suit inventory in the department-store chain's urban locations.
- Advertising on Spanish-language network television can give advertisers an average 20 percent hike in sales among Hispanic-American consumers, compared to a similar campaign on English-language broadcast networks, according to a pilot study by Skunkworks of New York.
- After a three-month grassroots protest urging CompUSA to advertise with African-American–oriented media, the nation's largest computer retailer last month decided to hire an African-American-owned advertising firm and offer store discounts to the protesters. The campaign against CompUSA was orchestrated by popular radio personalities and the BET host, Tavis Smiley.

- A week later, American Airlines, "in an effort to better serve its target markets," announced plans to name an African-American–owned advertising agency its national agency of record. "As a leader in the airline industry, we recognize that we operate in a global environment consisting of diverse markets," said Tom Morris, American's managing director of advertising. "Selecting an African-American agency to help with our communications efforts will enable us to better serve the African-American markets."

Challenges to Ethnic Media

Ethnic-media outlets have their own set of challenges. Key executives within minority media, and the ad community that best knows them, say they are working to counter advertiser resistance and dispel what they call a faulty conventional wisdom.

In the last three years, some 165 Hispanic-American publications with a combined circulation of 9.4 million have put together a one-stop shopping program for advertisers wishing to reach Latinos with national media buys. Called the Latino Print Network, the sales arm of the National Association of Hispanic Publications (NAHP), it is also conducting studies about the buying habits and economic standing of Hispanic-Americans. Andres Tobar, NAHP executive director and CEO, is optimistic that the organization's approach will mean "a more equitable share" of money for print and also will help members gain against Spanish-language TV.

Madison Avenue, says Dr. Andrew Erlich, of Woodland Hills, California-based Erlich Transcultural Consultants, "is a reflection of society, and it would be real easy to make them into the bad guys. But I think the issue here is one of human nature. It has to do with all humans being ethnocentric, that 'My way is the only way that has any value.'

"This has everything to do with innovative thinking, management, and creativity in the world of advertising, which is supposed to be about creative processes."

Cable Television and the National Association of Minorities in Communications Study

The cable industry knows it has a problem: A study released this year by the National Association of Minorities in Communications [NAMIC] concluded that cable, like most American industries, is dominated by white men.

"Any company that prides itself in having an ear to the ground and knowing what the consumer wants must have an employee makeup that reflects all the types of people in society. Otherwise, you're faking it," MTV Networks chairman and CEO Tom Freston told the press in 1999, adding that 20 percent of his company's work force are minorities. "But the higher you go, the fewer there are, and that's not unusual, but it is unacceptable."

"I think our industry understands the issue intellectually and is starting to understand it emotionally—meaning it becomes part of your being and not something you are forced to think about," said Nick Davatzes, A&E Networks president and CEO.

The National Association of Minorities in Communications study, which surveyed 15 cable companies representing 53 percent of the work force, concluded that while the overall minority population is about 30 percent, minority representation in positions in cable's uppermost management, senior VP to CEO at nonethnically targeted programming companies, is only about 5 percent. That 5 percent is made up of 12 minorities, nine of whom are men.

As for cable operators, the study found that minorities make up 7 percent of upper management—a total of six minorities with the rank of senior VP and above.

The study also polled NAMIC's membership and found minorities perceived discrimination in company policies and practices with respect to industry conferences, training programs, social networks and career opportunities. And about one-third of minority respondents do not believe their senior management or their department's management are committed to diversity.

"The movement into management or upper management has been nonexistent for blacks," said one 35-year-old African American woman working in a regional office of a cable network. "I recently interviewed for a position. After my interview they changed the criteria for the position and said I did not qualify."

If cable seems a calcified old-boys network, the study points out that the industry's shortcomings mirror the rest of American business, and that the existence of the study proves that cable is addressing the dilemma.

"There isn't a company out there that's deliberately slighting minorities, but we are a long way from the point at which we can say that everybody has an even opportunity," said Spencer Kaitz, president of and general counsel for The Walter Kaitz Foundation.

"In general, the media business is woefully behind," said Freston, who when asked why said, "People tend to hire people they are comfortable with, and unless they are forced to change that pattern you end up with a *de facto* semi-closed society. It takes some jolts and reprogramming to get off that mark."

The National Association of Minorities in Communications also points to a 1998 study that found ethnic groups increased their spending from 1995 to 1998 by 17.6 percent for African Americans, 17.7 percent for Asian Americans and 15.5 percent for Hispanic Americans. African Americans control buying power of $400 billion, followed by $270 billion for Hispanics/Latinos and $220 billion for Asians. "Anybody who doesn't see the need to meet the needs of minorities just doesn't have a clue," said Freston.

For both African Americans and Hispanics, entertainment is one of the top three areas that account for the increases in expenditures. For instance, African Americans subscribe to premium cable at nearly twice the rate of whites (45 percent to 26 percent), followed by Latinos (35 [percent]).

"We want to have as many voices as possible in the creative process," says Richard Plepler, HBO's executive VP of corporate communications.

A 1999 study by the Strategy Research Corp. reported that more than one-half of Hispanic households in the U.S. have some form of multichannel-video service, through cable, direct-broadcast satellite or larger satellite dishes. That number goes up to 75 percent of homes in top Latino markets such as Los Angeles and New York.

Specialty recruiting firms are working with companies, who, like MTV Networks, A&E, HBO and others, have established diversity councils that report directly to top management. Comcast has a VP of diversity and Time Warner Cable, AT&T and Cox Communications have large diversity initiatives in place. Companies have also hired outside consultants, and some are toying with the idea of compensating employees who help recruit minority job candidates.

. . . One has only to consider the wide diversity in minority groups themselves. What does it mean to be Latino, Asian, black? Each group has a long history, a widely varied population.

"It seems like such a simple thing on its surface, but I have found that changing behavior is more difficult than I had thought," Freston said.

Source: By Jim Cooper. ©1999 ASM Communications Inc. Used with permission.

CASE STUDY: NEWSPAPER PUBLISHING
AND ETHNIC AMERICANS

Twenty years ago, the American Society of Newspaper Editors (ASNE) looked across the nation's newsrooms and determined that to better represent their increasingly multicultural constituencies, they needed to become more racially and ethnically diverse. The association, made up of ranking editors from newspapers large and small, set a benchmark: by the year 2000, the number of minorities working in newsrooms would mirror the U.S. minority population.

Newspapers vowed to aggressively recruit African-Americans, Hispanic-Americans, Asian-Pacific-Americans, and Native Americans. Minority scholarships, intern programs, and training initiatives were instituted. Recruiters began traveling to conventions for minority journalists and minority job fairs. Editors and publishers took every opportunity to extol the importance of "accurately reflecting the community," while touting their own unwavering commitment to the cause. Diversity was hot.

Despite their good intentions, newspapers must now admit that they fell short—way short. Today, racial and ethnic minorities make up just 11.5 percent of newsroom employees nationwide, according to ASNE, compared with 28.4 percent of the U.S. population. (Shockingly, 380 newspapers that the association examined reported having *no minority representation whatsoever.*)

In 1998, ASNE was forced to adjust its 2000 goal and now hopes newsrooms can reach parity with the general minority population by the year 2025.

Jolted by the industry's dearth of achievements, the Newspaper Association of America (NAA) recently was moved to issue its first statement on diversity, urging members to redouble diversity efforts and suggesting strategies for boosting their numbers. Six in ten newspapers today have diversity goals, according to the NAA. Meanwhile, the association reports that just 18 percent of full-time newspaper employees across all departments are minorities, compared with 24 percent of the U.S. civilian workforce who are minorities. Larger newspapers, however, have better representation: those with circulations of greater than 50,000 are 27 percent minority, compared with the 7 percent minority workforce of newspapers with circulations of less than 10,000. "If diversity is to happen, it means a critical mass of folks have to believe it's important," said Toni Laws, NAA senior vice president of diversity. "Newspapers have to see themselves as agents for change, just as they have been agents for change throughout their existence."

Yet advances have been made, especially in news coverage of minorities. "You don't find the kinds of racially charged headlines and racially biased reporting, especially in the South, that you found in the '50s and '60s," said Reginald Stuart, corporate recruiter for San Jose, California–based Knight Ridder Inc. and former national president of the Society of Professional Journalists. "You can say there's been phenomenal progress in the . . . whole presentation of news."

But sad to say, more diverse ranks don't always translate to stellar news coverage. "There's a tendency at some papers for a minority to join the staff and cop the company line. That creates a homogenized perspective on the news, and that's not what we're here to do," said Jean Thompson, associate managing editor/staff development for Times Mirror Co.'s *Baltimore Sun.* "We have to recognize that every single person—male or female, gay or straight, black or white—is going to bring something different to a story that makes us a healthier, stronger newspaper, and that also makes for an article that rings true."

Of some 400 newsroom employees at the *Sun*, 17 percent are minority, up from 12 percent a dozen years ago. "Our goals at the *Sun* are to better reflect our readership and to hire great journalists of all different backgrounds," Thompson said, noting the city's 65 percent African-American population and its fast-growing Hispanic-American and Asian-Pacific-American communities.

Charlotte Hall, vice president/managing editor at Times Mirror's *Newsday* of Long Island and chair of ASNE's diversity committee, also links staffing with coverage. "You can't do the kind of journalism that's relevant to an increasingly diverse population unless you have a diversity of backgrounds and cultures in the newsroom," she said. *Newsday*'s newsroom last year was 21.4 percent minority, up from 11.1 percent a decade earlier. So far this year, 72 percent of the department's new hires have been members of minority groups, compared with 54 percent last year, according to Hall. *Newsday*, like many other newspapers, has also refashioned its content to cater to diverse audiences—adding a Latin-American news page and creating such beats as immigration, aging, and Hispanic affairs. Last year, a series of reports, "The Health Divide," examined the health care disparity between whites and blacks.

Jose Bertlos, vice president/diversity for the nation's largest news-paper publisher, Arlington, Virginia–based Gannett, says his company is "serious about bringing in more diverse talent and moving them up the line." In fact, the publisher of *USA Today* and the *Detroit News* can point to real progress. As of last year, its total minority representation had grown to 26.1 percent, up from 12.3 percent in 1980. Minorities hold 19.3 percent of the company's top-management posts, up from 8.8 percent in 1980. Minorities make up 27 percent of Gannett's news board and 15 percent of news management.

Sometimes, even companies with a strong commitment to diversity suffer setbacks. Knight Ridder, publisher of the *Miami Herald*, *San Jose Mercury News,* and *Philadelphia Inquirer*, this year ranked twenty-second on *Fortune*'s list of the best U.S. companies for minorities. The company boasts that 27.7 percent of its 22,000-person workforce are minorities, including 16 percent of its managers. The torch-bearing media behemoth even adopted the slogan, "Diversity. No Excuses."

But executives across the industry realize that newspapers' very survival clearly depends on their relevance to a mass audience—an ever more diverse audience. "If newspapers do not reflect what this country is about over the next twenty or thirty years, there will be fewer people using the product," said Veronica Jennings, project manager/content development for *Newsday* and former diversity chair of ASNE. "America is changing . . . and if we're going to attract young people coming up in this multicultural world—as readers, as advertisers, as potential newspaper professionals—they must see themselves reflected in the newspaper."

CASE STUDY: MAGAZINE PUBLISHERS ASSOCIATION (MPA)

A *Mediaweek* diversity survey conducted in 1998 by Fairfield Research, a media research firm, and human-resource company Raymond-Karsan Inc. clearly pointed out the lack of minority hiring for professional editorial and publishing positions. People of color—black, Hispanic-American, Asian-Pacific-American, or Native American—account for only 6.1 percent of professional staff in both large- and small-circulation titles.

Of the country's top 300 magazines, only 6.1 percent of staff on the editing side were people of color; and on the publishing side, only 6.7 percent were reported as nonwhite. Minorities consisting of black, Hispanic-, and Asian-Pacific-Americans are projected to make up 28.4 percent of the population next year, according to the U.S. Census. In 2050, these groups will make up 46.6 percent of the population. Currently, African-, Hispanic-, and Asian-Pacific-Americans have an estimated combined spending power of nearly $650 billion, according to the FCC.

"I don't think editorial directors and publishers have realized how important and lucrative the market can be for them," said Isabel Valdés, president of Cultural Axis Group of Axis Worldwide, a Los Angeles–based marketing research firm. "Right now, they are doing good business, but they are going to leave the door open to competitors that take away readers."

"A big part of magazine business is advertising and reaching people with disposable income," said William Sutton, president of the National Association of Black Journalists and deputy managing editor at the *Raleigh News and Observer.* "And just like most businesses, if you don't take care of the customer and you don't continue to broaden your base, you will die."

Publishers live in the now and see diversity as "a challenge of the future," said Vaughn Benjamin, vice president of Workforce Diversity for the Magazine Publishers of America and vice president of Media Credit Association. "Except, when tomorrow comes, publishers will need to be prepared."

A joint MPA–Yankelovich Partners survey has revealed the industry's current mind-set, and not surprisingly, the results indicated that for many publishers diversity has just not been top of mind. Of the companies surveyed, only 32 percent said they have implemented some sort of diversity program or training. And though 44.8 percent believe a diverse workforce offers different perspectives and approaches to work, only 10.3 percent have infused that corporate mentality into their workplace.

But it's not all bad news. The MPA study noted that 74.1 percent of respondents said they would make their offices "extremely" diverse in the next five years. And both the MPA and various publishers are already beginning to put those programs in place.

"We really let editors and publishers make their own decisions," says Ruth Diem, Hearst Magazines' vice president and director of human resources. Hearst Magazines publishes *Good Housekeeping*, *Esquire*, and *House Beautiful.* "We have not had a culture that has forced people to make hiring decisions of any kind, and in a sense that's what you have to do." Still, Hearst, under magazine president Cathleen Black, created an internship program three years ago, of which a third of the twenty-five slots are given to minorities. Time Inc. also has in place a number of corporate internship programs, including the Don Logan Associate Program, named for Time Inc.'s president and CEO, which recruits bachelor-level graduates into titles such as *Time* and *Fortune* or corporate jobs on the publishing side. A comparable program exists on the editing side, as well.

Even so, most companies have seen little progress at the midmanagement level and above, those positions of power and influence that can affect a magazine's editorial direction and its bottom line. The result has been that top-level minority talent and editorial content devoted to minority interests remain in various ethnically targeted magazines. *Essence*, *Black Enterprise*, *People en Espanol*, and *Latina* are proof that if publishers effectively seek out minorities and diversify their content, both the executives and readers will follow.

Beyond attending diversity fairs and college recruiting for entry-level jobs and internships, a number of publishers insist that finding professional-level minorities is not easy. The publishing pool is just too small. "It's not there because the talent pool just hasn't evolved where people have the experience of ten years or fifteen or twenty years of experience to do the jobs," said John Fennell, Hachette Filipacchi Magazines' chief operating officer. "It is a concern."

"Magazines, like many industries, are composed primarily of relatively small businesses," said Thomas Ryder, chairman and CEO of the Reader's Digest Association. "We can't as individual companies compete very well for highly talented ethnic minorities. They go typically to bigger companies that recruit aggressively at schools around the country."

In response, the MPA this August kicked off a workforce diversity initiative that will seek out talent at all levels. Wesley Brown & Bartle Company, a New York–based diversity recruitment firm, has been hired—with an initial $500,000 budget—to create a prescreened database of minority applicants from outside the magazine industry. The growing talent pool consists of both entry-level and professional-level candidates for editing and publishing positions. "We need to find the people who have the skills to be successful in magazine publishing, either on the ad-sales side, the circulation side, production and editorial from other related industries," said former MPA president Donald Kummerfeld who helped launch the industry initiative. "We think it will take some time to build up, but over a period of time it will make a difference."

The MPA program is being funded in part through the Reader's Digest Association, which set up a challenge grant ranging from $200,000 to $500,000 per year, with the amount dependent on whether both a recruitment and an internship program are set up. Those companies that join must agree to a five-year commitment. Most of the larger MPA members and a number of smaller members have donated money or have pledged to do so, including Hachette, Hearst, and Time Inc. So far, the recruiting process has started across campuses, but an MPA internship program is still under discussion.

"This [initiative] is catch-up, to be perfectly honest, but dividends get paid fast here," Ryder said. "The biggest symbol of all is when management throughout the industry makes a commitment to it. And, frankly, I think we're about there. I think it's about to happen."

POISED FOR GROWTH: MARKETING ON THE ETHNIC INTERNET

We are at the cusp of the third greatest revolution in mankind's history. There was the Agricultural Revolution and the Industrial Revolution, and now we are at the very beginning of the Information Revolution.

This third revolution rewards those who control and process information. It gives them a competitive advantage and a road to national affluence.

It is defined principally by its power to unlock the potential of markets, to transform retailing, to make businesses more profitable, and to create unimaginable wealth for a privileged few.

But I believe that this latest economic revolution means much more. It should be defined, first and foremost, by its power to unlock the potential of all of our people—by its power to educate our poorest children, to empower people with disabilities, to uplift impoverished rural and urban communities, and to repair and revitalize the fabric of our communities.

—from "The Great Equalizer," remarks of William E. Kennard, chairman, Federal Communications Commission, in his speech delivered at The Supercomm 2000 International Dinner, Capital City Club, Atlanta, Georgia, June 5, 2000

An Interview with Larry Tuckett

Larry Tuckett is director of ethnic marketing for Luminant Worldwide and a leading expert on trends in the ethnic Internet.

Schreiber: Demographic material shows that Hispanic-, Asian-Pacific-, and African-Americans are rapidly gaining access to the Internet, even though much-publicized gaps still exist and both Hispanic-Americans and African-Americans lag behind whites in the amount of time they spend on-line.

As the devil's advocate let me ask you first, why pay attention to doing business on the ethnic Internet? Why shouldn't marketers just bide their time and wait until most minority consumers have Internet access at home?

Tuckett: The macro is this. Minority groups are rushing to the Web because they're not finding programming off-line, on radio and TV, that addresses their needs, tastes, and desires.

The NAACP has been criticizing TV networks, for example, saying there are not enough blacks presented in prime-time programming. Despite the plethora of general-market magazines, radio stations, TV programs, movies, and cable, you are going to be hard-pressed to find a lot of information and content that addresses your needs and your community if you're black, Hispanic, Asian, or Native American.

More and more ethnic and minority people are looking toward the Web for that. It is a very democratic place where they can not only be content consumers but be content *producers*.

Schreiber: So the Internet speaks more authentically to minority and ethnic consumers?

Tuckett: There is real opportunity to reach them there, which is why so many advertisers and marketers are embracing the Internet to reach multicultural markets. The Web, after all, is about narrowcasting. More than any other medium, it allows a company to understand what the consumer thinks about their brand, company, product, or service. The Internet allows that company to track what consumers are doing—what they are clicking on and what they are not clicking on. The marketer can know how long the consumer is on a site, read what consumers post on bulletin boards, and even talk to customers in real time in chat sessions. This allows access to the consumer that can't be achieved in any other medium.

And the marketer gets that feedback in real time. If you run a TV ad or a print ad, you may not know for a few months how effective it was. If you run an ad campaign on the Web, you know immediately how many people have seen it, how many people were interested enough to click on it, how long they stayed on that site, and in many cases, whether an actual purchase was made. There is also the next stage of engaging the consumer, allowing the marketer to enter into a one-on-one dialogue with the potential consumer through E-mail marketing campaigns, another macro issue.

Schreiber: If you are a marketer and have not yet gotten started on the Internet, either through hosting your own site or through advertising on other sites, what's the best way to begin?

Tuckett: Well, if you haven't yet gotten started, the first step is to realize that unless you get started soon, you're probably not going to be in business five years from now. You know about the demographics in this country. People are waking up to them. Here on Madison Avenue, every major advertising agency has formed an ethnic marketing division.

One of the hottest things they are looking for is on-line ethnic marketing expertise. Advertisers have awakened to the $1.3 trillion buying power of the multicultural market, and they are looking for creative ways not just to reach but to connect and start building relationships with them. The Internet represents one of the most viable ways.

Regarding how to get started, I can only make a partial answer, because it is important to engage some people who have real expertise in Internet marketing to minorities. Start by hiring or retaining people with appropriate expertise. I've sensed and observed, with major advertisers like financial institutions and automotive companies, that because they haven't done ethnic marketing before, they are very eager to avoid mistakes. And that's good. They are aware of how savvy consumers are. They don't want to get responses from minority consumers like: "Well, you've ignored me and my community for all these years, now all of a sudden you show up and you want my money?"

The reason to hire an agency is to get it right. Otherwise, you run the risk of doing "drive-by marketing." Therefore you need to hire someone who knows that space community and how to form the right relationships. The Internet is a good place to form relationships. I've heard in focus groups and in all kinds of feedback that when black people or Hispanic people are on the Web, they don't see themselves first as black or Hispanic. They see themselves as Web surfers first and as members of their communities second. The Web is an equalizer and a good place to reach people if you can do it appropriately.

Schreiber: And there is money to be made today in E-commerce, not only in the years to come.

Tuckett: There is nowhere else that you can connect with consumers so effectively, so early in the buying cycle. For example, suppose you are a marketing company. You could make a deal with amazon.com so that every time someone orders a book on how to furnish, buy, or finance a new home, your lending company is offered the opportunity to talk to that consumer. That way you can connect with them early in the buying cycle. Marketers who do ethnic marketing have the rare opportunity to form such alliances on the Internet—alliances that would be crazy in the off-line world. Why would a lending institution form a strategic alliance with a bookstore? It makes absolutely no sense off-line. But on the Internet it makes perfect sense.

The Digital Melting Pot

Shopping is important to African-Americans, and now we're seeing that compared to white consumers, blacks use the Internet more for gathering information about products and shopping than for leisure, indicating there's a huge e-commerce opportunity out there for marketers willing to go after them.

—Hal Quinley, executive vice president,
Yankelovich Partners, quoted in *Advertising Age*,
November 29, 1999

In its 1999 study, *The Digital Melting Pot*, Forrester Research revealed that multicultural consumers often lead the country on key measures related to Internet usage. For example, 64 percent of Asian-Pacific-American and 36 percent of Hispanic-American households are on-line at home, versus only 34 percent of Caucasian-American households. (African-American households are the lowest at 23 percent but are expected to enjoy the fastest growth in 1999.) Asian-Pacific-Americans (56 percent) and Hispanic-Americans (49 percent) are more likely to do research about products and services on-line than Caucasians (48 percent). Similarly, more Asian-Pacific-Americans (21 percent) and Hispanic-Americans (11 percent) conduct financial transactions on-line than Caucasians (9 percent).

The multicultural consumer universe is smaller than that of the mainstream population, but it is growing, while the mainstream population is at a virtual standstill.

Prevailing Factors in Computer Ownership

According to the U.S. Department of Commerce (DOC), computer ownership has soared for all groups in the last fourteen years. The rate of ownership has grown rapidly for all demographic groups: at least fivefold across races and ethnic groups, and more than fourfold across all age groups and all educational groups, for example.

While ownership has increased for all groups, certain characteristics continue strongly to determine the rate of growth and the likelihood of a household owning a computer. Income, race, and education level, for example, continue to closely correspond with the computer penetration rate.

At the same time, age and employment status are beginning to become less significant variables, particularly, as seniors and those not in the labor force buy computers with increasing frequency. In 1984, 2.5 percent of households 55 and older owned personal computers (PCs), compared to 15.5 percent of 35–44-year-olds. In 1998, 25 percent of seniors owned PCs. Whether a family has children is also becoming a less significant determinant of whether the household owns a computer.

In 1984, nonfamily households were particularly unlikely to own PCs (3.7 percent), followed by family households without children (5.1 percent). In 1998, these two categories of households are still less likely to own computers than households with children but nevertheless now buy computers at a far higher frequency (27.5 percent and 43.2 percent, respectively).

The Ownership Divide

The rate of growth has also had a more significant impact on some groups than others. Those that were most likely to own PCs in 1984 were especially likely to own them in 1998, even though they may have experienced a lower rate of growth than other groups. For example, for the highest income group (those earning $75,000 and above), ownership grew nearly fourfold (from 22.1 percent to 79.9 percent). While the growth rate for the lowest income group (those under $5,000) was nearly tenfold during the same period, only one of six households at this income bracket owned computers in 1998.

The trend of seeing the "computer-rich get richer" means that the digital divide among groups is widening over time. The 20-percentage-point difference that existed between the highest and lowest income levels in 1984 has now expanded to a 64-percentage-point difference. What was a 15-percentage-point gap in 1984 between those with a college degree and those with elementary education became nearly a 61-percentage-point gap in the year 2000. These trends will continue until the relative growth rates among the least-connected Americans significantly surpass on a sustained basis the growth rates for the more connected.

Profiles of the Most- and Least-Connected Americans

According to DOC statistics, certain households have continued to own PCs at higher rates: those earning higher incomes, those with college degrees or higher, households consisting of married couples with children, households located in the West region of the country, and those that are employed.

One significant change has occurred based on race and ethnic origin. In 1984, white households accounted for the highest computer penetration rate; in 1989, they were surpassed by other non-Hispanic (i.e., Asian-Pacific-American, Native American, and Inuit) households, which held an even more significant lead in 1998.

In examining the least-connected households earning lower incomes, those with lower education levels, those located in the South, and those under the age of twenty-five have consistently had lower computer ownership rates. In particular, households earning low incomes and living in rural areas have repeatedly reported the lowest penetration rates. Rural African-American households have also remained the least likely group to own a PC (2.7 percent in 1984, 17.9 percent in 1998), followed by Hispanic-Americans living in central cities (3.1 percent in 1984, 21.4 percent in 1998).

Overall, race remains closely correlated with computer owner-ship. In 1984, white households owned nearly twice the number of PCs as African-American and Hispanic-American households. Other non-Hispanic households trailed white households, on the other hand, by only 0.4 percentage points. Between 1984 and 1998, white households' penetration rates increased approximately fivefold, and all other race and ethnic groups experienced approximately a sixfold increase. Because of their similar growth rates, white households continued to own computers at a rate roughly twice that of African-American and Hispanic-American households in 1998.

The Digital Divide

In general, underserved groups (such as low-income users) and rural areas have fallen farther behind the modem ownership leaders in their respective categories in recent years. Who is the most connected and who the least? DOC data affords some illuminating answers.

Those Americans enjoying the greatest connectivity today are typically high-income households. Generally, the most highly con-nected groups are whites or Asian-Pacific-Americans—middle aged, highly educated, and employed, some married with children—most often found in urban areas and the West. Conversely, the least connected generally remain low income or not employed; African-American, Hispanic-American, or Native American; senior in age or single par-ent (especially female headed); little educated; central city or especially rural households. These profiles generally prevailed during 1989–97, albeit some changes occurred (e.g., the South fell into last place among regions).

Here's more in-depth information on who is connected and who is not.

- **Income**
  From 1989 through 1997, modem ownership increased for all income levels. Penetration rose tenfold in income brackets below $20,000 and increased at a decreasing rate in the higher income brackets, registering growth of 4.2 times at the $75,000 and over bracket. Despite greater growth rates by the lower-income households, the percentage-point gap between lowest and highest penetration (for the $5,000–9,999 group versus the wealthiest households) grew from 13.4 percentage points in 1989 to 56.5 percentage points in 1997. During this period, rural areas generally experienced greater growth than central cities and urban areas but generally still trail the other two.

- **Race and Origin**
  During 1989–97, household modem penetration rose in every category of race or origin. White, African-American, other non-Hispanic, and Hispanic-American each grew eightfold or more. Because white and other non-Hispanic households started from a higher proportion, the digital gap has widened considerably compared to African-Americans and Hispanic-Americans. For example, the front-runner "other non-Hispanic" group (Native Americans, Aleuts, Inuits, Asian-Pacific-Americans) outdistanced African-Americans and Hispanic-Americans by more than 22 percentage points in 1997, compared to 2.0 and 2.22 in 1989. That pattern generally held whether their households were rural, urban, or central city, although white households have the highest penetration in rural areas (24.6 percent).

- **Education**
  During the eight-year period from 1989 to 1997, the digital gap mushroomed to more than a fivefold increase (from an 8.6 to a

Internet Access Gaps Widen

The digital divide among certain demographic groups and regions of the country continues to persist and in many cases, widen significantly, according to the National Telecommunications and Information Administration. Minorities, low-income persons, those with less education and children in single-parent households—particularly when they reside in rural areas or central cities—are among the groups that lack access to information resources. Although more households are gaining access to new technologies, some groups are falling even further behind.

Households with incomes of $75,000 or higher are twenty times as likely as those at the lowest income levels to have Internet access and nine times as likely to have a computer at home. Whites are more likely to have access to the Internet from home than blacks and Hispanics are from any location. The gaps between white and Hispanic households and between white and black households were six points wider in 1998 than they were in 1994. In 1998, 32.4 percent of white households, 11.77 percent of black households, and 12.9 percent of Hispanic households had Internet access. Only among households with incomes of $75,000 or higher has the gap between white and black households narrowed (by six points); that between white and Hispanic households in this income range has increased by five points.

From 1997–98, Internet access increased 52.8 percent for white households, 52.0 percent for black households, and 48.3 percent for Hispanic households. The role of race or ethnic origin is highlighted when looking at similarly situated families. A white, two-parent household earning less than $35,000 is nearly three times as likely to have Internet access as a comparable black household and nearly four times as likely as a Hispanic household in the same income category.

Digital divides based on education and income have also increased. From 1997–98, the divide between those at the highest and lowest education levels increased 25 percent and that between those at the highest and lowest income levels increased 29 percent.

Source: "Falling Through the Net: Defining the Digital Divide," National Telecommunications and Information Administration, U.S. Department of Commerce, Washington, D.C.

46.3 percent-point difference) between households of the lowest and highest educational levels. This result can be explained largely in terms of the very low penetration rates exhibited by

the less-educated households in 1989. This pattern generally
holds in rural, urban, or central city areas, with the largest disparity in rural environs.

- **Household Type**
  The ownership of modems by all types of households grew
  substantially during 1989–97, registering sevenfold gains or
  more. Households comprised of a married couple with children
  eighteen years old or younger led all other categories (4.9 percent in 1989, 42.5 percent in 1997). Single-parent households
  with children lagged considerably; female households with children trailed all others throughout the period (1.0 percent in
  1989, 15.4 percent in 1997) but grew fifteenfold—faster than
  any other category. The digital gap expanded from 3.9 percentage points to 27.1. Both types of single-family rural households
  with children registered only a 0.5 percent modem penetration
  in 1989 but rocketed more than thirtyfold by 1997.

- **Age**
  Modem ownership in each age bracket grew approximately
  sevenfold or more. Middle-aged householders (ages 35–54) led
  all other categories, equaling more than 35.0 percent in 1997.
  Senior citizens exhibited the lowest penetration throughout the
  period, registering 13.2 percent in 1997. However, the seniors'
  elevenfold growth rate in modem ownership exceeded all other
  brackets. Between 1989 and 1997, the digital gap in terms of
  percentage points increased by roughly sixfold between the two
  groups. Urban middle-aged householders possessed the highest
  ownership rate (+36.0 percent), while rural seniors had the
  lowest penetration (11.2 percent) but the greatest growth rate
  (almost 13.0 percent from 1989–97).

- **Employment**
  Modem ownership rose more than sevenfold for both the
  employed and unemployed, and more than fourteenfold for the
  many-faceted not-in-labor-force category. In 1997, the highest
  penetration occurred among the urban employed (34.5 per-

cent), while the lowest gauge belonged to the not-in-labor-force category in rural areas (9.0 percent). From 1989 to 1997, the digital gap increased from a 3.6- to a 21.7-percentage-point differential. The greatest growth during the period 1989–97 occurred in rural America for the employed and unemployed, and in urban areas for the not-in-labor-force.

- **Region**
  The West exhibited the highest modem penetration in both 1989 (4.5 percent) and 1997 (30.8 percent), and no region experienced less than a sevenfold increase. The digital gap grew modestly, from 1.9 percentage points to 6.4. Whether in areas that were rural, urban, or central city, the Midwest grew more than any other region, bumping the South into last place. Rural areas frequently experienced greater growth rates than their urban or central-city counterparts but often fell farther behind in percentage-point differentials in urban-rural comparisons.

What We Can Learn from the DOC's Findings

The DOC's study of the years 1984–1998 reveals a number of promising patterns. While telephone penetration rates stabilized, the traditional "have nots" (including households with lower incomes, lower education levels, under age 25, or of certain minorities) have become more connected over time. Nevertheless, these groups are still less likely than other households to have a telephone.

Internet access has become more common among households of different demographic characteristics. Most significant, Hispanic-Americans and African-Americans, while lagging behind whites in Internet use and access, are "signing on" and using the Internet at a rate that surpasses whites by several percentage points.

Despite these patterns of growth, the information "haves" have dramatically outpaced the information "have nots" in their access to electronic services. As a result, the gap between these groups—the digital divide—has grown over time.

CASE STUDIES

With new Internet offerings appearing on the scene almost daily, a comprehensive list of Internet Web pages and services would not be possible to include here.

One good thing about the Internet is its accessibility and openness. Even if you pick up this book months or even years after it is published, the ethnic and multicultural Internet always stands ready for your inquiry.

For the purpose of this book, however, I will list only a small group of select Internet sites that meet two criteria. First, they currently are state-of-the-art, high-quality Internet services. Second, they seem likely to stand the test of time and remain on the scene for years to come. Visit these sites both for their own sake and because the many ads and links they incorporate will lead you to other Internet sites that address their particular constituencies.

Top Hispanic Sites
- Quepasa.com is a pioneering, high-quality site for Hispanic-Americans. Interestingly, it is available in both Spanish- and English-language versions, making it relatively convenient for English-speaking Americans to discover the depth and richness of the Latino Internet.

  A typical visit to quepasa.com's home page will uncover breaking news and media-related stories, and many interesting human-interest stories. Beyond the home page lies an interesting and useful mix of resources tailored for the Latino audience, including stock quotations, chat rooms, message boards, games, news, health-related stories, job ads, links to stores (that host pages in both English and Spanish), education, sports news, and even a Latino "recipe box" to help Latino parents plan the evening meal. As with Yahoo! and other more mainstream sites, quepasa.com allows its users to set up hosted E-mail accounts and home pages.

  All in all, quepasa.com's presence serves as ample evidence of the vibrant Hispanic Internet.

- Yahoo! en espanol (espanol.yahoo.com) is the Spanish-language version of Yahoo!
- Starmedia.com is another portal positioning itself as a Hispanic alternative to Yahoo!
- Latina.com, the Web site of *Latina* magazine, offers another successful site tailored for the Latino woman and is at present an excellent object lesson in how well a multi-featured Latino site can be structured and produced. Also available in either Spanish or English, latina.com offers a rich, vibrant mix of features and articles.

  Notably interactive, it offers readers the opportunities to send questions to the magazine's experts in many fields. If you would like to see how many mainstream Web merchants are advertising on ethnic sites, latina.com is well worth a visit.

- Yupi.com, a portal launched in 1999, is positioning itself as the Hispanic alternative to Yahoo!
- Ehola.com is another portal in direct competition with yupi.com.

Notable African-American Sites
- BlackVoices.com, owned by Chicago's Tribune company, is arguably the highest-quality, most full-featured African-American site on the Internet today. BlackVoices.com hosts a large and active membership community; becoming a member entitles readers to receive free on-line newsletters and advisories. Members can also take advantage of job listings, chat rooms, and other features.

  The site offers a virtual laboratory—and an ever-evolving lesson—in how Internet advertising works since there are at least five or six applet ads on the site each day. Site visitors and members can buy books and beauty products, and even book travel cruises.

  It's worth not only visiting BlackVoices.com but joining, too, because the site's outreach is outstanding, with E-mail welcoming messages, news alerts, and other community

messages that come from the site. Once you join the
BlackVoices.com community, you really feel part of a neighborhood. That's an effective stance to take and a precursor of
success for any Web page—African-American or otherwise.

- MSBET.com, BET's Web site, a joint venture with Microsoft
Network, is a full-featured site with an emphasis on entertainment. Microsoft's presence and financial backing may give
MSBET.com the durability and staying power it needs to
remain a Web presence for the long term. Also, the fact that
many new computer owners will sign up for the Microsoft
Network as their Internet service provider may give the site
significant penetration with African-American consumers.

- NetNoir.com, often cited as the most popular black-oriented
Internet site, offers "channels" that are organized around topics such as travel, health, sports, and families. NetNoir.com is
a partner of Internet giant America Online, giving it penetration and durability on par with MSBET.com.

- BlackFamilies.com, owned by Cox Interactive, offers black
families advice on finance, health, and parenting. It also provides links to local businesses offering child care and other
services.

- GlobalMecca.com, launched in 1999 by Roderick Robinson,
a Wharton School graduate with big plans, aims to position
itself as the preeminent site for African-Americans. It is
ambitious not only in plans but in execution, featuring a lit-
erature channel that presents books by and about African-
Americans, contributions by top black executives, and
information business topics such as raising seed capital.

- The Black World Today (tbwt.com) has often been cited as
the most sophisticated of sites created for and by African-
Americans. The emphasis here is on more than topical issues,
message boards, or chats; it is a page that reflects a wider
spectrum of black-related issues. Polls are conducted and the
site offers links to visitors' Web pages. The featured articles
are varied and sophisticated, with a range of political and
human-interest articles (once including a personal evaluation

of the movie *Hurricane* by Lloyd Kam Williams and an article on moral responsibility by Hugh Price).

• Blackenterprise.com, the on-line presence of the distinguished *Black Enterprise* magazine, stands coequal with *Fortune, Forbes,* and other business publications in the breadth and scope of the information provided. A class act on many levels, it is worth visiting both for its features and for the advertising it contains.

Bookmark blackenterprise.com and visit it regularly. It is a great way to keep tabs on the upscale African-American Web.

• EverythingBlack.com, an Internet search engine, was launched in 1997 with a listing of 300 black-oriented Web sites. By late 1999, EverythingBlack.com listed over 4,000. The black Internet is seeing explosive growth.

Top Asian-Pacific-American Web Pages

• AsianWeek.com, the Web site of the prestigious *AsianWeek* magazine, may have fewer ads and bells and whistles than other ethnic sites, but it has considerable depth and a good range of offerings. A typical visit will offer news and media stories, bulletin boards, chat rooms, arts reviews, and a searchable archive of older articles. Another useful item for potential event sponsors is the calendar of events. All in all, a good solid site and one worth visiting often to take the pulse of the Asian-Pacific-American community.

• ABCflash.com offers a terrific gateway to many links throughout the Asian-Pacific-American community. Its home page is light on visible advertising but rich on links to advertisers. You'll also find profiles of notable Asian-Pacific-Americans, summaries of news stories pertaining to Asian-Pacific-Americans, profiles of companies run by Asian-Pacific-Americans, and many articles on lifestyle and the arts. There are few gateways that offer a better glimpse of trends and interests within the Asian-Pacific-American community.

Chapter Eleven

MULTICULTURAL HEALTH CARE

> The growing multicultural nature of the U.S. and other markets accentuates the need for individualized care and a wide range in the choice of medications available to prescribers. Greater awareness of the importance of health-related cultural differences will help policy makers both in government and in the private sector to understand that pharmaceutical diversity must keep pace with the cultural diversity of the patient population.
>
> —from *Pharmaceutical Marketing and Cultural Diversity* by Richard Levy, Ph.D., and John Hawks, National Pharmaceutical Council, Reston, Virginia, 1995

On April 17, 1999, the headline of an article by Holcomb B. Noble in the *New York Times* declared, "Health Care Systems in the U.S. Called Separate and Unequal." The article went on to describe a shocking disparity in the quality of health care enjoyed by Americans. Middle-income blacks, Hispanic-Americans, and whites had significantly different attitudes toward health care, Noble wrote. This reality has been confirmed by statistics gained through new research sponsored by the Morehouse School of Medicine in Atlanta and the New America Strategies Group.

The study resulted from a telephone survey of African-Americans, Caucasians, and Hispanic-Americans from coast to coast, residing in urban, suburban, and rural areas. The group of respondents was equally divided among men and women. All respondents had health insurance, their ages ranged between 21 and 65, and all had household incomes in the range of $20,000 to $60,000.

This book proudly reports the findings of that groundbreaking study. They represent a call to action, a real opportunity where effective marketing can result not only in success in the marketplace but in significant health and lifestyle benefits for many members of the new America.

Mainstream Versus Minority Health Care: Separate and Unequal

Forty-five years ago, the U.S. Supreme Court voted unanimously to overturn a law allowing segregated schools, stating separate educational systems were inherently unequal. Government officials and civil rights activists believed *Brown v. Board of Education* would go a long way in ridding this country of the ills that divided the races, and to an extent it did. However, some disparities, such as health care, must be bridged by other means.

One battle still being waged is closing the gap in health care: minorities in this country still suffer disproportionately when it comes to illness, disease, and death. Closing the health care gap is imperative because by 2040 minorities of this country, growing seven times faster than the white population, will account for 53 percent of U.S. citizens. This means much of our nation could suffer from serious but treatable diseases, and thus turn America from one of the world's healthiest nations to one of less desirable state of health.

The Morehouse School of Medicine and the New America Strategies Group–sponsored Multiethnic Healthcare Survey indicates that the health care gap is not based solely on economics (70 percent of minorities have some form of health insurance) but also because minorities are not receiving culturally relevant health care treatment information needed to address their unique medical profiles and cultural needs. Indeed, important differences exist among America's major ethnic groups in concepts of disease, patient and provider communication styles, and beliefs about medications. Additionally, research has shown that many medicines may be more effective and freer of side effects for some races than for others. It is vital that America's health care infrastructure be aware and act on this information.

Despite the fact that 70 percent of minority respondents have health insurance coverage, the Morehouse School of Medicine and the New America Strategies Group survey revealed that

- Caucasians are between 10 and 20 percent more likely to report chronic or long-term health problems than are Hispanic-Americans or African-Americans. This indicates that members of some minorities do not have chronic conditions adequately controlled.
- Multiethnic America represents 25 percent of the overall population but bears a disproportionate amount of the morbidity and deaths due to disease in America.
- Seventy percent of minorities use health care maintenance organizations (HMOs), meaning they typically see general practitioners, even though their diseases often require a specialist's care.
- African-Americans were less likely to believe there is a cause-and-effect relationship between diet and health.
- When a primary physician is not available, African-Americans are more likely to opt for emergency-room care (50 percent) than Caucasians (41 percent) and Hispanics (39 percent), indicating a gap in continuity of care.
- More than one-third of African-Americans who take a prescription drug do not always take it as directed, indicating that African-Americans may lag behind in their understanding of the effects of improper use of medication.
- African-Americans are less likely to believe generic drugs are as good as name brand drugs.

An Opportunity to Profit by Helping People

The increasing attractiveness of the multicultural marketplace for health care marketers should help focus attention on the health care gap and begin to close it. At 25 percent of the population, ethnic Americans represent a $25 billion pharmaceutical marketplace based on 1996 U.S. drug manufacturers' $98.6 billion total sales. Additionally, according to the New America Marketbasket Index, a study commissioned by True North Communications, multicultural America's expenditures for health care have grown three times faster than whites' between 1995 and 1999. The following paragraphs analyze the multicultural health crisis:

- **Heart Disease**
  One in four Latinos die because of heart disease, states a study conducted in 1998 by the National Heart, Lung, and Blood Institute of the National Institutes of Health and Univision Communications Inc.

- **Stroke**
  The number three killer and major disabler of Americans is stroke. The 1995 death rate for stroke was about 71 percent higher for black females than for white females. Each year companies devise more novel means for treating and detecting cardiovascular problems, but most of these are offered from specialists. Over 70 percent of African-Americans and Hispanic-Americans use HMOs, however, and therefore may not have access to specialists.

- **Cancer**
  Cancer is the second-leading cause of death in the United States, accounting for more than 544,000 deaths each year. An estimated 7.4 million Americans have or have had cancer, and about 1.4 million new cases were diagnosed in 1997. For minorities the outcome of cancer is bleak. Blacks have a cancer death rate of 171.6 people per 100,000, versus 127 Caucasians per 100,000.

- **Breast Cancer**
  The American Cancer Society projected in 1998 that 112 white women per 100,000 will be diagnosed with breast cancer and 27 will die, compared to 95 black women per 100,000 diagnosed and 31 of them projected to die. Some health professionals say black women mistakenly believe that breast cancer is a

Minority Health Fact Sheet

- The average African-American lives nearly seven years less than his white counterpart.
- The death rate for stroke is 71 percent higher for black females than for whites.
- The diabetes rate is twice as high among Hispanic-Americans and African-Americans as the national average.
- The average years of healthy life are eight years less for African-Americans than for whites.
- Black men have the highest rate of prostate cancer in the world.
- Hepatitis B is more prominent among Asian-Pacific-Americans than the rest of the U.S. population.
- The risk of developing mental health problems is four times greater for African-Americans and two times greater for Hispanic-Americans than for whites.
- African-Americans have a 40 percent higher chance of dying from coronary heart disease.
- Although minorities make up 25 percent of the population, they account for 54 percent of all AIDS cases.

white person's disease. The estimated number of breast cancer cases in 1998 was 178,800. Although the breast cancer mortality rate has remained stable over the past twenty-five years, the rate has significantly increased in African-American women over fifty years of age. Mortality associated with breast cancer can be reduced by about 30 percent with the use of proper screening techniques. But health professionals state that, although many black women are the caretakers of their families, they often neglect themselves.

- **Lung Cancer**
Tobacco is linked to three million deaths a year worldwide. The U.S. Surgeon General's office has predicted that if current usage patterns continue, by the year 2020 the toll will be ten million deaths a year.

While the number of smoking teens overall has risen by a third since 1990, officials are seeing the rates double for black males. The incidence rate for lung cancer in black men is 50 percent higher than for white men, 110.7 versus 72.6 per 100,000 people.

- **Prostate Cancer**
  The rate of prostate cancer is about 37 percent higher in black men than in whites, and blacks are more likely to develop the disease at an earlier age. Researchers state that many black men diagnosed with prostate cancer allowed either ignorance or a macho attitude to deter them from medical checkups, which include a digital rectal exam and routine blood screening. Some men reported a belief that prostate cancer was a venereal disease with sexual connotations. Health professionals should recommend support groups to all men, but particularly minority men, who suffer from this disease to help them deal with the psychological aspects.

  In the early stages of the disease, there are no symptoms. Annual checkups are necessary to detect this cancer early. If detected in the early stages, the chance of treatment and full recovery is greatly increased.

- **Cervical Cancer**
  While Hispanic-American women are less vulnerable to breast cancer, they are more likely to develop cervical cancer than their black or white counterparts. Cervical cancer is increasing among black women as it decreases among white women.

- **AIDS**
  HIV infection and AIDS are leading causes of death for all people between 25 and 44 years of age. Between 650,000 and 900,000 Americans are estimated to be living with HIV infection.

  AIDS disproportionately affects minority populations. While racial and ethnic minorities comprise approximately 25 percent of the total U.S. population, they account for nearly 54 percent of all AIDS cases. While the epidemic is decreasing in some populations, the number of new AIDS cases among blacks now surpasses the number of new AIDS cases among whites.

During 1995 and 1996, AIDS death rates declined 23 percent for the total U.S. population, while declining only 13 percent for blacks and 20 percent for Hispanic-Americans. Researchers believe contributing factors for these mortality disparities include late identification of disease and lack of health insurance to pay for very expensive drug therapies. The cost of efficacious treatment runs between $10,000 and $12,000 annually. Additionally, some people feel that because the disease is ultimately fatal, there is no reason to diagnose it or get treatment for it.

Blacks now account for more than 57 percent of all new HIV infections. Among those aged 13 to 24, the rate is 67 percent.

Hispanic-American teenagers aged between 13 and 17 had the highest proportion of reported AIDS cases, 46.5 percent compared to 27.2 percent for blacks and 21.9 percent for Caucasians.

- **Infant Mortality**

Although infant mortality in the United States has declined steadily over the past several decades, the United States still ranks twenty-fourth in infant mortality compared with other industrialized nations.

Infant mortality rates vary substantially among and within racial and ethnic groups. Infant death rates among blacks, Native Americans, and Hispanic-Americans in 1995 and 1996 were well above the national average of 7.2 deaths per 1,000 live births. For blacks, the infant death rate was 14.2 per 1,000 in 1996. That is nearly 2.5 times that of white infants, 6 per 1,000 in 1996. The overall Native American rate was 9 deaths per 1,000 in 1995, but some communities had infant mortality rates approaching twice the national average. Similarly, the overall Hispanic-American rate was 7.6 per 1,000 live births in 1995, but Puerto Ricans had an infant mortality rate of 8.9 per 1,000 live births in 1995.

In 1996, 84 percent of white pregnant women, compared to 71 percent of black and Hispanic-American pregnant women, received early prenatal care. There was a higher incidence of preterm births among black mothers than white mothers, 17.7 percent compared to 9.7 percent.

- **Diabetes**
Diabetes is the seventh-leading cause of death in the United States, affecting nearly sixteen million people. However, only half of the people affected have been diagnosed.

The prevalence of diabetes in blacks is approximately 70 percent higher than whites, and the prevalence in Hispanic-Americans is nearly double that of whites. The prevalence of diabetes in Native Americans is more than twice that for the total population, and at least one tribe, the Pimas of Arizona, has the highest known prevalence of diabetes of any population in the world.

Amputation related to diabetes occurs 2.3 times more often for African-Americans than for Caucasians, and glaucoma leading to blindness occurs seven times more often in African-Americans than in Caucasians.

- **Immunology**
The reduction in incidence of vaccine-preventable diseases is one of the nation's public-health success stories. But more can be done. Childhood immunization rates are at an all-time high, with the most critical vaccine doses reflecting coverage rates of 90 percent. However, older adults are at an increased risk for many vaccine-preventable diseases. Approximately 90 percent of all influenza-associated deaths in the United States occur in people 65 and older, the fastest-growing age group of the population. Reduction of deaths in this age group has been hindered by a relatively small rate of immunizations.

Meanwhile, an estimated 45,000 adults die of infections related to influenza, pneumococcal infections, and hepatitis B despite the availability of safe and effective vaccines to prevent these conditions and their complications. There is also a disproportionate rate of influenza, pneumococcal infections, and hepatitis B in minority and underserved populations. The rates of African- and Hispanic-Americans who currently use immunizations remain low.

Economics Is Not the Sole Reason for Health Care Inequality Among Minorities

According to the findings of the Morehouse School of Medicine and the New America Strategies Group Multiethnic Healthcare Survey, the widening gap in health care between people of color and white America is not due solely to economics but to the lack of culturally relevant health care treatment and medical information designed to effectively reach the nation's fastest-growing populations.

People of color in this country have an increased incidence of death from cancer, coronary heart disease, and HIV, indicating that there are two Americas when it comes to health care. There is a widespread perception that all people have the same access to health services, observed researcher Dr. Louis Sullivan, president of Morehouse School of Medicine and former U.S. Secretary of Health and Human Services. But when people get sick, they are very different, and that is reflected in the number of minorities who become ill or are injured, and in the number who die from those illnesses and injuries.

Dr. Sullivan noted that individual members of the health care enterprise who recognize the reality of the new American mosaic and reach out to specific groups with focused messages and programs will be the winners. The multicultural population in this country is growing at seven times the rate of the white market, and it needs to be treated with a different and greater level of care and responsiveness by health care decision makers.

The study was the most extensive health care survey concerning the health attitudes of people of color. It showed that important differences exist among America's major ethnic groups in concepts of disease, patient and provider communication style, and beliefs about medications. These differences have strong implications for public sector policy makers and strategic planning and marketing for health care providers and pharmaceutical companies, for which minorities represent a $25 billion annual market.

The study also revealed that 61 percent of Hispanic-Americans feel it was very important to have a doctor of the same ethnicity, compared to 28 percent of African-Americans who felt it was important to have a black doctor.

The Morehouse School of Medicine and the New America Strategies Group Multiethnic Healthcare Survey Highlights

- African-Americans were the most likely to have HMO coverage (67 percent) and Caucasians the least likely (47 percent).
- African-Americans were less likely to believe there is a cause-and-effect relationship between diet and health.
- African-Americans were more likely to get information from health newsletters and from TV advertising and programs than were Caucasians or Hispanic-Americans.
- Hispanic-Americans named fewer sources of information than other groups.
- African-Americans were more likely than other groups to think relatives were reliable sources of health information. Hispanic-Americans considered medical-based sources (doctors, pharmacists, nurses, and hospitals and clinics) less reliable than other groups.
- The overwhelming majority of the respondents considered themselves to be in either excellent or good health (84 percent). However, African-Americans were less likely to feel that way (80 percent) than were Caucasians (87 percent) and Hispanic-Americans (86 percent).
- African-Americans were more likely to have been seen by a doctor within the past year (85 percent) than Caucasians (76 percent) or Hispanic-Americans (30 percent).
- Caucasians were likely to require frequent medical attention (24 percent) compared to African-Americans (31 percent) and Hispanic-Americans (30 percent).
- Caucasians were more likely to report chronic or long-term health problems (27 percent), and Hispanic-Americans were the least likely to complain of chronic problems (16 percent).
- This was also true for spouses: 18 percent of Caucasians reported that their spouses had a chronic medical problem, while only 10 percent of African-Americans and Hispanic-Americans had spouses with chronic problems.
- Only one in five respondents who reported having chronic or long-term health problems named diabetes (21 percent) or high blood pressure (21 percent) as the problem.
- African-Americans were more likely to name both diabetes (31 percent) and high blood pressure (27 percent) or high blood pressure alone (21 percent) as the problem.

- African-Americans were more likely to opt for the emergency room (50 percent) versus 41 percent for Caucasians.
- Hispanic-Americans were more likely to opt for another doctor (40 percent) than African-Americans (30 percent) or Caucasians (34 percent).
- Most (81 percent) Caucasians had a Caucasian physician, while only 40 percent of Hispanic-Americans had Hispanic-American physicians and only 27 percent of African-Americans had African-American physicians.
- Those in PPO plans are more likely to have a doctor of their own ethnicity (56 percent) than those in HMOs (46 percent).
- About one in four African-Americans (28 percent) considered it important that their doctor be of the same ethnic group as themselves versus one in nine (11 percent) Caucasians, who considered it important.

Commenting on this finding, Dr. Rene Rodriquez, president of the Interamerican College of Physicians and Surgeons, representing 39,000 Hispanic-American physicians, said, "The reasons for the health care gap are complex, but they can be solved. This study shows that we have to provide treatment and information to minorities in cultural terms and language they understand and trust. At the same time, we need to recognize that hospitals throughout the country are actively decreasing the number of minority physicians being trained. This policy threatens to further reduce the already low percentage of African-American and Hispanic doctors."

CASE STUDY: MARKETING FOOT-CARE PRODUCTS TO HISPANIC-AMERICANS

When a major manufacturer of foot-care products contacted Alternative & Innovative Marketing (AIM) to explore the possibility of marketing its products more aggressively and effectively within Hispanic-American markets, they were embarking upon a field of endeavor that was entirely new to them. This health-product manufacturer, an established brand among mainstream American consumers, was about to make its first targeted effort toward ethnic consumers.

Why were they suddenly interested in approaching Hispanic-American consumers? Why, after long periods of targeting only mainstream white consumers?

The answer, of course, was that they saw the opportunity to make significant profits by bringing their product before an entirely new audience. In part, their thinking was driven by information such as in Table 11.1 and then again, by statistics shown in Table 11.2.

Perhaps even more interesting, research conducted by AIM determined an unusually promising opportunity in targeting Hispanic-American consumers. Research quickly determined that Hispanic-American consumers out-index (in other words, they buy more product in key foot-care product categories) white consumers. Tables 11.3 and 11.4 show the anatomy of this very promising market opportunity.

Table 11.1 Eighty-Three Percent of Hispanic-Americans Are Concentrated in the Top Twenty Markets

1	Los Angeles	6.4 million
2	New York	3.6 million
3	Miami	1.4 million
4	San Francisco/San Jose	1.2 million
5	Chicago	1.2 million
6	Houston	1.1 million
7	San Antonio	1.1 million
8	McAllen–Brownsville	0.8 million
9	Dallas–Fort Worth	0.8 million
10	San Diego	0.7 million
11	Fresno	0.7 million
12	Phoenix	0.7 million
13	El Paso	0.7 million
14	Albuquerque	0.7 million
15	Sacramento	0.6 million
16	Denver	0.4 million
17	Philadelphia	0.4 million
18	Washington, D.C.	0.4 million
19	Corpus Christi	0.3 million
20	Boston	0.3 million
	Total	23.5 million

Table 11.2 Ninety Percent of the Hispanic-American Population Live in Ten States

1	California	10.5 million
2	Texas	5.5 million
3	New York	2.9 million
4	Florida	2.2 million
5	Illinois	1.2 million
6	Arizona	1.0 million
7	New Jersey	1.0 million
8	New Mexico	0.8 million
9	Colorado	0.6 million
10	Massachusetts	0.4 million
	Total	26.1 million

Table 11.3 Hispanic-American Research Identifies Opportunity

Foot-care conditions suffered or experienced in the past twelve months

Foot Care	Hispanic-American Index Against General Market
Heel pain or heel spurs	214
Foot discomfort caused by shoes	144
Itchy or burning feet or toes	136
Dry, cracked, or peeling skin on feet or toes	133
Foot perspiration or wetness	120
Tired, aching legs or leg fatigue	120
Corns on feet	117
Shin splints or shin pain	117
Foot odor	111

Next, in planning its effort to sell more of its products to Hispanic-American consumers, this foot-care company identified its key geographic markets. It determined, and quite rightly so, that if it were to meet with success in Los Angeles—the number one Hispanic-American market in the continental United States—they would be doing very, very well. Also, penetration in San Antonio and Houston—the top two Hispanic-American markets in Texas—would represent still more market penetration within the Hispanic-American community.

Table 11.4 Hispanic-American Research Identifies Opportunity

Hispanic-Americans out-index the general population on the use of most
over-the-counter foot-care products.

	Indices of Foot-Care Products Purchased
Ingrown toenail relievers	25
Corn removers	33
Callus cushions	33
Heel cushions, pads, or cups	33
Foot moisturizers or exfoliators	43
Cushioned insoles	50
Ball-of-foot cushions or pads	50
Pumice, beauty stones, or files	80
Athlete's foot medications	88
Foot sprays or powders	100
Bunion cushions	100
Medicated powders on feet	133

But where did they start their marketing efforts? In Miami. This
represented a good strategic choice because Miami, for many reasons,
represents an excellent test market. First, there is a large Hispanic-
American community in Miami. Second, one of the primary objectives
of this campaign was to maximize store-level penetration and visibility. Here again, Miami was an excellent choice. In Miami, mass retailers could be found (Wal-Mart, Kmart, Target); drugstore chains (Rite
Aid, Eckerd, and Walgreens); and a variety of food stores—both large
chains and smaller independents. So Miami clearly represented an excellent test market.

The foot-care product manufacturer made some very wise choices
and decided not to begin by marketing its entire range of products to
Hispanic-American consumers. For its initial efforts in marketing to
Hispanic-Americans, the decision was made to focus on only four of
its key products: products for odor and wetness; products for corns, cal-
luses, and bunions; insoles and underfoot pads; and creams and pow-
ders to combat athlete's foot.

What kind of marketing would be used to approach these
Hispanic-American consumers in Miami? AIM decided the most suc-

cessful overall campaign would incorporate the following elements: TV, radio, and print advertising; multi-brand promotions; public relations; in-store education programs; consumer promotions; event-centered and mobile marketing; celebrity endorsements, including and especially sports figures; and grassroots marketing and community involvement.

In an effort to find culturally relevant programs that would speak compellingly to Latino consumers, AIM also negotiated and secured an endorsement from a popular and respected soccer player, a famous international soccer star. It seemed clear to AIM and the foot-care product company that soccer and foot-care products were a natural mix. This kind of thinking represents the kind of good, synergistic thinking that makes for good advertising campaigns. The soccer-related theme offered logical extensions to in-store and mobile marketing campaigns. Specifically, a mobile soccer-goal installation was created and taken to retail outlets in the test markets. Youngsters could try to kick a ball through this goal, while their parents were picking up product samples and talking to company representatives. Along with educational benefits, this promotion both generated a lot of fun and excitement and created brand awareness at major Hispanic-American festivals and retail parking lots. In short order, Hispanic-American consumers in the target markets encountered the product in a very immediate and compelling way.

In-store education formed another key element of the campaign. While youngsters kicked goals outside the store in the parking lot, parents, aunts, uncles, and grandparents could visit specialized counters inside to receive product samples, coupons, and educational information on better foot care. A variety of materials were created to help support this effort, such as brochures and flyers about good foot care.

At the same time, other promotions were put in place, including a professional program that helped deliver product information to health care professionals. Among the elements of this campaign were

- a bilingual direct-mail program to pharmacists who catered to Hispanic-American consumers
- a bilingual, educational foot-health brochure, which was distributed to podiatrists in test markets

- the incorporation of bilingual podiatrists into community events and the mobile marketing program

How well did that initial effort go in Miami, Florida? Did the company achieve results that merited further efforts in assessing the Hispanic-American markets? Indeed they did. In fact, during 1997 and 1998, the program was rolled out nationwide, and over 150 events were staged. The results—which are proprietary to AIM and cannot be reproduced in this book—greatly exceeded the foot-care manufacturer's expectations and goals. By doing good within the Hispanic-American community, this company established itself as the brand of choice among Hispanic-Americans where foot-care products are concerned. And that position is unlikely to be challenged by any other company in the foreseeable future.

CASE STUDY: PROJECT SOUL

Glaxo Wellcome's Program in Harlem in Response to the HIV/AIDS Emergency

Project SOUL, a peer-to-peer educational program, was initiated in 1999 to reduce the aggressive spread of HIV/AIDS in the Harlem community. In recognition of the ravaging of African-Americans by HIV/AIDS and the call by the Congressional Black Caucus to declare the HIV/AIDS epidemic among African-Americans a public health emergency, Glaxo Wellcome, a leading research-based pharmaceutical firm, launched this program to reduce the spread of HIV/AIDS through education and medical access in the Harlem community.

Project SOUL is a grassroots program developed to mobilize the African-American community around HIV testing, diagnosis, and treatment, relying on peer-to-peer influence within the community so that genuine trust and an environment of open communication could be established and maintained. The program fostered HIV/AIDS awareness and helped those affected gain access to the health care system.

Project SOUL was launched in the Harlem community, where, like African-American communities nationally, the spread of

HIV/AIDS Fact Sheet: African-Americans

- African-Americans have been profoundly and disproportionately affected by HIV and AIDS. Through December 1997, African-Americans represented 36 percent (230,029) of the 641,086 cases reported, although they represent only an estimated 13 percent of the total U.S. population.
- Researchers estimate that 240,000–325,000 African-Americans are infected with HIV. Approximately 1 in 50 African-American men and 1 in 160 African-American women are believed to be infected with HIV. Of those infected with HIV, it is estimated that 93,000 African-Americans are living with AIDS.
- In 1997, more African-Americans were reported with AIDS than any other racial or ethnic group. Of the total AIDS cases reported that year, 45 percent (27,075) were reported among African-Americans, 33 percent (20,197) were reported among whites, and 21 percent (12,466) were reported among Hispanic-Americans.
- Among women and children with AIDS, African-Americans have been especially affected, representing 60 percent of all women reported with AIDS in 1997 and 62 percent of reported pediatric AIDS cases for 1997.
- During the period from January 1994 through June 1997, African-Americans represented 45 percent of all AIDS diagnoses but 57 percent of all HIV diagnoses. Among young people (ages 13 to 24), 63 percent of the HIV diagnoses were among African-Americans.

Source: Centers for Disease Control and Prevention

HIV/AIDS has been rapid, aggressive, and unrelenting. It has become the number one cause of death among African–American men and women between the ages of twenty–five and fifty–five.

"While statistics indicate that HIV/AIDS has declined in the majority community, it is increasing precipitously in the minority community with a profound, disproportionate impact on the African-American community. We are very pleased, therefore, to sponsor this program in Harlem aimed at reducing the spread of this devastating disease," said Dean Mitchell, vice president, sales and marketing, Oncology/HIV at Glaxo Wellcome.

Harlem State Senator David Patterson added, "I welcome this program to Harlem, and I am extremely enthusiastic about its potential for reducing the spread of AIDS in this community. I salute Glaxo Wellcome for this much-needed AIDS initiative."

Manhattan Borough President and former Harlem Council member C. Virginia Fields said, "Any program initiative to help reduce the spread of this devastating disease in the Harlem community is welcome. Glaxo Wellcome's responsiveness is an example of the private-public partnership we need to fight this disease."

Project SOUL partnered with two respected community institutions: The Balm In Gilead, a national organization that works through black churches to stop the spread of HIV/AIDS in the African-American community, and The Momentum AIDS Project, one of New York's oldest and largest AIDS service organizations and the only agency in New York City providing people with AIDS hot meals, pantry bags, and support services in a communal setting in their own neighborhoods.

"Project SOUL, with its strategic utilization of trained HIV–positive counselors who are on therapy ... holds an abundance of promise for reducing the spread of HIV/AIDS through education," said Dianna Williamson, MD, a Harlem-based HIV specialist.

Eric Peters, an HIV–positive education counselor for Project SOUL, said, "I feel so strongly about Project SOUL because it brings awareness to the underserved community. We are not only delivering HIV awareness in a comprehensive and down-to-earth fashion, we try to help them gain access to the health care system and follow up with them to assist everyone we come in contact with overcome their barriers to treatment and receive quality care."

Project SOUL Partners

The Balm In Gilead

The Balm In Gilead is a national organization that works through black churches to stop the spread of HIV/AIDS in the African-American community. It mobilizes churches to become community centers for AIDS education and compassion. The Balm In Gilead organizes the

Black Church Week of Prayer for the Healing of AIDS in March, which in 1999 included more than 5,000 churches and was endorsed by every major black church denomination and caucus.

The Balm In Gilead is the only national organization that works exclusively to educate and organize black churches to address AIDS. The organization is endorsed by over ten national black church denominations and caucuses, including the eight-million-member National Baptist Convention and the nearly four-million-member African Methodist Episcopal Church.

The Momentum AIDS Project

Founded in 1985, The Momentum AIDS Project is one of New York's oldest and largest AIDS service organizations, and the only agency in the city providing men, women, and children living with HIV/AIDS with hot meals, pantry bags, and support services in a communal setting in their own neighborhoods. Most of Momentum's clients are low income, and many are either homeless or inadequately housed. Currently, Momentum provides approximately 2,000 clients with lunch and dinner, seven days a week at twelve programs in Manhattan, Queens, Brooklyn, and the Bronx.

Food and nutrition are the centerpiece of Momentum's services, as wasting diseases and poor nutrition are leading contributory factors in AIDS–related deaths. Food and nutrition services have been shown to help delay the onset of full-blown AIDS in those infected with HIV. Additionally, Momentum's congregate meals provide a social setting for people who are often otherwise isolated or disenfranchised. A shared meal, counsel, good friends: these are Momentum's gifts.

WHAT WILL THE BUSINESS
OF THIS CENTURY
LOOK LIKE?

What is this new America?

This book began with this question. After having shared information and insights that shed light on that question, it is time to ask a second question: What will new American *business* look like? How will it operate? What will its priorities be?

We invited Victor Edozien of The Asaba Group to share his views. Victor, a seasoned strategy consultant, is originally from Nigeria. He started his career as an engineer at United Technologies. Then he went to business school and joined the Ford Motor Company. After Ford, he joined The Lucas Group, a corporate strategy consulting firm. At The Lucas Group, he led numerous growth strategy projects, which have led to substantial growth in revenue and profits for private equity and Fortune 500 clients.

Recently Victor helped launch The Asaba Group, a strategy consulting practice focused on developing pragmatic winning growth strategies in the multicultural environment. The goal of The Asaba Group, headquartered in Boston, is to help corporations, private equity investors, and portfolio companies enter and prosper in the new markets.

Victor Edozien's Insights for Businesses in the New America

How should a company seek success in America's growing multicultural markets? I will answer this disarmingly simple question in an equally simple way. A company should think about entering the new markets in the same way it would think about entering a new market abroad. You begin by asking three strategic questions:

1. What are the relevant market segments (size and defining attributes)?
2. What is your unique value proposition to these segments? How well do your products fit the needs of the target consumers?
3. What are the optimal channels to fulfill the requirements of the target segments?

Suppose you decided to sell your products in Vietnam. How should you undertake your marketing efforts? You wouldn't simply go there with your products, place advertisements in Vietnamese electronic media and magazines, and expect to succeed. You would begin by asking the three key strategic questions.

Yet many American businesses approach ethnic markets without asking these same strategic questions. These businesses proceed by spending money and time placing ads. They view ethnic markets as only a *downstream tactical initiative*. Over and over again, mid-level marketing and brand managers are charged with making decisions about the ethnic markets although they lack clear knowledge on how to approach them. These managers have defaulted to hiring ethnic advertising agencies and placing ads in what the agencies have defined as "culturally relevant" media. Creative content in the ad is typically an African-, Asian-, or Hispanic-American face. These, in most instances, may be the same ads used in the mainstream media. And they think the job is done.

This approach reflects the prevalent attitude that ethnic marketing is really an afterthought, something that comes after your mainstream marketing efforts. The result? A number of nonstrategic, uncoordinated efforts that get very little incremental revenues or fail to build lasting customer loyalty.

Let's reconsider how you would go into Vietnam and try to achieve market success there. (The same questions might be asked about China, Eastern Europe, or any emerging market.) If you followed the current practice—hiring an ethnic-oriented agency and placing some ads—you would sell some product because there is always latent demand in any market for products that meet the needs of consumers. But are these sales the true potential of the product? Would these practices get the sales and return on investment (ROI) you should expect from growing markets?

To achieve success you must find answers to the questions mentioned earlier:

1. **What are the relevant market segments (size and defining attributes)?**

   Remember, not every Vietnamese will buy your product. It's more likely that a target segment, perhaps two million Vietnamese, will potentially buy what you have to sell. They're your relevant market segment. Taking things further, you can divide the potential two million target consumers. You may determine that within that group there is a segment that will buy your premium product and another segment that will buy your value product.

2. **What is your unique value proposition to these segments? How well do your products fit the needs of the target consumers?**

   What products will these consumers want? Keep in mind that the desired products may be somewhat different from those you have in your current portfolio.

   Back to our example, in Vietnam, you might identify two unique customer segments to target: upscale consumers and more general, value-oriented consumers. You wouldn't view the Vietnamese population as monolithic. Yet here in America, some corporations market to African-, Asian-, or Hispanic-Americans through a monolithic lens. Suppose you are a manufacturer of fine dinnerware entering the Vietnamese marketplace. There may exist a consumer segment, which will desire high-end, premium dinnerware. You might look at your product portfolio and say, "What product do I have in my portfolio that is high-end fine china?" Then you might say, "Okay, I have some elegant gold-encrusted patterns that might meet the needs of the consumer." Or you might do even better and say,

"The patterns that will sell best must be unique and culturally relevant to that population. I can't position something in my existing lineup as what they want."

So you can take the product and make incremental changes so that it is relevant to the high-end Vietnamese customer segment. This is all about ensuring optimum fit between your products and the target customer.

3. **What are the optimal channels to fulfill the requirements of the target segments?**

In order to sell product, you must make it available where the target customer will most likely seek it. In our example, high-end Vietnamese consumers will seek the product in the high-end channels, for example, fine department stores. Similarly those seeking your value product would look for it at the mass-market retailers. This same principle applies to ethnic markets.

The key for corporations is understanding that multicultural marketing is not simply taking existing products and advertising them to your target consumers through appropriate media; you must determine the appropriate products and place them in the relevant channels and markets.

Bringing It Back Home

It is critical to take a strategic approach and not simply spend money advertising in appropriate media. You should always consider the following three fundamental questions:

1. How big is the market opportunity?
2. What are the relative consumer segments?
3. How do those segments overlap with my product portfolio?

Many marketers find themselves in the unfortunate position of saying, "I'm spending all this money in the ethnic segment, but I have no idea whether I am making any sales." When marketers express this concern, it is because they have not addressed these fundamental marketplace questions, which must be asked before going into any market.

And more logical questions follow.

Is Your Infrastructure Up to the Job?

What portions of your existing infrastructure can you leverage when pursuing the new multicultural market opportunity?

If you are going after an ethnic segment within the United States, certain elements of your existing infrastructure you can leverage and some you cannot utilize in their present form. You might use the same distribution channel and maybe the same sales force. But you have to ask, is that the right way to proceed? Or is some new kind of thinking required?

As an example, consider the following marketing problem, which can be quite revealing. Suppose you are a skin-care company and you have products of high potential usage by African-Americans—for example, an effective remedy lotion for razor bumps. African-American men have a very high incidence of razor bumps and ingrown hairs on their skin after shaving.

If your company already has a product that addresses this problem, how well are you reaching African-American consumers? Do they have to go to Macy's or another department store to purchase your product? If so, is that the optimal channel for selling your product?

No. The sales you're getting through such general distribution channels are just general-market sales. To tap the real potential of the African-American market, you have to repackage your product so that it becomes culturally relevant to African-American consumers. For example, you might put an African-American cultural image or some other relevant message on the packaging. (Interesting to note, you can use the same product that is already in your lineup.)

How many African-American men have razor bumps? Fifty percent share of that market with a focused product will more than pay for the investment in packaging and distribution because you are selling the same product.

The next question is, how do you distribute the product? The best way will be through barber shops and beauty shops that cater to African-Americans because, in general, African-Americans do not get their haircuts or shaves at typical mainstream salons and boutiques. Instead, they have their own hair-care channel, which is unique and different from going to a typical salon. Thus, you should sell your appropriately packaged product through all those beauty locations used by African-Americans.

Then you begin to advertise your product through African-American print and electronic media. You are no longer in the position of saying, "I'm running some ads, but I don't know how effective they are or if they are generating sales."

African-Americans are brand loyal, so you are also building strong customer franchise and loyalty. Once an African-American consumer knows you have a product that works and it's sold at the point of need—barber shops—then you have achieved lifetime value in that customer. The consumer knows you have a product he needs and it's available at the time of need.

With lifetime value, you can extend your "share of wallet." African-Americans, like all Americans, have a variety of needs for skin-care products, such as body creams, deodorants, or astringents. Once you are under way, you can grow your presence and "own" that customer in a particular product/commodity category.

Take It One Step Further

The next question is, what is your operating model? The operating model is all about people, systems, and business processes. This is where the multicultural market strategies and approaches need to mesh with corporate diversity initiatives. In corporate America, diversity initiatives are implemented independently with no links to the realities of the multicultural marketplace.

Companies talk about diversity. But they talk about multicultural marketing on another track entirely. Corporate executives think, "Corporate diversity is a good thing...the right thing to do." But these same executives also wonder, "Does diversity make sense from a business point of view?"

More important questions, however, need to be asked: How can we get the most ROI from the economic potential in the multicultural markets? and next, How can we link our recruitment, hiring, and retention of ethnic minorities to that multicultural market opportunity?

Go back to the skin-care company example. If you are able to develop and package a skin-care product for African-American men and sell it through appropriate distribution channels, you should logically go on to ask, "Who should be our marketing and sales manager for this skin-care product?" and then define the competencies for that position through a multicultural lens.

The competency definition for the position might be someone who understands the skin problems that are unique to African-Americans and who can go to the salons and barber shops to build the required channel relationships.

What emerges is a competency definition that consists of the required marketing and sales capabilities. But in addition, it defines an individual who understands African-American culture and can relate to African-American merchants. It's very likely that the individual to fill this position will be an African-American.

The candidate profile stops being a race-based definition and becomes a competency-based definition. Nine out of ten times that competency definition defines an African-American individual, even though there is nothing about race in the profile. Your skin-care company might well end up with a Caucasian who can do the job. But whomever you select must understand and be able to relate to that marketplace.

The Benefit to Your Company

Now that you are entering the multicultural marketplace and hiring for needed competencies, you will much more likely be interviewing and recruiting appropriate diversity candidates. In just a short time, the need to search for appropriate minority candidates diminishes. You are attracting a strong set of multicultural-oriented candidates because you have defined competency job profiles that fit their profiles.

Over time, this kind of thinking permeates your organization. It defines competencies everywhere in the business process. For example, if customers have a problem with one of your lotions and there is a toll-free number on the bottle for customer service issues, who will they

reach when they call? Will the people who answer the phones understand African-American skin-care needs? The representatives at the call
center need to understand. And if you define the competencies for those
positions, chances are you will no longer have all Anglo-Americans
answering the phones. You will have some African-Americans who
match your market.

And with sophisticated phone answering systems now available,
you can have a message that says, "If you are calling about such-and-
such a product, press one now . . . " and routes that call straight to an
African-American representative who understands the cultural nuances
of the customer.

By defining human-resources needs based on competencies, you
get beyond the kind of thinking that dictates, "I need ten blacks, three
Hispanics, four women." And you can use this approach at a higher level
in the organization. Who will be your vice president of customer service? Or the manager for call centers? More and more, to address your
markets, you will need people at all levels who understand the cultural
nuances of your consumers. Your entire organization may well begin
to have a multicultural flavor.

If you have a sizeable and growing African-American market, for
example, you can go to your research and development (R&D) department and say, "We need four new products for our evolving African-
American market." You will need to have R&D employees who
understand the marketplace and African-Americans. So, soon you are
hiring biochemists who are African-Americans. This is how corporate
diversity recruitment initiatives are linked with multicultural market
opportunities—and with your business processes and competencies.

You are moving from race-based definitions to competency-based
definitions, which are much more effective and needs based than saying, "We have quotas." Incidentally, if your company is ever questioned
about its minority hiring, you can point to the competencies you are
hiring for and how you are filling them. No one will ever question your
activities.

On a grander scale, America is increasingly becoming a multiethnic majority country. Population experts forecast ethnic minorities

at 40 percent or more of the general population by 2010. Some early population statistics forecast California to become the first state to have an ethnic majority population by 2001. The more multicultural and flexible an organization is, the more adaptive and better it will perform in the future.

Linking corporate diversity to the market opportunity makes business sense. It becomes a holistic system; everything is linked together—how you deploy your resources versus the market opportunity. And it all makes sense.

SAMPLE MARKETING PROGRAM PROPOSALS

We encourage you to spend some time reviewing the seven marketing plans that are reproduced for you here. They represent real plans—actual "decks" for proposed marketing plans—targeted to ethnic Americans.

Some of these proposals, after modification and cooperation with the corporate clients, were implemented; others were not. In all cases, the names of the corporations and products have been changed before inclusion in this book.

By adapting the approaches and methodologies from these plans, you will greatly increase the chances of achieving success in your own multicultural marketing initiatives.

Sample Proposal 1:
African-American Marketing Support
Recommendation for Trans-Continental
Bus Company

The Opportunity

- Strengthen relationships and expand business with the growing African-American marketplace, a market that will account for over 30 percent of the total U.S. population growth through 2005
- Merchandise good works to enhance positive perception among Trans-Continental employees and other key audiences (e.g., special interest groups, regulators)
- Build linkage with corporate cosponsors and co-op partners to create synergy and cost-efficiencies and extend program reach

African-American Market Characteristics

The African-American marketplace is distinctly different. African-Americans

- prefer African-American spokespeople and role models
- support marketers who respectfully acknowledge their beliefs and cultural values
- require messages that demonstrate an elevated level of cultural awareness
- align with programs that strengthen the foundation of the African-American community and are a source of civic pride
- respond to a targeted media approach

Target Market Psychographics

African-Americans increasingly base their buying decisions on two questions:

1. What are you giving back to the community in exchange for my patronage?
2. Is this the best value and quality for my dollar?

Situation

- Unlike many companies, Trans-Continental's past and future have been inextricably linked to America's multicultural populations.
- African-Americans represent almost 30 percent of Trans-Continental's total business, more than double their representation in the U.S. population.
- Additionally, African-Americans comprise a full third of Trans-Continental's drivers and half of their station personnel.
- America's significant demographic shifts (ethnic Americans are growing at seven times the rate of the general market) favor Trans-Continental's business—heavily weighed to multicultural Americans who seek convenient, cost-efficient transportation provided by the bus.
- To maximize both short- and long-term marketplace expansion, it will be important to continue to build and strengthen the African-American consumer market (AACM) relationships through a strategic, targeted approach that is linked to community-based initiatives that both "package" Trans-Continental services as relevant, attractive "products" and embrace the cultural imperatives of the AACM. This will demonstrate respect, cultural awareness, and the responsiveness to specific customer needs—key "buy" factors.
- These relationship-based marketing initiatives can be cost-efficiently leveraged to drive significant visibility primarily through public relations (PR), networking, and co-op promotions.

Objectives

- Build current business, gain long-term market expansion, and increase brand loyalty among African-Americans
- Drive visibility and positive perception of African-American initiatives among Trans-Continental employees

- Position Trans-Continental as a good career choice and encourage qualified African-Americans to consider employment potential

Audience

- Deliver specific program messages to Trans-Continental's two key audience sectors among African-Americans: (1) college students, and (2) "destination-bound" African-American travelers (families, individuals, church members)
- Prioritize sectors, beginning with college

Markets

Atlanta
Detroit
Washington, D.C.
Philadelphia
Baltimore
Chicago
New York
Los Angeles
Dallas–Fort Worth
San Francisco–Oakland

Strategy

- Develop customized segment programs that deliver key travel and lifestyle-related messages and (new) services that are targeted to the specific needs of high-interest audiences among African-Americans
- Create linkage with affinity groups, key networks, institutions, etc., whenever possible, to provide credibility and cost-efficient outreach
- Build preemptive programs that the competition will find difficult to duplicate

College Market

Execution

1. Support Heritage Bowl Sponsorship
   - Develop customized Heritage Bowl travel package (e.g., hotel, meals, other incentives), and merchandise to potential student attendees from both away team and other historically black colleges within the league
   - Merchandise through unique promotions in local college newspapers and radio stations: Win your own Weekend Jam for you and three of your friends—all-expense-paid trip and $1,000 (each) spending money for the lucky winners
   - Additionally, merchandise travel packages through PR, special group discounts for fraternities, linkage with on-campus affinity groups
   - As run-up to Heritage Bowl, produce mini-band concerts using Trans-Continental bus stations as venue to promote travel packages to both the campus and the general community; select key markets for events

2. College Market: Trans-Continental's Going Places
   - Introduce Trans-Continental Going Places program—a destination-related discount travel program that identifies, packages, and delivers the ultimate in (low-cost) weekend excitement for college kids
   - Explain what it is: provides on a monthly basis a calendar of travel opportunities specifically chosen to appeal to college kids—packaged by Trans-Continental to deliver the most fun—along with the best price and the most convenience (include, whenever possible, low-priced hotel accommodations in overall price); buses leave from or near campus; each trip is a party from start to finish; sign up through student organizations; travel with your friends; receive special discounts, premiums whenever possible
   - Choose and promote destinations within traveling distance of key campuses

Cosponsorships and Co-op Programs

- Build Going Places program "packages" with key hotel partners—Travelodge, Sleep Inn, Holiday Inn, Hampton Inn—to deliver convenient, low-cost transportation and lodging packages for students
- Cross-promote partnerships in PR, networking, co-op advertising
- Explore cosponsorship programs with corporations that seek to reach the college market (e.g., Reebok, Fila) and that would sponsor event packages (e.g., NCAA Tournament) and contribute equipment and apparel to college teams in return for exposure

Trans-Continental Going Places

- Sample package destinations are
  - Philadelphia Greek Picnic
  - Virginia Beach Labor Day Weekend
  - Syracuse Annual Greek Freak
  - Tri-State Step Show
  - key football and basketball games and tournaments (NCAA)
  - *Essence* Music Festival
  - NCAA Annual Convention
  - Whitney Young Classic
  - Orange Blossom Classic
  - Indiana Circle City Classic
  - homecomings: (e.g., Howard, Hampton, Morgan State, etc.)
  - sorority/fraternity meetings: Delta, AKA, Zeta, Omega, Kappa, etc.
- Trans-Continental's Going Places would include student summer travel discount pass: unlimited travel June–August; similar to "Eurail Pass" and "Visit the family" home travel holiday packages.
- Program would be merchandised through college newspapers and radio stations and monthly "Going Places" flyer or newsletter distributed at key campuses.
- Cosponsorships would be sought among campus Greek organizations and athletic and affinity groups to lend credibility, drive awareness, and increase sales.

- Whenever possible, Trans-Continental would seek to offer on a discounted basis its travel services to campus groups based on their special needs, e.g., team travel to games.

Markets
- Southeastern region
  - –Atlanta
  - –New Orleans
  - –Mobile, AL
  - –Memphis
  - –Hampton, VA
  - –Norfolk, VA
  - –Jackson, MS
  - –Washington, D.C.
  - –Baltimore
- Detroit
- Philadelphia
- New York
- Dallas–Fort Worth

"Destination Bound" African-American Travelers
Execution: Overall "Destination Bound" African-American Travelers
- Umbrella program would package "marquee value" African-American travel destinations (based around travel to culturally relevant, highly desirable places and events) and merchandise both the special packages and the overall benefits of "choosing Trans-Continental for your travel needs" for the overall African-American consumer marketplace.
- Offerings would include both travel and hotel within one convenient package.
- Program attractiveness would be based on both the unique selections and low-cost packages.
- Program would be branded Trans-Continental Gateway Travel.

Execution: Trans-Continental Gateway Travel

- The Trans-Continental Gateway Travel program will make it possible for African-American families, singles, young people, retirees, etc., to learn about and cost-efficiently travel to a variety of highly desirable destinations with special packages available only through Trans-Continental.
- Trans-Continental Gateway Travel will be marketed in key African-American markets and will feature travel packages to the following example destinations:

  –*Essence* Music Festival

  –New Orleans Jazz & Heritage Festival

  –Atlanta (weekend tour package)

  –Disneyland, Disney World

  –Historic Black College Tour (for parents and students; special discount)

  –NCAA Tournament

  –Bayou Classic (for alumni)

  –Universal Studios Tour (California)

  –National Council of Negro Women—Family Reunions

  –Jackie Robinson Afternoon of Jazz

  –Hollywood Bowl

  –Atlanta Art Fair

- These packages—many of which would be copromoted by destination partners (and hotel partners) in their own advertising—would be positioned as seasonal opportunities, with a different schedule for each season. They will also be announced through publicity and be accompanied by a Trans-Continental Gateway Travel brochure that would be widely distributed through direct mail to hundreds of affinity groups. The brochure would encourage their members to sign up for the Gateway Travel Pass, which would entitle them to additional discounts.
- Additionally, Trans-Continental would be positioned as "official carrier" of key national and regional church groups, working with groups on customized packages and special discounts.

- Sponsorship and package deals would be negotiated with key groups to offer relevant Gateway Travel packages: family reunions, African-American Women on Tour, etc.

Execution: African-American Marketplace

- Trans-Continental Gateway Travel would be promoted and merchandised through its unique, proprietary "Travel Tips" column—The Trans-Continental Gateway—that would run as editorial in key black newspapers and magazines nationwide. An audio version would be produced for radio airing on black stations in the major markets. Ideally, an African-American celebrity (well-traveled) would be hired to become a PR spokesperson and perhaps "author" of the ongoing column.
- Program would be accessed around 1-800-GATEWAY where prospects could call in and get the latest information on packages, discounts, etc.
- As discussed, there is a significant opportunity for copromotions with event promoters and marketers: *Essence* Music Festival, New Orleans Jazz & Heritage Festival, clubs, resorts, etc. All have promotion channels to cross-merchandise and sometimes budgets to advertise on Trans-Continental's moving billboards.

Marketing Plan: USP Pagers for Building Share in the African-American Consumer Market

Marketing Objective
- Drive the African-American consumer target to call 1-800-USP-PAGE or visit a USP Phone Mart to activate pager service
- Increase sign-up for multimonth agreements

Target Audience
- Teens, 12–17
  - –fifty percent of all teens purchase their own pagers
  - –are product (and brand) influencers
  - –understand and appreciate power of the product
- Adults, 35–49 with children
  - –self-purchase—potential for gifts
  - –purchase for teens (50 percent of all kids have beepers purchased by parents)
  - –are most likely "guardian" of teen's bill

Product Targeting
Potential for enhanced revenue-product targeting

- Current overall product focus drives numerical pagers against teens and alpha pagers toward adults
- However, African-American teens
  - –desire to have the latest in technology
  - –aspire to set trends and be on cutting edge
  - –are already familiar with simple pagers

We recommend targeting the alpha-numeric version to both teens and adults:

- Teens
  - provides cutting-edge technology; teens are early
    technology adapters
  - negligible cost differential
  - parents and guardians will appreciate the feature
  - it's what adults use
- Adults
  - allows for customized messages
  - security issue for children—day care, latchkey, etc.
  - enables multiple-party communication

Program Strategy

The USP pager will be positioned as a "hero," value-added element in people's lives.

- adds value to people's lives by providing them with both new and important information
- allows busy and fragmented families to keep in touch

Program Components

- Acquisition—develop messages and proprietary programs that drive ownership of the product
- Retention—drive resubscription and, in the future, upgrades through various loyalty programs

Teen Program Criteria

The program will enhance lifestyle, enable access to the latest information, and give discounts on "stuff" they want.

- As a USP customer, teens will be entitled to lifestyle benefits including the latest news in music and happenings, discounts, merchandise, and rewards for use.
- Teens want to be "the first to know."

- Teen urges are immediate; teens demand instant gratification.
- Style and functionality are key.
- Cost is low for such a service.

Teen Program

- Creates promotional radio campaign with a top teen radio station in each key market
- Combines product giveaway with partnered information system to build sign-ups
- Grants access to radio station–sponsored concerts, tickets, appearances, etc.
- Ties owning a USP pager with what's hot and new in music and entertainment
- Creates a demand for USP-branded pagers
- Centers radio promotion around the USP unique product attributes and pager's unique attributes
- Cross-promotes at pager stores

"USP on the 411"

- Sets up a yearlong program with four promotional windows
- Is supported by radio advertising, promotions, point of sale at pager sales, and direct mail
- Features a call to action by offering teens membership in a club with discounts and merchandise in exchange for a minimum three-month contract—prizes and discounts include discounts on CDs (Sam Goody's) and apparel (Tommy Hilfiger), Blockbuster certificates, etc.
- Will offer other benefits over the course of the year:
  - Once a month, members get beeped by the radio station to listen to new music by a favorite artist—available only to USP customers.
  - Members are also eligible for random "Mystery Beeps" for cash and concert tickets.
  - "Super Beep" will happen once annually at random in each market. No one will know when the beep will happen, so excitement can be built over the course of the year. Prizes

might include dinner in New York City with Chris Rock, a weekend on the set of *Vibe Live*, or being Sinbad's personal guest at the Cancun Jazz Festival.

Adult Program Criteria

The program will provide value, convenience, child safety, and peace of mind, and help "manage" busy lives.

- USP customers are *entitled* to lifestyle rewards including discounts, merchandise, rewards for use, and peace of mind.
- Customers have greater ability to control family activities.
- Program allows for closer contact with the extended family.

"USP Family Ties" Adult Program

Program's goal is to contact targeted adults in each market with a direct-mail offer and radio promotions.

- Takes advantage of parental desire to maintain contact with children
- Combines multiple pager acquisition with high-perceived value offers: "Buy a pager for yourself, get additional pagers for your family members at a discount"
- Uses print format to effectively explain alpha-numeric function
- Reinforces message and validates purchase through radio promotions
- Creates demand for USP pagers and service in a market with larger families

The yearlong program with four promotional windows will be supported by direct-mail and radio promotions.

Direct mail features a call to action by offering adults the opportunity to purchase multiple pagers at a discounted rate—two for one is simplest deal. In addition, the program will offer membership in a USP club with discounts and merchandise in exchange for additional subscriptions, renewals, etc. Prizes such as discounts on movie tickets, videos from Blockbuster, gas coupons, Dine Around certificates, etc., will be offered.

DJ-driven promotions also serve to educate adult users on pager capabilities and provide a fun validation of purchase. Pagers will be given away to random callers over each promotional period. Pager winners will then be "beeped" over the course of the program; if they answer the page, they will win additional pagers.

Geography
Of the fourteen USP target markets, the following are the most heavily populated African-American markets:

Los Angeles	488M
Houston	458M
Dallas	297M
Cleveland	235M
Columbus	143M
Tampa–St. Petersburg	117M

Source: U.S. Census Bureau

However, a second-tier markets list should also be explored for base-level support, e.g., bill stuffer by zip code.

The Media Solution
Radio
- Use the high-affinity medium of radio to reach both adult and teen markets
  —number one medium against the African-American target
  —higher usage and response indices
  —most cost-effective way to reach scattered target
- Product giveaways in radio cross-promotions
  —trade of product for mention strengthens deal for both
  —radio personalities provide third-party endorsement

Direct Marketing
- Use targeted mailings to African-American adults
  —Seasonality—post-holiday, Kwanzaa, Black History Month, and key consumer electronics retail period

> –May–June (eight weeks)—prime gift-giving season, prior to
> summer recess, greater control needed over kids, graduation,
> Mother's and Father's Days
> - Key purchase time frames for teens
> –August
> –Back to school—new fashions, new schedules to develop
> –November–December (four-week flight)—holiday season

Customer Retention Programs

USP Club membership: These loyalty programs (teen/adult) reward customers for using the USP pager service—the heavier the usage, the greater the incentive: movie and restaurant discounts; retail discounts (video, music, clothing, consumer electronics); free prepaid USP phone cards; discounted pager fees.

Customer Retention Programs for Teens   Teen newsletter communicates pager information to teens in a fun and involving way, "USP on the 411."

- offers phone number to call for latest music, new music monthly
- tells teens of new and useful technology
- puts teens at the forefront of high tech
- allows for corporate testing of new products and concepts with interactive forum
- creates a forum for loyalty incentives

Customer Retention Programs for Adults   Direct communications serve to deliver promotional offers and pertinent security information.

- coupons, discounts
- notification of pager and other USP deals
- handy tips for using the pager and new technology
- corporate testing of new products and concepts with interactive forum

Public Relations Support
- Support programs with local market public relations in key African-American print and broadcast media

—introduce teen program with a new music party, hosted by the radio station

—introduce adult program with a media relations program to outlets discussing parental security concerns

- Use local market spokesperson to increase awareness
- Develop and offer bylined USP column to targeted African-American consumer market media outlets, offering pager tips, latest technology, and security advice
- Coincide public relations efforts with promotional windows

Sample Proposal 3:
Marketing Program for a
Telecommunications Company

The Opportunity

Telex can reap major benefits by developing a targeted approach to the African-American consumer market (AACM).

- African-Americans will respond to a targeted effort from a major and respected marketer.
- African-Americans are heavy users of cellular telephone services, but there's room for growth.
- African-Americans comprise a large and growing segment of the total U.S. population and are particularly important in key cities.

The African-American Marketplace

- Largest single minority group: 13 percent of U.S. population
- Thirty-four million people; growing to over 40 million by 2010
- Highest combined buying power of any ethnic group: $324 billion and growing
- Over 43 percent are solidly middle class ($25,000+ household income)
- Double the population growth rate of white Americans; will account for 30 percent of the total U.S. population growth through 2005

Sources: U.S. Census Bureau; U.S. Bureau of Labor Statistics

African-American audiences are different from nonethnic Americans. First, the demographics are different. African-Americans

- are younger—average age of 29, versus 34 for total United States
- are likely to be single—57 percent are single, versus 39 percent for total United States
- have larger families—average family is 3.5, versus 3.2 for total United States
- have more female-headed families—about 50 percent, versus about 20 percent for total United States
- live mostly in urban areas and in the South—58 percent of African-Americans live in central-city areas; over half of all African-Americans live in the South

Second, the attitudes are different:

- Home and family are more likely to be the main source of satisfaction—39 percent say home provides all or almost all of their satisfaction, versus 25 percent of nonminorities.
- Church and religion are far more important than to the nonminority population—73 percent say religion is very important, versus 47 percent of nonminorities.
- Education is a "stepping-stone" to a better life—78 percent say "the best thing a young person can do is to go to college to prepare for a career," versus 69 percent of nonminorities; 61 percent say the value of education lies in its ability to help a person get ahead, versus 42 percent of nonminorities.
- African-Americans seek out community connections—77 percent agree strongly that they feel the need to become more involved in the lives of their communities, versus 61 percent of nonminorities.
- African-Americans respond to and support networks in their personal and professional lives.

Sources: Yankelovich/Burrell; Market Segment Research; Nielsen

African-Americans Communicate Through Networks

Hundreds of organizations and membership networks are within the African-American community. Their importance derives from generations ago—pre–civil rights when there were "two Americas." These networks were formed to enable African-Americans to travel, conduct business, gain information, and feel connected. Today, most African-Americans still belong to a variety of these ethnic-based groups with a much higher incidence and loyalty than the general market. In most cases, greater credibility is attached to information endorsed by one's membership group rather than by the general market.

Sources: Yankelovich/Burrell; Market Segment Research; Nielsen

Guidelines: Marketing to the African-American Consumer Market

- They prefer African-American actors and role models. Seventy percent say they're more likely to buy when African-American actors are featured. They are very responsive to African-American celebrity endorsements.
- They align with events that focus on their cultural heritage. For example, Kwanzaa, a holiday based on African-inspired social practices, is now celebrated by more than fourteen million African-Americans.
- They support marketers who support things they believe in. African-Americans prefer to buy from marketers who support cause-related programs focused on their communities.
- They require a targeted media approach. While they watch a lot of television (73.5 hours/week, versus 48.5 nationally), they aren't watching the same shows as nonminorities. Compare the top ten picks of non–African-Americans to African-Americans—there's only one show in common.
- Above all, they seek respect. More than 60 percent say respect is why they favor one retailer over another.

Sources: Yankelovich/Burrell; Market Segment Research; Nielsen

African-American Ownership of Cellular Phones Is Widespread

Many African-Americans (21.8 percent in 1996) already own cellular phones, although with an index of 86 versus the total market, there's still room for growth. African-Americans are heavy users of a range of telephone services. Thirty-seven percent of African-Americans call at least one other country in a typical month. African-Americans call an average of twenty-two different domestic numbers in a typical month. African-Americans index very high on telephone services such as caller ID and call waiting.

Sources: Yankelovich/Burrell; Market Segment Research; Nielsen

The Program
Objectives
- Position Telex as the leader in cellular services within the AACM
- Drive enrollment within the AACM
- Preempt competitive inroads with the AACM
- Establish long-term relationships in the AACM

The Approach
Build a marketing communications template that can be executed in key AACM markets.

Background
- Despite the high degree of interest in community issues and activities, an easy-to-access, single source of information for the African-American community on a local market basis does not exist. As a company that provides communication as its product, Telex should have the appropriate technology in place. Therefore it is appropriate for Telex to position itself as the community provider of this information.
- As a commodity product, the following strategy addresses an opportunity for Telex to enhance and differentiate its services.

"The Neighborhood Buzz": How It Works
"The Neighborhood Buzz" is a product-enhancement communications network offering timely information available only to Telex cellular customers. The information, updated every two weeks, will offer a full spectrum of calendar events and exciting opportunities from sports and

entertainment to church and education events. As an added incentive, special retail values will be offered as a result of strategic alliances with various companies (e.g., Mobil Oil, Blockbuster Video, JCPenney, Tower Records, quick-service restaurants).

Special Retail Offers

- Free Domino's Pizza—consumer will receive a certificate good for a free, large, one-topping, classic hand-tossed Domino's Pizza and a two-liter bottle of soda (or retail equivalent). Consumer can use it for delivery or carryout at any participating Domino's location.
- Free Loews/Sony Theatres movie tickets—consumer will enjoy two free general admission tickets to be used at any participating Loews/Sony Theatre.
- Discount on a CD at Tower Records—consumer will receive a $10 certificate to be used on any CD at participating Tower Records stores.
- Free $10 Mobil Go Card—consumer will get a $10 Go Card good for gas or merchandise at all participating Mobil locations.
- Free Blockbuster Video rental—consumer will receive a certificate good for a free rental of any Blockbuster Video movie to be used at any participating Blockbuster location.
- Discount on JCPenney merchandise—consumer will receive a $15 certificate good on any merchandise at participating JCPenney stores.

Media Outreach

Sign-up advertising promoting "The Neighborhood Buzz" will be delivered through African-American radio stations and newspapers. Radio was selected for its ability to provide good coverage, be promotional, and tie into retail outlets. Newspapers were selected for their ability to extend the reach of radio within the African-American community and for their willingness to provide editorial and promotional support for new information and products targeted to the communities that they serve. A response mechanism (800 number) will be built into the media so that the consumer can call and sign up.

Promotional Activity

Increase trial of Telex's cellular products by using live radio remote events in or near appropriate Telex phone mart locations. Each radio remote would feature Telex and include the following: one live two-hour remote with the top DJ in each market and "goody" bags that contain gifts—special discount coupons to be immediately used to buy the product in participating outlets. Radio stations will provide other giveaways such as concert and event tickets, bumper stickers, and assorted other promotional items to draw consumers to the location of the remote and therefore to the retail outlet. "Available at store X" tags will be run on the radio spot and in the newspaper advertisements. Targeted stores will have special pricing that coincides with the live remote events.

Public Relations

This program would be positioned and presented as a community service to help organizations and community groups inform and promote their activities and events to the AACM. National and local media would inform the AACM about the community aspects of "The Neighborhood Buzz":

- Provides communications platform for organizations and community groups
- Allows organizations the opportunity to get valuable cellular products that can help in the operation of their organizations; this will be done through sign-up drives among their members; a certain number of sign-ups will yield a designated amount of equipment
- Sponsor conferences and conventions of select key organizations; focus could be on updating technological advances in the cellular business, which could be helpful in business and personal lives

Summary of Benefits
- Creates unique proprietary channel
- Provides true community services
- Builds economic base for community
- Provides incentive to buy

Sample Proposal 4:
Marketing Program for Pizza Masters

Urban America: Where It's At

- A large, growing, and increasingly attractive marketplace
- A growth opportunity for Pizza Masters to build business for today and tomorrow

"411" on the Urban Market: Me of the New America

Large

- One in four Americans is a member of a minority group

Growing

- Will jump to one in three in approximately ten years; by 2040 minorities will be 53 percent of America: a "minority majority"

Increasingly Influential

- African-Americans are the largest and fastest-growing group and are the acknowledged trendsetters across the full spectrum of American popular culture, including entertainment—movies, music, fashion—and sports. Eighteen to thirty-four-year-old urban males are the key drivers; trends often extend to general market.

The Opportunity

- Develop a large, loyal customer base within the urban market
- Build Pizza Masters' share of market among urban young adults aged 18 to 34, with a male skew

- Use Pizza Masters' new Full Meal pizza introduction as the platform for this new increased market share and ongoing loyalty

The Urban Market—Especially African-Americans—Loves Pizza

There is significant opportunity to grow Pizza Masters' business by bringing Pizza Masters' urban patronage up to, say, the national African-American norm:

- African-American Pizza Masters' patronage is 100 index.
- Overall African-American pizza consumption is even stronger: 115 index of pizza restaurant patronage and 129 index of pizza purchase at the grocery store.

To win a larger share of the urban pie, mount a program that celebrates and respects the urban culture. Developing programs geared to the urban consumer market will significantly contribute to achieving these goals. And, programs that are successful in the urban marketplace have crossover potential in the general market; they can add value and support Pizza Masters' overall marketing initiatives.

Business Situation

The Challenge

The urban market is a significant potential growth area for Pizza Masters. But it's a definite marketing challenge with a fiercely competitive marketplace and entrenched competition.

Success depends on developing breakthrough products and marketing programs:

- Provide attractive products: the new Full Meal pizza appears to be the "right" product for the marketplace
- Differentiate the brand with innovative, high-impact marketing
- Develop creative, cost-effective programs that support the overall "global" branding but can be strategically positioned to the "urban" marketplace and implemented at a local level

The marketing challenge will be to make Pizza Masters' pizza the preferred choice among young urban adults.

- Deliver immediate sales: give urban youth a reason to choose Pizza Masters' Full Meal
- Develop long-term brand preference: add Pizza Masters' Full Meal pizza to their food preference menu
- Increase Pizza Masters' overall visibility, stature, and sales within the young, urban market and counter competitive acceleration

Program Criteria

Needs to be a "Home Run"—a breakthrough, preemptive, high-impact program that

- Feels "big" and national yet delivers significant local impact in key urban markets
- Drives store traffic and builds sales
- Builds relationships: designed to develop long-term loyalty as well as immediate sales
- Becomes ownable: cannot be preempted by competition
- Showcases youth-oriented values: creativity, energy, enthusiasm
- Plays to young adults' desire for their own community and their own identity
- Is interactive: offers active customer involvement
- Makes good business sense
- Is cost-efficient
- Can be repeatable: a perennial program to build Pizza Masters' Full Meal pizza equity year after year, not a "one-off"
- Has "legs": a catalyst for major retail promotions, public relations, advertising, and word of mouth; builds "buzz"

Geography

The urban male can be reached efficiently in these top markets:

New York	Houston
Los Angeles	Washington, D.C.
Chicago	Philadelphia
Detroit	Memphis

Atlanta   San Francisco–Oakland–San Jose
Dallas–Fort Worth   New Orleans
Baltimore   Miami–Fort Lauderdale
Raleigh–Durham

Target Audience

Understanding the Urban Male: The American Trendsetter Urban males ages 18 to 34 offer a dual attraction. They are "hungry" consumers, a growing market, and are a key influencer group with the general market. Addressing the lifestyle needs of the trendsetting 18 to 34 urban male will serve to build Pizza Masters' brand and product loyalty not only among that group but for surrounding segments as well: "wanna be's" (12-to-17-year-olds) and "wish I still were's" (+35 with similar psychographics).

Reaching the Urban Marketplace: Selling Through Empowerment and Meeting Their Needs

- The urban audience respects and responds favorably to companies that empower rather than simply sell by telling them what to do, say, think, or buy.
- A core group of style makers is forging the way in today's mainstream culture. They desire to have the latest, aspire to be cutting edge, and are responsible for setting trends—especially in entertainment and fashion, which often go mainstream.
- They are major consumers of entertainment in all its forms, overconsuming in relationship to their numbers. For example, African-Americans represent 13.3 percent of the population but buy almost 30 percent of all movie tickets, overindex in "music" purchases (both CDs and concert tickets), and index at 200 in many fashion and apparel categories.

Program Positioning

Build a unique, preemptive position for Pizza Masters not only as provider of the best-tasting food—Full Meal pizza—but also as an enabler and a catalyst with the urban market, making it possible for that market to enjoy the things it most likes to do in ways that are easier, more exciting, and more fun.

Key Strategy: Relationship Marketing

Why Relationship Marketing for Full Meal Pizza?

- It meets consumers on their own ground:
  - —makes product and company part of "lifestyle"
  - —creates an experience
  - —appeals to all the senses
  - —encourages participation and feedback
  - —leaves a lingering impression
- Old paradigm: the product responds to the environment
- Today: the product acts upon the environment—who, what, where, when, how, and engagement

By simply being a Pizza Masters' customer and enjoying the great taste of Full Meal, the consumer will get access to a selection of highly desirable entertainment and fashion-related experiences and unique opportunities.

Key Program Drivers

- Deliver lifestyle-based rewards and incentives
- Build the program around empowerment: offer target market the opportunity to use the program as a platform "to be heard"
- Develop dynamism and impact with linkage and program support through strategic alliances with urban market icons and media
- Support program with a synergistic mix of traditional and nontraditional media: TV, urban radio, grassroots—urban street teams, local sponsorships

Product

- A new product from Pizza Masters that features toppings "to the max," delivering the ultimate in snackability and craving
- Special appeal to the nontraditional customer—not "business as usual"

But what does Full Meal mean to the young, urban market?

- Marketing program will empower the urban market—within Pizza Masters' parameters—to tell us what Full Meal means to them.

- Program provides an interactive platform for relationship building.

Positioning Full Meal for the Urban Market
- When consumers have Full Meal, they have the advantage, best, latest, and greatest.
- Program tracks with urban male trendsetter psychographics.

Entertainment Program: What It Is
The Full Meal Party is a unique major urban market program that celebrates and rewards the lifestyle preferences of urban trendsetters as defined by entertainment, fashion, and sports. Pizza Masters' Full Meal Party will be informed by urban culture so it will both reflect and capture the attitudes and feelings of today's urban trendsetters. It is an interactive, multitiered, state-of-the-art marketing initiative, geared toward satisfying the desires of urban youth, which

- Empowers the urban consumer to choose urban lifestyle icons and offers incentive purchase with choice of highly appealing lifestyle enhancements
- Enables participation in an exciting and unique sweepstakes with once-in-a-lifetime prizes
- Uniquely positions Pizza Masters as a company that understands, respects, and celebrates urban lifestyle

Program Elements
- Relevant: "This is me"
- Participatory: "I play a role"
- Exciting: "I wouldn't miss it"
- Relationship derived: "I couldn't be here without you"
- Works on a variety of levels by
  —interacting with consumers
  —encouraging purchase and repeat purchase and store visits
  —positioning Pizza Masters and Full Meal pizza in the minds of urban youth
  —providing a foundation for future urban efforts—program "builds" year after year, becoming even bigger in second year

Awards and Ultimate Sweepstakes

Pizza Masters creates first-of-its-kind urban "people's choice" award. Participants vote for Full Meal Pizza Awards in each of four categories: movies, TV, music, and sports. The Pizza Masters' Full Meal Pizza Awards winners, those icons receiving the highest votes, would be announced or would appear on a major late-night TV show (promotional partner). Entry form will feature Full Meal pizza discount coupons and other Pizza Masters' offers.

Awards Nominees

Movies: Men
> Omar Epps
> Isaiah Washington

Music: Men
> Blackstreet
> Maxwell

TV: Men
> Jamie Foxx
> Kadeem Hardison
> LL Cool J

Sports: Men
> Keyshawn Johnson   Emmit Smith
> Michael Jordan   Tiger Woods
> Glen Rice

Movies: Women
> Vivica Fox   Jada Pinkett
> Regina King   Lela Rochon
> Nia Long

Music: Women
> Aaliyah   Lil' Kim
> Da Brat   Salt-N-Pepa
> Missy Elliot

TV: Women

Brandy	Robin Givens
Stacey Dash	Queen Latifah

Sports: Women

Lisa Leslie	Sheryl Swoops
Rebecca Lobo	Venus Williams

Sweepstakes   Casting a ballot in the Pizza Masters' Full Meal Pizza Awards automatically enrolls the participant in the Pizza Masters' Sweepstakes. Ballots are available in stores, with delivery or carryout, or call 1-800-MEAL.

Multilevel prize structure   Ultimate Prize: The Ultimate "Delivery" Vehicle
   one-of-a-kind customized Hummer
   Sony Satellite Navigational System
   Nintendo video games
   selection of TV, video games, or VCR on built-in headrest
      screens
   liquid crystal control panel
   Fifty-CD disc player, AM/FM stereo radio
   Internet equipped

Winners
- Grand prize: winner and guest will appear on a leading late-night show and receive backstage passes. They also win a spectacular Full Meal Weekend in the coolest city in the world—Hollywood, where they will be chauffeured from clubs to TV and movie studios, attend the Pizza Masters' Pizza Party with the show's cast, and receive a $5,000 wardrobe and $1,000 Pizza Masters' Cash.
- Second prizes: three lucky winners will be flown to New York City to choose their own Pizza Masters' CD collection (100 discs) at the Virgin Music Superstore in Times Square.

- Third prizes: twenty-five people will win Pizza Masters' Movie Passes, entitling the winners and a guest to go to one free movie a week for a year.
- Fourth prizes: 100 people will win a custom-designed Pizza Masters' two-piece warm-up suit.
- Runners-up: 1,500 runners-up win Pizza Masters' caps and free pizza coupons good for one free Full Meal pizza.

In addition to sweepstakes enrollment, Pizza Masters will offer customers a selection of lifestyle rewards. The customer chooses what fits his or her interest: Pizza Masters' custom CD compilations, Pizza Masters' Movie Cash (movie passes), and Pizza Masters' custom designer clothing. The more frequently a customer patronizes Pizza Masters and purchases Full Meal pizzas, the greater the discount on each reward. Other benefits include self-liquidating premiums (purchase with purchase) and "free with X number of Full Meal pizza purchases" (gift with purchase). Thus, Pizza Masters' Full Meal Party delivers both a "chance to win" and the potential for further rewards.

Media Support Program

Objective
- Support and leverage visibility for eight- to twelve-week Pizza Masters' Full Meal Party promotional campaign beginning March 1998 in fifteen top urban markets
- Generate program impact at launch and sustain exposure through strategic alliance with top urban TV personality or program
- Gain additional support from local TV affiliates that will run promotional schedules
- Drive local visibility with radio—the key medium of choice among urban audience, ages 18 to 34—and leverage TV alliance by creating tie-ins with DJs and icons and maximizing exposure through promotions
- Build grassroots-community-level visibility with Street Teams and sponsorships
- Generate third-party endorsement and local exposure via public relations and local tie-ins

Why Keenen Ivory Wayans?

- Keenen has visibility among urban males, ages 18 to 34; he has the highest Q rating on TV with this audience.
- His highly rated TV show offers Pizza Masters a promotional platform.
- He offers a strategic alliance with Pizza Masters.
- This is a preemptive opportunity for Pizza Masters.
- The promotional alliance delivers highly cost-effective media, provides affiliate support in key urban markets, and promises a potential long-term relationship.
- Full Meal becomes the "official pizza" of the Keenen Ivory Wayans show.
- Approximately four national thirty-second TV advertisements per week are run on the Keenen Ivory Wayans show, featuring the uniqueness of Full Meal pizza and its appeal for this marketplace.
- Pizza Masters will have the exclusive rights "to cater" Full Meal pizzas to the studio audience of the Keenen Ivory Wayans show. Prior to the show, Pizza Masters delivery trucks will pull up and offer Full Meal pizzas to Keenen audience members. The audience members eating Full Meal pizzas would be taped; Keenen would make mention of this, possibly playing the tape and "playing up" Full Meal pizza.
- Pizza Masters' Sweepstakes will be promoted with Keenen TV affiliates in the fifteen key markets.
- Over a two-week period, four twenty- or thirty-second TV spots per day will announce the Pizza Masters' Sweepstakes and feature Full Meal pizza and Keenen.
- Keenen will establish a special Full Meal seating section where specially selected audience members who dress, look, and act with the attitude fitting with Full Meal pizza will sit. Keenen will make reference to this seated area similar to Arsenio Hall's "Dog Pound."

Urban Radio: Full Meal Promotions in Key Cities

- Use the high-affinity medium of radio to reach the elusive urban youth segment

–the number one medium for reaching the urban target
–higher usage and response indices
–most cost-effective way to reach scattered target
- Keenen "informs" radio spots
- Product giveaways in radio cross-promotions
–trading product for mention strengthens deal for both
–using radio personalities provides third-party endorsement
- Use sixty-second radio spots rotating between product and promotion advertisements
- Run radio commercials on urban stations in the top fifteen markets with the top rating for men and women ages 18 to 34
- Run radio spots between 3:00 P.M. and midnight and on weekends (strongest time period for target)
- Run commercials in conjunction with RadioScope, the premier urban radio entertainment magazine on air that features the latest on the biggest stars (Over the past ten years, RadioScope has featured celebrities, issue-oriented reports, as well as insightful looks at film, television, and books.)
- Have RadioScope customize news segments to talk about Full Meal pizza
- Have RadioScope network remotes travel through urban neighborhoods giving away tickets to upcoming concerts and Full Meal pizza coupons and information

Taking It to the Streets
- Urban Street Teams would be used to create further awareness of Pizza Masters' Full Meal Party and provide advance visibility for Full Meal pizza in key urban markets.
- Local market urban influentials ages 18 to 34 would serve to saturate the market on a grassroots level by distributing pizza coupons and promotional materials at sports events, college games, clubs, concerts, and movie theaters.
- Street Teams designed to build store traffic, word of mouth, buzz, and excitement at music stores, barber shops, malls, etc.

College Intercollegiate Athletic Association (CIAA) Promotion

- Promotion targets males ages 18 to 34 with one of their favorite pastimes: sports.
- The CIAA tournament finals have over 40,000 fans per game.
- Eighty percent of TV viewership are African-Americans 18 to 34 years old.
- Eight games from February 26–28 will feature Full Meal pizza at the game and on network TV.
- Promotion includes
  - Full Meal logo on a 4 × 10 foot rotating floor sign
  - a display booth where Full Meal pizza can be sampled or coupons distributed
  - television signage
  - opening and closing billboards
  - full-page four-color ad in the tournament program
  - two public announcements sponsored by Pizza Masters
  - two halftime sponsor interviews with key players
  - one in-program segment with sponsor logo and identification
  - two 4 × 6 foot banners on site
  - category exclusivity

Public Relations (PR) Extends the Message

- Launch Pizza Masters' Full Meal Party with major press announcement on both the national and local market levels in key urban print and broadcast media
- Leverage Awards—Pizza Masters asks urban America to name local candidates to gain exposure in local markets
- Announce winners toward end of promotion on Keenen Ivory Wayans show and through national and local PR

Program Benefits

- Marketplace impact: Pizza Masters' Full Meal Party has the legs to generate significant marketplace impact in both sales and visibility.

- Increased franchisee support—special promotion and Keenen involvement provide motivational element
- Increased consumer demand
- Increased consumer loyalty for Pizza Masters: more "special-ness" with urban young adults and brand differentiation
- The program is repeatable toward building long-term growth in sales and profits.

What Pizza Masters Should Expect from the Full Meal Party

- Urban consumers will say more often:
  - "Pizza Masters understands me and fits the way I live."
  - "I like Pizza Masters for making this program possible."
  - "Pizza Masters really has a heart."
  - "Pizza Masters has done for me what others haven't."
  - "Pizza Masters helps me have more fun than anyone else."
- Franchisees and local restaurant managers will say more often:
  - "Pizza Masters' programs bring people to my stores."
  - "This Pizza Masters' program makes me a local hero."
  - "This promotion is tailored for my own market."

Sample Proposal 5:
Marketing Program
for Crown Motors

The Opportunity
- Build sales for Crown Motors with the growing African-American marketplace
- Make competitive inroads against current favored brands among African-American consumers

Objectives
- Differentiate Crown Motors vehicles among African-Americans
- Create dealer incentive programs to drive traffic and test drives
- Develop loyalty initiatives to increase repeat purchases

The Big Picture
America is entering a period of profound change. To put it simply, the world's leading nation will change from a 25 percent minority population to a minority-majority. This kind of unprecedented, rapid shift will influence all institutions, from politics to plays, from entertainment to education, from leadership to leisure.

> —Eric Miller, "From Melting Pot to Magnet: The New American Diversity," *American Demographics*, December 1994

The new America involves an unprecedented economic and cultural shift:

- Minority groups now make up 25 percent of the U.S. population—33 percent by 2010 and 53 percent by 2040.

- The age of the melting pot is past. Enter the American mosaic, where each minority group retains its own identity as it contributes to the whole picture.
- Marketers who recognize the presence of the new American mosaic and who reach out to specific groups with focused messages and programs will be the winners.

African-Americans are today's most important ethnic group:

- Largest single minority group: 33.6 million consumers
- Double the population growth rate of white Americans
- Will account for 30 percent of the total U.S. population growth through 2005
- Highest combined buying power: $324 billion, up 25 percent since 1990

Situation Overview

As Americans move into the millennium, they are placing a premium on balancing work and play.

- The trend is toward an increasing value placed on travel, leisure, and quality time.
- African-Americans are gaining ground quickly in key economic and quality-of-life measurements.
- African-Americans claiming the American Dream are increasingly securing the "good life"—upscale recreational activities historically the domain of the general market (e.g., leisure travel, skiing, golf, cycling, tennis, scuba diving).

Marketing Strategies

There is an opportunity for Crown Motors to underscore the trend toward the increasing participation of African-Americans in the good life. By aligning the Pathfinder, a recreational vehicle, with the upscale travel and leisure activities of the growing African-American middle class, Crown Motors can support the values of this marketplace. This can build a linkage and a preemptive positioning for Crown Motors that symbolizes the lifestyles and values of this growth market segment.

Crown Motors Good Life Program

Overall program goal is to create linkages and preemptive positioning for Crown Motors with the African-American middle class through exclusive access to the Good Life program. The Good Life program is a lifestyle-based continuity program that enables African-Americans to enjoy a wide range of specially selected sports, travel, and entertainment opportunities with greater convenience and cost-effectiveness.

- Programs are targeted to both Crown Motors owners and prospects in key urban markets.
- Activities and programs are featured that index high against middle-income African-Americans.
- The Pathfinder Series programs would offer discounts and special access to these activities including leisure travel, skiing, golf, cycling, tennis, scuba diving, etc.
- All offers are activated with an 800 number.
- Via a quarterly mailing to owners and prospects with point-of-sale collateral at dealerships, customers gain special access to activities such as
  - ski trips: annual Black Skiers Summit
  - tennis tournaments: American Tennis Association
  - golf programs
  - Black Enterprise Celebrity Classic Festivals
  - New Orleans Jazz & Heritage Festival
  - *Essence* Music Awards
  - Caribbean cruises
  - national sporting events: NCAA, World Series, NBA championship games
- Special automobile-related Crown Motors merchandise are offered, including bicycle racks and ski racks

The Good Life Guide

What The Crown Motors Pathfinder Good Life Guide is an extension of the Crown Motors Pathfinder Series, offering greater depth and additional information.

How

- Newsletter or mailer highlighting key travel and leisure opportunities targeted to African-Americans, courtesy of Crown Motors, building on Pathfinder Series and offering greater depth and additional information
- Editorials offering how-to tips on travel and leisure activities
- On-line Internet Good Life Guide linking Crown Motors' site to Web pages and sites featuring relevant activities

Why

- As a metaphor for the aspirations of this growing market segment and their increasing interests in a wider range of leisure-related activities, these programs can build significant linkage for Crown Motors with the emerging black middle class.
- Unique. Offers distinct competitive advantage differentiating Crown Motors in the minds of African-American target group.
- Value added. Participants will say, "I couldn't have done this without you."
- Continuity programs build ongoing loyalty.
- Good Life Guide enhances the interactive relationship between Crown Motors and African-Americans.
- It creates bonds with key African-American organizations.

Sponsorships

What   A portfolio of organization, event, and venue sponsorships of African-American cultural and entertainment events providing special access to upscale "Good Life" activities will be developed.

How   Sample events:

U.S. Open: Arthur Ashe Children's Day
Gala celebrations: NAACP Image Awards
Black Filmmaker Foundation premieres and parties
Black History Makers Awards Dinner
Sinbad's Caribbean Seventies Summer Jam

Why

- Offers on-site visibility for Crown Motors
- Gains third-party endorsement from trusted organizations
- Acquires access to targeted mailing lists
- Is preemptive versus competitive
- Makes a statement about and builds relationships for Crown Motors with the aspirations and goals of this key target market
- Gains recognition externally and within Crown Motors system with high-profile news and events heralding special programs (public relations initiatives)
- Sends messages focused on specific deals and incentives directly to owners and prospects through direct marketing
- Targets ads in key African-American media in top ten markets
- Draws attention to offers and discounts through attractive materials at the point of sale

SAMPLE PROPOSAL 6:
MARKETING PROGRAM FOR A CONSUMER PACKAGED-GOODS COMPANY

Package Goods Inc. Ltd. Multicultural Marketing Objectives

Build Package Goods Inc. Ltd. products as the brands of choice among African-Americans:

- Deliver immediate sales: give the African-American consumer market (AACM) a reason to choose Package Goods Inc. Ltd.'s brands over others
- Develop long-term brand preference for Package Goods Inc. Ltd. brands within the AACM
- Preempt competitors concerning the AACM segment
- Build Package Goods Inc. Ltd. minority employee pride, motivation; support recruitment, retention
- Enhance Package Goods Inc. Ltd. "corporate image" among nonconsumer audiences including security analysts and business partners
- Increase Package Goods Inc. Ltd.'s overall visibility, stature, and sales within the AACM and counter competitive acceleration

Program Criteria
Breakthrough, preemptive, high-impact program needs to be a "Home Run."

- Feels "big" and national, yet delivers significant local impact in key urban markets
- Drives store traffic and builds sales
- Builds relationships: designed to develop long-term loyalty as well as immediate sales

- Is ownable: cannot be preempted by competition
- Showcases African-American values: sense of accomplishment, energy, enthusiasm, success
- Reflects AACM desire for their own community and their own identity
- Is interactive: offers active customer involvement
- Makes good business sense:
  —cost-efficient
  —repeatable; perennial program to build Package Goods Inc. Ltd. brands equity year after year; not a one-off
  —has legs: a catalyst for major retail promotions, public relations, advertising, and word of mouth; builds buzz
- High quality; meets Package Goods Inc. Ltd.'s "gold standard"

Geography

The AACM can be reached efficiently in these top markets:

New York	Houston
Los Angeles	Washington, D.C.
Chicago	Philadelphia
Detroit	Memphis
Atlanta	San Francisco–Oakland
Dallas–Fort Worth	New Orleans
Baltimore	Miami–Fort Lauderdale
Raleigh–Durham	

Target Audiences

- Primary target: women, 18 to 49 years old
- Secondary target: families with children

Program Positioning

The program will build a unique, preemptive position for Package Goods Inc. Ltd. not only as offering the highest-quality consumer products—key brands—but also as an enabler and a catalyst within the AACM community to build a greater sense of respect, pride, and achievement for African-Americans (see Figure A.1).

Figure A.1   Why an Interactive Program?

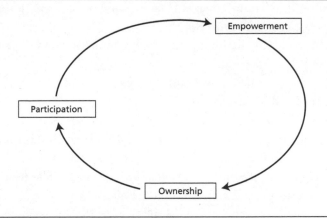

Key Strategy

Relationship marketing to build consumer view: consumers will think, "Simply by being a Package Goods Inc. Ltd. brand consumer I'll help to support not only local community goals but also contribute to the long-term success of both my own family and that of other African-Americans nationwide." Key program drivers

- Deliver lifestyle-based rewards and incentives
- Build the program around empowerment; offer target market the opportunity to use the program as a platform "to be heard"
- Develop dynamism and impact with linkage and program support through strategic alliances with urban market icons and media partners
- Support program with a synergistic mix of traditional and nontraditional media: TV, urban radio, local sponsorships, and national print

Program Concept: Package Goods Inc. Ltd. American Dream Awards

This urban cause-related marketing program celebrates the achievements of ethnic Americans in improving the quality of their lives as defined by attainments across a spectrum of private and public sector arenas—an urban "Horatio Alger" award. It offers recognition and support to help others build toward greater achievements in the future.

> I have learned that success is to be measured not so much by the position that one has reached in his life as by the obstacles which he has overcome while trying to succeed.
>
> —Booker T. Washington

Recent Multicultural American Dream Index showed that ethnic Americans are capturing the American Dream three times faster than nonethnic Americans.

Accelerating growth rate at which African-, Hispanic-, and Asian-Pacific-Americans have been improving their quality of life over the past ten years—obtaining mortgages, owning their own small businesses, earning college degrees—is outpacing that of nonethnic Americans by well over 300 percent.

If current trends continue, ethnic Americans' share of participation in these American Dream categories will reach parity with nonethnic Americans within ten years.

Multicultural American Dream (MCAD) Index: Quality Versus Quantity

- MCAD demonstrates that ethnic Americans are accessing the means to prosperity at a much faster rate than is generally recognized (counter-intuitive).
- Previous studies have highlighted quantitative gains; MCAD focuses on qualitative progress.
- MCAD can regionalize future studies.

Strategic Alliances

The program will reflect the endorsement of key national groups that support minority progress. These include, but are not limited to

> The Minority Business Development Center of the U.S. Department of Commerce
>
> The President's Initiative on Race: One America for the 21st Century

The President's Summit for America's Future
Turner–Time Warner: Trumpet Awards

The American Dream Awards: Celebrating Urban "Horatio Algers"

- Both at a local-market (retail) and national level the program will focus attention on outstanding multicultural achievers who have made real progress in both their own and the lives of their neighbors through acts of courage and commitment.
- Working with local retailers and media partners (TV, radio, and newspaper), chambers of commerce, and key urban not-for-profit groups, the program will recognize and honor these urban "Horatio Algers" both locally and nationally.
- Local recognition will derive from media visibility for the winners (public relations, salute ads), and national exposure will come from public relations, public service announcements, and visibility at the Trumpet Awards, the nationally televised TBS program that celebrates African-American achievers.
- Program positions Package Goods Inc. Ltd. brands and customers as supporting—through a cause-related marketing platform—the success of multicultural Americans.
- Consumers will have the opportunity, through entry forms at retail displays, to
  –vote for their choice of national achievers and local awardees
  –enter the Package Goods Inc. Ltd. American Dream Award Sweepstakes and win free tickets to the Trumpet Awards television program, full or partial college scholarships, trips to ethnic heritage festivals, ethnic magazine subscriptions, computer equipment, etc.
–get discount coupons for selected Package Goods Inc. Ltd. products that are supporting the Package Goods Inc. Ltd. American Dream Awards program through a cause-related contribution tied to brand purchase

Trumpet Awards

- Airing on the TBS Superstation, the Sixth Annual Trumpet Awards honor African-American icons in fields as diverse as law, medicine, politics, and entertainment.
- 1998 ceremony, hosted by Gladys Knight and Robert Guillaum, honored General Colin Powell, Wynton Marsalis, Whitney Houston, and baseball legends Don Newcomb and Larry Dobe.
- TBS, seen in more than 73 million homes, is the most-watched network on cable.

Marketing Support

- Announce with national kickoff press event in New York featuring an advisory council comprised of Package Goods Inc. Ltd. management, multicultural icons from the public and private sectors, key cabinet officials (e.g., General Colin Powell, secretary of education, secretary of commerce), retail partners, etc.
- Launch and feature announcement of national award candidates; announce sweepstakes
- Support in-store point of sale with national and local market radio, newspapers, national freestanding inserts, and national and local public relations tied to release of regional versions of the Multicultural American Dream Index
- Announce winners with local and national press conferences and appearances on Trumpet Awards
- Showcase and position Package Goods Inc. Ltd. brands within a program that provides real recognition and support for multicultural Americans (role models)
- Offer "hero" positioning for local retailers as cosponsors
- Provide a broad platform for a wide and growing spectrum of Package Goods Inc. Ltd. brand sponsors
- Offer a program that annually builds in impact
- If desired, offer the opportunity for cosponsors: e.g., airlines, hotels, computer companies, etc.

Execution Strategy

- Launch three-month effort that actively seeks, recognizes, and rewards achievers
- Establish high-profile, regional-based celebrity and personality partners to help build program awareness and momentum throughout the three-month period
- Include private and public sector leaders in outreach and winner selection process
- Establish market-specific chamber of commerce (or regional chapter) and other not-for-profit tie-ins that offer fund-raising opportunities as an added promotional value to both sponsors and affiliate stations
- Structure program with a series of publicity vehicles that attract both additional sponsor interest and audience attention
- Launch announcement
  –announce outreach through press conference in New York
  –include celebrity personalities to kick off national award competition
  –outline national and regional outreach efforts
  –outline key nonprofit and sponsor partners
  –outline timeline and rewards for both national and regional winners
  –define criteria for winners (national and local), e.g., motivation, determination, innovation within limited resources, unique impact on individuals, special circumstances, etc.
  –target media: national print, radio broadcast, TBS cable partners nationwide, top-tier black media, concentrated regional broadcast and print in "key markets"
- Regional celebrity publicity events

Execute regional mini-events that add direct community longevity and awareness for program announcement: include area celebrities and nonprofits as appropriate, support sponsor interests, conduct event at retail level, establish strategic point-of-purchase locations

- Possible regional celebrities include
  –Chicago—Michael Jordan, Phil Jackson, Buddy Guy, Mike Ditka, John Malkovich, Gary Sinise, Laurie Metcalf

–New York—Roberta Flack, Al Roker, Regis Philbin, Ed
   Koch, Paul Shaefer
–Los Angeles—Magic Johnson, Edward James Olmos, Paul
   Rodriguez
–Detroit—Aretha Franklin, Berry Gordy, Bob Seger, Grant Hill
   (Detroit Pistons), Mayor Dennis Archer
• Judge selection as news opportunity
–establish "civic panel" of strong community leaders in the private and public sectors to determine program winners
–leverage panel members as spokespersons in news
–include local affiliate on-air personalities or anchors as panel
   members
• Public service announcements to maintain momentum and
   awareness
–create series of national and regional public service spots for
   TV and radio to encourage program participation, increase
   Package Goods Inc. Ltd. connection to program, and maintain program momentum throughout three-month period
–access both area celebrities and judges in campaign
• Regional award celebrations
–conduct community spirit luncheons, receptions, or dinners in
   each target market
–design as strategic community-relations platform
–invite area celebrities and panel leaders as participants
–publicize as news opportunity on regional basis
–develop customized collateral materials that support both
   regional affiliates and sponsors
–encourage sponsors to leverage events as cross-marketing
   opportunities (direct, advertising, etc.)

Program Benefits

All this will create for Package Goods Inc. Ltd. brands

• Marketplace impact—Package Goods Inc. Ltd. American
   Dream Awards has the legs to generate significant marketplace
   impact in both sales and visibility.

- Based on size, scope, and outreach to millions of consumers, the sponsor will gain positioning as America's largest single private sector initiative to both recognize and support ethnic Americans—and to offer multicultural Americans an invitation to buy Package Goods Inc. Ltd.'s consumer products.
- Incremental volume
  —increased retailer support; local media involvement provides motivation
  —increased consumer demand
- Increased consumer loyalty
  —more "specialness" with urban consumers
  —brand differentiation
  —repeatable toward building long-term growth in sales and profits
- A relationship-based, strategic initiative with the power to deliver the competitive edge for Package Goods Inc. Ltd and open and build a new and growing market

What Package Goods Inc. Ltd. Should Expect from the American Dream Award Program

- Urban consumers will tell you more often:
  —"Package Goods Inc. Ltd. understands me and fits the way I live."
  —"I like Package Goods Inc. Ltd. for making this program possible."
  —"Package Goods Inc. Ltd. really has a heart."
  —"Package Goods Inc. Ltd. has done for me what others haven't."
- Retail partners will tell you more often:
  —"Package Goods Inc. Ltd. programs bring people to my stores."
  —"This Package Goods Inc. Ltd. program makes me a local hero."
  —"This promotion is tailored for my own market."

SAMPLE PROPOSAL 7:
BRAND-BUILDING FOR A
LATIN-AMERICAN MINERAL WATER

Let's examine a successful marketing campaign that was undertaken by Alternative & Innovative Marketing (AIM) in Escondido, California, for a Latin-American brand of mineral water that was eager to rebuild its market share among Hispanic-Americans.

The Goals

The assignment was to rebuild the brand in the United States by rebuilding its share in the Hispanic-American market. A well-known brand in Latin America, San Pedro ranks among the top five of all mineral waters bottled in Latin America. For several years during the early 1990s, the brand was imported and aggressively marketed in the United States. Then, due to a change in U.S. distributors, the brand disappeared from the United States for several years.

To accomplish San Pedro's goal of rebuilding the brand and increasing its market share in the U.S.–Hispanic marketplace, some specific challenges needed to be addressed:

- During the time San Pedro was out of the U.S. marketplace, several smaller, well-accepted Latin-American competitors had entered the market and began to take San Pedro's position and shelf space.
- The new U.S. distributor was handling many imported brands; among them all, San Pedro was seen as a smaller, secondary priority behind these "more important" brands.
- The route-to-market channels that the distributor had set up were targeted to mainstream retail outlets rather than to those that catered to Hispanic-American consumers.

- "Grey market" product (cases of illegally imported San Pedro) was coming in from Mexico.

Implementation

The San Pedro name still had a very high level of awareness and prestige in the Hispanic-American marketplace, especially in the southwestern United States. Therefore, extensive advertising efforts to drive consumers to purchase would have been premature if they could not find the product at retail.

So these steps were undertaken:

1. Retail outlets were identified that catered to Hispanic-American consumers in key areas. Instead of rolling out nationally, San Pedro was best equipped to cover only certain geographic areas effectively. Therefore, the decision was made to first target the most important Hispanic-American markets—starting in Los Angeles.
2. Distributors were identified to supply those retail accounts.
3. The brand was relaunched to distributors, wholesalers, and retailers of various classes of trade (grocery, mass, food service, and entertainment). Sales programs were devised, including incentives and display programs such as special pricing, etc.
4. Retailers were offered in-store marketing and coupon support to move product.
5. A Spanish-language in-store demonstration program was created to drive sales.
6. The message was taken right to the market. San Pedro developed a "mobile merchandiser" for the key market (Los Angeles) to visit and merchandise retail locations Wednesday through Friday and participate in consumer sampling events and grassroots activities on the weekends.
7. The program was supported with radio advertising during the summer and key Hispanic-American promotional periods.
8. An aggressive monitoring program was launched to shut down grey market product coming across the international border.

Results

The brand began to grow again in the United States. Within only eighteen months, sales grew from 0 to 60,000 cases monthly.

A Major Sports Franchise Builds Its Presence in the Hispanic-American Community

Let's examine another campaign undertaken by AIM that helped a major California-based baseball team build ties to the Hispanic-American community.

Of course, given the high concentration of Hispanic-Americans in California—not to mention the many extraordinary Latino baseball players who have been in the game for decades—baseball teams have long enjoyed a high level of awareness from U.S.–Hispanic consumers, especially Hispanic-Americans of Mexican descent.

Still, one California team realized several years ago that in order to grow their fan base and franchise in their market, they needed to more aggressively develop new fans from the emerging market segments.

In an effort to promote greater outreach, the team's management contacted AIM. AIM's initial investigations of the team's intentions immediately turned up one extraordinary fact: a high percentage of Hispanic-Americans living within forty miles of the stadium have never come to a game.

Goals

In addition to attracting more Hispanic-American fans to the park, additional goals emerged:

- to develop new sponsorship revenues centered around Hispanic-American products and consumers
- to create an event to position the team as a sports franchise that cares about the Hispanic-American market
- to generate positive public relations about the team's commitment in the Hispanic-American market

- to generate revenues from both Hispanic-American consumers and advertisers interested in reaching the Hispanic-American market

An Event Is Created

With these goals in mind, the team and AIM developed and implemented a major event at the stadium: a one-day event that invited Latino fans to the stadium five hours before game time to enjoy a concert with Latino recording artists, meet the players, visit sponsor booths, and win prizes in a festival-like environment. The entire event was staged in the parking lot, and it was free with the purchase of a ticket to the game following the event.

Results

- In 1998, approximately 4,000 fans attended the event, for which a major bank and several retailers were the main sponsors. The team generated enough sponsorship revenues to cover the event costs. The event was covered by both Spanish-language and major English-language media.
- In 1999, over 5,500 fans attended the event. A major bottling company was the main sponsor, participating in retail tie-in programs that included point-of-purchase materials and a special contest at soft-drink displays in over 140 grocery outlets that cater to Hispanic-Americans. Over fifteen major sponsors were in the second-year activities. Again, English- and Spanish-language TV, radio, and print covered the event.